Peasants on the Edge

PEASANTS ON THE EDGE

Crop, Cult, and Crisis in the Andes

by William P. Mitchell

University of Texas Press, Austin

To my children, Sean and Nicholas,
and to
the memory of Gerald Freed

First Edition, 1991

Requests for permission to reproduce material from this work should be sent to Permissions, University of Texas Press, Box 7819, Austin, Texas 78713-7819.

♾ The paper used in this publication meets the minimum requirements of American National Standard for Information Sciences—Permanence of Paper for Printed Library Materials, ANSI Z39.48-1984.

Library of Congress Cataloging-in-Publication Data
Mitchell, William P., 1937–
  Peasants on the edge : crop, cult, and crisis in the Andes / by William P. Mitchell. — 1st ed.
    p.   cm.
  Includes bibliographical references and index.
  ISBN: 0-292-72145-5
  1. Indians of South America—Peru—Quinua (Humanga)—Agriculture. 2. Indians of South America—Peru—Quinua (Humanga)—Economic conditions. 3. Indians of South America—Peru—Quinua (Humanga)—Politics and government. 4. Peasantry—Peru—Quinua (Humanga) 5. Quinua (Humanga, Peru)—Religious life and customs. 6. Quina (Humanga, Peru)—Social conditions. I. Title.
F3429.1.Q56M58 1991
985'.292—dc20   90-47300
                                                          CIP

CONTENTS

PHOTOGRAPHS

FIGURES

TABLES

ACKNOWLEDGMENTS

MY INTELLECTUAL DEBT to Barbara Price is apparent. Dean Arnold, Nahid Aslanbeigui, Jane Collins, Rhoda Halperin, Robert Hunt, Gregory Knapp, Cynthia McClintock, Daphna H. Mitchell, Barbara Price, Pamela Rosi, and Bruce Winterhalder have been especially generous with their ideas and comments on various portions of the manuscript. Guy Oakes commented on chapter 1. Esther Goldfrank Wittfogel, Richard S. MacNeish and Karl Wittfogel commented on the ecological and farming material in an earlier manuscript. Jane Freed has provided invaluable help in editing the manuscript and made most of the botanical identifications and catalogued the agricultural and botanical samples from Quinua. Deborah Pearsall kindly checked the botanical identifications. Barbara Jaye has read the manuscript several times, helping me improve not only its substance but its grace. Figure 3 was prepared from a photograph by Dean Arnold (1975). Dean Arnold has also been most obliging in sharing his knowledge and other photographs of Quinua. Dennis Lewis drew figures 1 and 3. José Oriundo, Rachel Lax, and Todd Rutledge helped prepare the manuscript. Ralph Binder of the Monmouth College photography department prepared the photographs for publication. Hildegard Webb, reference librarian at Monmouth College, has been most helpful in tracking down even the most obscure publication. Linda Nelson and the rest of the computer staff at Monmouth College have been most obliging.

I am very grateful to my friends in Quinua and Lima for their hospitality, patience, and generous sharing of their lives. Pedro Oriundo has always been most gracious. I could not have completed this book without the help of Virgilio Oriundo, Herlinda Ramos, and their children. The people who have helped me are numerous. In Quinua,

X   ACKNOWLEDGMENTS

I especially thank my adopted parents—mama Vicenta and, now deceased, tayta Pascual—and my friends and assistants: Mamerto, Guillermo, Benjamin, Adrian, and Teofilo. Javier Coras, Andres Pariona, and Wilton Martinez were invaluable assistants in Lima. Enrique Herrera, Fernando Gonzales, Alex Diaz, and Alicia Grandon provided various documentary data.

The Foreign Area Fellowship Program, the Freed Foundation, the National Endowment for the Humanities, the National Science Foundation, the Monmouth College Grants and Sabbaticals Committee, the Fulbright-Hays Commission, and the wonderful students and alumnae of the Anthropology Department at Monmouth College financed various stages of the research, for which I am indebted. I developed some of my more global thinking while a resident at the Summer Institute on Global Education at Princeton University, organized by the Woodrow Wilson National Fellowship Foundation.

I wrote most of the book while teaching at Catholic University in Lima on a Fulbright. I have been helped immeasurably by writing in-country, and I am most grateful to the Fulbright-Hays Commission for its financial support and to my students and colleagues at Catholic University for their help.

I wrote this book in Teofilo Altamirano's home office in Lima, a pleasant place for work and reflection. I also thank him and Catholic University for the use of his computer. Luis Millones, as always, provided his help and encouragement.

I have published earlier descriptions of Quinua zonation in the *American Anthropologist*, the *Proceedings of the International Hill Lands Symposium*, and *Michigan Discussions in Anthropology*.

Peasants on the Edge

"Worse off we get, the more we got to do."

      —John Steinbeck, *Grapes of Wrath*

1.

THE TRANSFORMATION OF A PEASANT SOCIETY

MY RESEARCH in Quinua, an Andean town located in the Department of Ayacucho, Peru, began in 1966. The community has actively transformed itself since that time, a metamorphosis caused by the difficulties people have had to endure. Population has grown rapidly, but ecological and economic constraints have frustrated peasant attempts to expand farming to feed their larger families. Quinuenos have responded to these pressures by entering the nonfarm economy, becoming laborers and petty entrepreneurs, quickening their economic activity in whatever way they can. Large numbers of Quinuenos have migrated, both sending and receiving remittances.

Economic changes have led to social ones. The family is more dispersed, with members distributed widely over Peru and even foreign lands. The fiesta and peasant political systems, of fundamental importance in social organization in 1966, have altered in function and declined in importance. Almost all Quinuenos were Catholic in 1966, but many are Protestant today. Since 1980, moreover, the village has been convulsed by the violence of the Shining Path guerrillas (*Sendero Luminoso*) and subsequent government repression.

These social changes are unintended consequences of the ecological and economic forces at work in Quinua. As peasants entered the nonfarm economy, they began to divert income from providing elaborate fiestas by means of civil and religious posts known as *cargos* (a system that is well known in Latin America) to capital investments and subsistence food. Social mobility has improved for some, but not everyone has done well in the new economy. Poverty has worsened for many. The large numbers of young people educated for too few jobs have created a revolutionary climate of unfulfilled expectations.

Because the social upheaval in Quinua is similar to that in many other areas of the Third World, my analysis has wide application. Rising population growth and increased market penetration during the last quarter century have undermined many so-called traditional cultural forms in villages throughout Hispanic America and the rest of the world.

Anthropologists have generally ignored these phenomena, but we do so at our peril, for such forces are altering the world we study. It makes little sense to investigate the Andes as if the people are quaint holdovers from some Inca or pre-Inca past. They are not and we must pay attention to the dynamic forces that have created peasant life (cf. Weismantel 1988) and that are today transforming it.

The data from Quinua demonstrate the utility of materialist strategies focusing on ecology and economy to study change rather than idealist ones focusing on symbols and meanings. As we shall see, Quinuenos have transformed their lives in response to the exigencies of practical reality, modifying their beliefs and religion in the process. Peasants are not the conservative inhibitors of change sometimes depicted (e.g., Banfield 1958; Foster 1965; Harrison 1985), but rational people who adjust their behavior to the ecological, economic, and political reality around them. Such an approach has practical as well as theoretical utility. Planners and development agencies must look primarily to material reality if they are to have any impact on improving the lives of the people they want to help.

THE SETTING

Peru is extraordinarily diverse topographically and ecologically (Pulgar Vidal n.d.; Tosi 1960). The immense Andean massif is flanked by tropical forest to the east and desert coast to the west. Each of these zones is itself divided ecologically, creating a mosaic of differing climatic and vegetative zones within very short distances of one another.

Quinua lies in the Andes mountains. Most of the Peruvian sierra or highlands is too high or dry for human habitation, and the major centers of population have been located in a few semiarid plateaus or valleys since aboriginal times. Quinua and the Ayacucho Valley comprise part of what is sometimes called "the Andean trapezoid," a group of five highland departments that are among the poorest in the country. Peasants speak Quechua, chew coca leaves, and dress in what is offhandedly described as "Indian" clothing, but which is in fact derived from Spanish colonial styles (Mitchell 1987a).

The coast, a narrow flat desert, lies to the west of the sierra. Although small in size, the coast dominates contemporary Peru economically and politically. The capital of Lima is located here. Containing one-third the population of Peru, Lima produces most of the gross national product (Matos Mar 1984:59). Peasants are aware of the coast's economic dominance, and they have flocked to Lima and other coastal areas in search of work.

The third major geographical zone, the tropical forest, begins east of the sierra. Peruvians divide the tropical forest into two zones: the beginnings of the forest on the lower eastern slopes of the Andes known as the *montaña* and the tropical floor called the *selva*. Tropical forest inhabitants produce fruits, peanuts, lumber, and coca leaves. Many highland people have begun to settle in the *montaña*, colonizing areas said to have been uninhabited, but in fact populated by culturally distinct native groups. The world demand for cocaine has fueled some of this settlement; many desperately poor peasants have migrated there from the highlands to participate in growing the coca plant or the manufacture and distribution of its drug (NACLA 1989).

THE AYACUCHO VALLEY AND QUINUA

Quinua lies 34 km northeast of the city of Ayacucho, a one-hour trip by truck. The setting is spectacular mountain and valley, surely one of the world's most beautiful panoramas (see figure 1). The town sits atop a ridge on the eastern wall of the Ayacucho Valley, overlooking steep gorges and broken terrain. The city of Ayacucho (sometimes called by its old name, Huamanga) lies on the valley floor in the distance, hard to see except for the white airport runway on the edge of town that slashes the grayish earth.

To the west the steep, arid and snowless mountains of Huancavelica and the continental divide form a wall of gray, brown, red, and purple peaks. The hues change throughout the day as the sun plays on the earth's minerals, picking up different colors and illuminating areas formerly in shadow. Sunset creates a special splendor of red, pink, and purple peaks, but since the tropical sun sets very quickly, the display is all too brief. Quinuenos obtain salt, potatoes, and animal products from this area. Lima, unseen but nonetheless prominent, lies beyond these mountains. Lima is only about 175 air miles away from the city of Ayacucho, but the rugged terrain imposes a trip of about twenty-four hours in an omnibus and more than a week on foot.

Far to the north a silver band marks the Rio Cachi (Salt River) and the Huanta Valley. The Rio Cachi drains into the Rio Mantaro, which empties into the Rio Apurimac, then the Amazon and finally

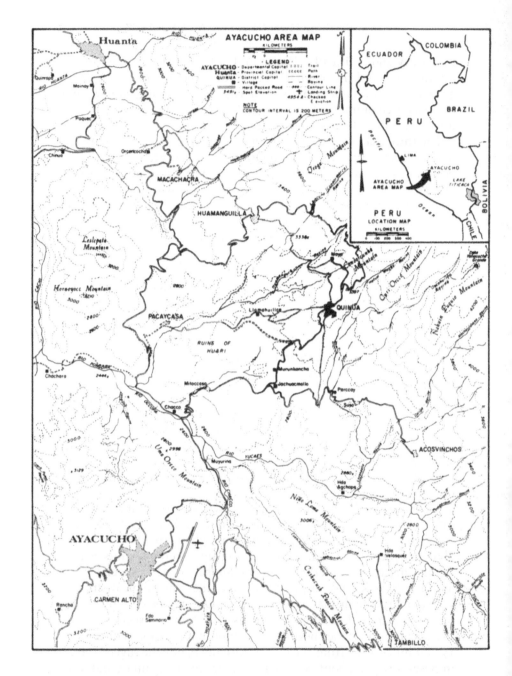

Figure 1. Ayacucho area map

Aerial view of Quinua, with the moist forest in upper portion of the photograph. (Photo of the Peruvian Servicio Aerofotográfico Nacional)

the Atlantic Ocean on the other side of the continent. The Mantaro Valley and its city of Huancayo lie north of Huanta. This economically vibrant region often provides Quinuenos with work and markets. Huancayo cannot be seen from Quinua, but its presence is nonetheless evident in the clothing, speech, and music adopted by Quinua's young. The regional music of Huancayo—"happy music" according to the listeners—has replaced the music of Ayacucho in daily listening and at most fiestas; young people are emulating the styles and music of an area seen to be progressive and exciting.

Quinua is connected to Ayacucho and the Mantaro Valley by a road (the *carretera central*) visible in the distance on the valley floor (Rivera 1971:179–189). Constructed in 1924, this dirt road was Quinua's major motor route to Lima until 1974. The trip to Lima on this road is grueling. In good traveling weather, one arrives in Huancayo (257 km) about fourteen hours after leaving Ayacucho and in Lima (258 km more) after another nine hours. In the rainy season the trip may take days. In 1974 to commemorate the Battle of Ayacucho the government paved this road and opened a new one (*la vía de los libertadores*) that connects the Ayacucho Valley to the coast at Pisco. This is a better road, but the trip to Lima (576 km) still takes about twenty-four hours in an omnibus.

To the east of Quinua, the land quickly rises to a sparsely inhabited, cold, treeless plain, broken by large igneous outcrops and highland tarns: small dark lakes that Quinuenos believe enchanted, containing spirits and the gold hidden from the Spanish conquerors. The road to the tropical forest follows this route. A traveler reaches the fertile valley and prosperous town of Tambo two and a half to three hours (when road conditions are good) after leaving Quinua in one of the trucks that ply the route. One arrives at the Rio Apurímac in the tropical forest *montaña* four to five hours later.

To the south lies the city of Ayacucho. Still farther south lie the high altitudes of Pampa Cangallo and the departments of Apurímac and Cuzco. Served by poor roads, these regions are less important sources of work for Quinuenos than Lima and Huancayo; many Quinuenos nonetheless travel to the south for trade.

Quinua is the name of both the central town and the district. The district contains some six thousand people, and the central town just under eight hundred. The town is the political, social, economic and ceremonial center for fourteen surrounding hamlets (*pagos*). The immediate environs of the town are divided into two barrios: Lurin Sayoc and Hanan[1] Sayoc, a two-fold division found throughout the Andes. The Inca capital of Cuzco was organized in a similar way.

The barrios are important residential and social divisions in Quinua. Each barrio has its own irrigation system (Mitchell 1976a) and until 1970 had separate peasant political organizations (*varayoc*).[2] The barrios are central to religious organization. They compete in giving annual religious fiestas, and each barrio has its own door to the church.

Despite its seeming isolation, Quinua has played a surprisingly central role in key events in the larger world (Mitchell 1987a). The ruins and refuse of the city of Huari, the capital of an empire that conquered much of Peru (ca. 600–1000 A.D.), covers most of the lower portion of Quinua. The ruins of an Inca fortress dating from the first half of the second millennium are found in the heights above the central town, commanding a view of the entire valley and controlling the ancient foot road linking the Ayacucho Valley to Tambo and the tropical forest.

In 1539 Quinua was the first site of the city of Ayacucho (then known as San Juan de la Frontera). The Spanish founders moved the city to the present location on the warmer valley floor two years later (Rivera Serna 1966). The Spanish left an indelible mark on Quinua and throughout the Andes, introducing new crops and animals and creating new economic, sociopolitical and religious forms (Stern 1982).

On December 9, 1824, General Sucre defeated Spanish forces on a pampa that lies above Quinua's central town. Latin Americans everywhere celebrate this Battle of Ayacucho, for it marked the final defeat of the Spanish in South America. A monument commemorating the event dominates the pampa. The battle was fought in an area of the pampa called *ayacucho* (corner of the dead), so named (or so legend tells) after an earlier battle fought there against the Inca. General Bolívar took the name of this place in Quinua and renamed the entire area the Department of Ayacucho.

While Spanish rule ended at the Battle of Ayacucho, urban domination did not. Quinua and other "native" communities continued to provide labor to the larger world, while that world dominated local production. Indeed, the Creole elite used independence to extend the hacienda system at the expense of Indian communities (Dobyns and Doughty 1976:165–168). Contemporary economic production in Quinua continues to take place in this larger regional, national, and international context. Outside forces affect local production and labor and modify local ecological and economic relationships. Quinuenos sell goods to outside markets, trading and buying over vast areas of Peru, even selling ceramics abroad. Most people born in the community are now forced to migrate, often working in the export sector and remitting money and goods to their families at home.

The city of Ayacucho is the regional center of commerce and schooling for many Quinuenos, who sometimes maintain dual residence in the town and the city. Quinuenos frequently have to travel there to arrange political, judicial, and ecclesiastical matters. The national capital, Lima, and the surrounding areas of the coast also draw Quinuenos, many of whom have lived there for years, while still maintaining fields and homes in Quinua. The city of Huancayo attracts fewer Quinuenos. In the international context the economic policies of the United States and the industrial world affect Peruvian industry and markets, and thereby the lives of Quinuenos.

The social classes of Quinua are formed in this extracommunal context. A small group of townspeople (*vecinos*) distinguish themselves from the majority of peasants (*campesinos*) (Mitchell 1979). Although sometimes expressed in racial terms of mixed blood (*mestizo*) versus Indian (*chutu*), the distinction derives rather more from political and economic control. Townspeople are not only farmers but the major merchants and school teachers. Until recently, they also had a monopoly on the necessary skills (fluency in the Spanish language, literacy, appropriate dress and bearing) to act as intermediaries with the national society. They were the district's political officials, able to manipulate their contact with the national government to maximize their own interests. Peasants, who in 1966 spoke only Quechua and were unable to read or write, were effectively excluded from this process.

These relationships have changed since 1966. Most Quinuenos go to school today. The young are bilingual. Townspeople have always maintained their status through access to commercial wealth, but new opportunities for the creation of such wealth have caused rapid changes in social status. Many of today's townspeople were once monolingual speakers of Quechua and have parents who are still unable to speak Spanish. These townspeople have altered their social status through the acquisition of schooling and wealth.

ECONOMIC AND SOCIAL CHANGES IN QUINUA

At the present time Quinua is very different from the town I found in 1966. Then nearly everyone was a farmer, engaging in some non-farm work, to be sure, but that work was much less important than it is today. There were few merchants and few people with schooling. People inside and outside of the central town obtained drinking water from the irrigation canals and lit their homes, if at all, with candles. The town was unquestionably Roman Catholic, the population devoutly celebrating village saints in the syncretic religion of the Andes with elaborate and costly fiestas. Peasants used participation in that fiesta system as an index of citizenship. Acceptance of fiesta posts (cargos) legitimized rights to land, labor, and water. Peasant political leaders helped to maintain the agricultural, political, and spiritual health of the community. Although this peasant political organization was on the decline in 1966, such leaders still organized communal work parties, maintained the irrigation system, punished people for crimes, and propitiated the saints and gods in one of the barrios. Townspeople used these political leaders and the fiesta system to appropriate peasant labor to work on public buildings, parks, irrigation canals, and other projects designed by and usually for the benefit of townspeople.

Today Quinuenos organize themselves in a very different way. The nonfarm economy is much more important in peasant production than it was in 1966. Young peasants are usually literate, unlike their parents. Most people born in the community migrate, some abandoning their fields and causing a decline in agricultural production. Those that remain have increased their cash-cropping, producing food for the growing city of Ayacucho. Others have become small capitalists, operating stores, peddling food to highway travelers, and driving small trucks to transport goods and passengers. Considerable numbers sell their labor to others, working in agriculture or as assistants to traders. Still others produce crafts, especially ceramics, for commercial sale. The commercialization of ceramics had already begun in 1966, but the number of ceramicists has jumped more than 900 percent: from less than fifty to more than five hundred. Quinua is consequently known worldwide for its ceramics, especially the little fired-clay Ayacucho churches. Quinuenos have also abandoned the fiesta system, and many have converted to Protestantism. The peasant political organization exists only in the memory of the old.

Signs of both new wealth and continued poverty are visible. Electricity lights the central town, and people there drink potable water. Some houses are more elaborate, with two stories, stucco fronts, and windows. Radios are ubiquitous and a few houses have television sets that operate on town current or car batteries. A few people own small trucks. At the same time, many have been unable to compete successfully for agricultural and nonagricultural resources. Income disparity is perhaps greater than it was before (McClintock 1983;

Wise 1986). Although most of the poorest Quinuenos flee to the cities, a hand-to-mouth existence, malnutrition, and high infant mortality are nonetheless the lot of many who remain.

THE SHINING PATH REVOLUTIONARY MOVEMENT

The Shining Path guerrilla movement well illustrates the social ferment in Quinua and Ayacucho. In May 1980, Shining Path started a war that has torn the Ayacucho area apart (Bonner 1988). The guerrillas began by hanging dead dogs on lampposts in various areas of Ayacucho (but not Quinua) and setting off explosives during the presidential elections. The fighting intensified gradually. The city of Ayacucho was terrorized in March 1982, when Shining Path staged a spectacular jailbreak, using dynamite and gunfire to free more than 300 prisoners.

In a pamphlet published in Spain, Shining Path has listed five aims (Palmer 1986; González 1986): (1) agitation and armed propaganda; (2) systematic sabotage and regular guerrilla actions to attack the symbols of the landowning bourgeoisie and state; (3) generalized guerrilla war and creation of a mass support base; (4) the conquest and expansion of the bases of support; and (5) the siege of the cities and the total collapse of the state.

Shining Path has tried to suppress cash-crop production and rural markets, hoping to disrupt food supplies to the cities (Baird 1985; Bennett 1984; DeQuine 1984; *Lima Times*, no. 416, April 15, 1983; Palmer 1986; Vargas Llosa 1983; *Wall Street Journal*, January 4, 1983). At first this tactic was partially successful (Mitchell 1986). Early in the war people sent fewer food parcels by bus from Ayacucho to Lima, but parcel volume returned to previous levels as people adjusted to the uncertainties of the war. Shining Path's opposition to nonhousehold agricultural production actually may have alienated many peasants. As we shall see, cash-cropping is an important peasant economic strategy.

Throughout the Department of Ayacucho, Shining Path has murdered political leaders, teachers, engineers, and ordinary peasants. They have threatened and killed those suspected of collaborating with the military. They have extended the war beyond Ayacucho. As many as 259 towns throughout the country were reported as without local authorities in May 1989; officials and police had fled in fear for their lives (*Lima Times*, no. 718, May 5, 1989).

The military has responded to Shining Path violence with an active counteroffensive, a "dirty war" that became especially severe in 1983, when the military routinely began to jail, torture, and kill people without a trial. In 1983 the government declared Ayacucho (and therefore Quinua) an emergency zone, a status that continues to the present. Constitutional guarantees are suspended and movement is restricted. Government is by military rule, in fact if not in name. The politico-military command in Ayacucho dominates the political process to such an extent that elected leaders have little authority (Americas Watch 1988:25–26). The central town of Quinua serves as a regional military post, and the police presence has increased from 4 men in 1966 to twenty-five to thirty men today.

The military command has also created peasant militia (*rondas campesinas*, or *montoneras*) in many communities to combat Shining Path. Quinua has refused to establish one, claiming the large police post is sufficient. Independent human rights groups (Americas Watch 1986; Amnesty International 1985:12–18) and many Quinuenos believe that these militia are vigilante groups, acting not against Shining Path but against neighbors with whom they have land disputes.

Many people have been killed in Quinua, but Quinuenos have

Plaza of the central town in 1987; note the barricades in front of the police post, one consequence of the guerrilla war.

often been uncertain of the identity of the killers. Most believe that the victims were innocent, caught in forces beyond their control. They attribute the deaths to a variety of groups: the military, guerrillas, bandits, narcotics gangs, and peasant militia from neighboring communities. The murder in 1984 of an entire family living in an isolated homestead on the prairie is blamed by some on Shining Path because a flag with a hammer and sickle was left by the bodies. Others discount the flag, saying it was a ruse, that a peasant militia had killed the family to avenge a land dispute.

Situations of political passion and arbitrary violence inevitably produce such confusion, and the uncertainty about so many of the deaths has caused some Quinuenos to attribute them to *pistacos* or *nacaq*. The belief in *pistacos* is widespread in the Andes (Ansión 1987). They are depicted as light-skinned and frequently bearded gringos[3] who kill peasants and sell their blood and rendered fat to Lima factories to run airplanes and other machinery. In September and October 1987, a rumor alleging an increased number of *pistacos* swept the Ayacucho region with terrible force. Quinuenos visiting me in Lima reported bodies found without arms, heads, or legs— clear evidence, according to them, of *pistacos*. They warned me not to visit Quinua, as people were very tense. Many people believed that the president of Peru had sold Ayacucho out to gringos (the *pistacos*) in compensation for not paying the national debt. The rumor unfortunately led to the murder of a young man from Huancayo who was suspected of being a *pistaco* (Ahora 1987; Degregori 1987); some Quinuenos claim he was actually a member of the military.

In spite of the general uncertainty, Quinuenos clearly blame the military for a number of specific deaths. Many believe the military responsible for the headless bodies that are occasionally found; they believe it is only the military who are interested in disguising their victims. They are especially suspicious about military involvement in an event early in the war. On July 16, 1984, a group of masked men entered Quinua in three trucks. They seized and tortured two young men who led them to the homes of twelve others in various parts of the district. All fourteen men were ultimately tortured and killed on a violent morning that left mutilated bodies scattered throughout the district, from the high altitude grasslands to the valley bottom. Most Quinuenos believe the masked men were the Peruvian antiterrorist forces (*sinchis*). Quinuenos say that some of the murdered youths were involved with Shining Path but that others were not. It is unclear what they mean by that involvement. The possibilities range from advocacy to active participation. One young man had the bad fortune to have been visiting his parents when the attack occurred—he neither lived in Quinua nor had anything to do with guerrillas but was nonetheless assassinated, as were the others, without a trial or any fair method to determine guilt or innocence.

Many Quinuenos, especially the young, have fled. In 1983, someone painted threats on the Quinua highway, causing several townspeople to flee to Lima. Other townspeople have settled permanently in the city of Ayacucho. Peasants have abandoned the higher altitudes for the safety of the central town, so that the high-altitude pastoral adaptation described below no longer exists. Parents have sent young sons to Lima or other areas of the coast to work or study. This has exacerbated agricultural labor shortages. Cash-crop production has diminished, although not to the extent desired by Shining Path. Tourism is nonexistent. Migrants in Lima are reluctant to visit Quinua for fiestas or agricultural work, fearful for their lives.

The situation in Quinua and Ayacucho improved temporarily after 1985. Some of the people who had fled to Lima returned, and some migrants began to travel to Quinua for agriculture and the September fiesta. Others, however, would not. One woman, who had cowered on a floor in Ayacucho as bullets flew over her head during the 1982 jailbreak, was so traumatized that she refused to leave Lima, even to visit her aged mother in Quinua. She may have been correct in her assessment. Since 1989, the situation has worsened and the violence is perhaps as great—or greater—than in 1983.

THEORIES OF CHANGE: IDEAS OR MATERIAL RELATIONS?

How do we explain the economic, political, and religious changes in Quinua? My theoretical orientation is materialist, a position proposing that ecological and economic adaptations determine the shape of a society, its social organization. Residence patterns, marriage and kinship, power relations, stratification, ideology, and religion reflect material reality. We can best explain the changes in Quinua by focusing on how the people provision themselves, how they deal with the tangible world around them: mouths to feed, work to do, expenses to meet, children to prepare for the world, governments and elites to deal with. Ideas, symbols, values, and beliefs are created and accepted by people as they work in the world and altered by them to reflect and codify these experiences. While ideas motivate the individual, evolutionary developments beyond the individual determine how widespread these ideas become.

Other social scientists answer the question of social variation (if they do so at all) by emphasizing ideas and mental structures. They collect data on myth, meaning, symbols, and beliefs, rather than births and deaths. The debate is an old one. The classic modern statement was framed by Weber, Tawney, and Robertson at the beginning of the twentieth century over the role of religious ideas in the evolution of European capitalism. Since I am concerned with the relationship between economic and religious change in Quinua, this controversy is directly relevant to my study.[4]

Max Weber (1958a [1904–05]) traced the origins of European capitalism to the ethic (or ideas) of Protestantism. His is not a simple idealist[5] argument, for he argued that the ideas of Protestantism were themselves the result of complex economic and other social forces (ibid.:183). Nonetheless, Weber viewed ideas as significant causal elements in the evolution of capitalism and considered the Puritan outlook "the most important, and above all the only consistent influence in the development" of the European "rational bourgeois economic life" (ibid.:174). This position in *The Protestant Ethic* has come to stand in the social sciences as the classic expression of the idealist position, regardless of Weber's caveats in this and other works.[6]

In *The Protestant Ethic* Weber was not concerned with the origin of motives of economic gain, which are found everywhere, but in the creation of a narrowly defined capitalism characterized by the separation of business from the household, the use of "rational bookkeeping" and "the rational capitalistic organization of (formerly) free labor" (ibid.:21–22). Sixteenth-century Calvinism and seventeenth-century Puritanism set the stage for this difficult social transformation by making thrift, hard work, and the pursuit of wealth moral obligations.

Tawney (1958 [1930], 1962 [1926]) is a sympathetic critic of the Weber thesis, but viewed it as "one-sided and overstrained" (1962 [1926]:316). Unlike Weber, Tawney emphasizes the primacy of economic forces over ideas, although he sees religion and other idea systems as facilitating the transition to capitalism. According to Tawney, incipient capitalism had developed in fifteenth-century Roman Catholic Italy and Flanders as a result of economic events, disproving any necessary association between Protestantism and capitalism. Full-scale capitalism flourished later in sixteenth- and seventeenth-century Holland and England because of the discovery of the Americas, which caused the creation of new wealth, the expansion of trade, and the rise of new social classes to political power (ibid.:66–79, 82–85, 278, 315–317). Protestantism, however, facilitated that transition.

Robertson (1959 [1933]) takes a decidedly materialist position and argues "that the spirit of capitalism has arisen rather from the material conditions of civilization than from some religious impulse" (ibid.:xvi). He criticizes Weber for overemphasizing the capitalist ideas in Calvinism and deemphasizing those in Catholicism (ibid.: 1–32). It was capitalism itself that caused both Calvinist and Catholic doctrines to become more capitalistic, not the doctrines that created capitalism.

As we shall see, the data from Quinua are consistent with the views of Tawney and Robertson. In Quinua economic changes clearly led to religious ones. Although I am not concerned with the transition to capitalism in Weber's sense (I am, after all, dealing with a peasant village), Quinua peasants have increased their participation in the cash economy and have distanced themselves from agrarian production. Many have changed their religious behaviors and values in the process, adapting their religion to facilitate the economic changes.

The Weberian emphasis on values and ideas in social change is an important contemporary position, especially in the literature on development (see DeWalt and DeWalt 1980; McClintock 1981; McKenna 1988; and Taylor 1979 for critiques of this literature). A veteran United States Agency for International Development (AID) official, for example, recently attributed Latin American underdevelopment to cultural tradition, resuscitating the "black legend" in which Spanish (as opposed to English) culture is seen as stultifying (Harrison 1985). Foster (1965) argues that the "image of limited good" inhibits peasant cooperation. Banfield (1958) stresses the atomistic nature of peasant society limiting change. Kirkby (1973) emphasizes the importance of social versus economic rationality in limiting present development of the full agricultural potential of Oaxaca, Mexico. Some authors have even evoked "blind tradition" to explain poor agricultural productivity in Peru (Christian Science Monitor, October 22, 1988; Mitchell 1988).

The contemporary idealist tradition in anthropology, however, generally emphasizes symbols, structure, and meaning (cf. Turner 1967) rather than values per se. Material reality is nonetheless often ignored or deemphasized. Sahlins (1976), in his influential book Culture and Practical Reason, for example, has argued for the primacy of symbolic meaning, even suggesting that ecological selection "originates in cultural structure" (208).

Some anthropologists currently working in the Andes employ symbolic and structural analyses. Although there are major differences between these theoretical positions, Andeanists tend to incorporate both approaches in their work without making formal distinctions between them (cf. Isbell 1978). Their work differs from mine and that of other materialists in that they focus on the role of ideas, mental structures, and the personal interpretation of events by the participants (cf. Isbell 1988 and the critique by Ferguson 1988a, 1988b).

Many of these works suffer the methodological weaknesses common to the genre. The question of falsification receives little attention, and underlying structures and meanings are often established through tortured metaphors and similes (see Keesing 1987 for an excellent critique). Some authors (Platt 1986; Rasnake 1988:205–207), for example, invoke sexual symbols without telling us if their informants agree with their interpretations or why the authors choose sexual rather than other meanings. Structuralists have variously described Andean thought as concentric (Isbell 1978), quadripartite (Platt 1986), and triangular (Harris 1986). Which is it? What do the authors mean by these terms? What does it mean "to think in squares" (Platt 1986:255)? Western culture places great emphasis on the number three (for example, in the concept of the Trinity), but Western thought is by no means triangular. Similar caution in interpretation must be applied to the Andes. While Platt is correct in calling our attention to the cultural use of four corners in the Andes, it is doubtful that it has profound significance in structuring thought. Drinking behavior (is there anything more Andean?) is by no means "quadripartite." It is a one-on-one activity that links people into a chain of dyadic acts. The ritual kinship established through godparenthood (compadrazgo) is also dyadic—not square, nor triangular, nor concentric.

Careful use of structural, semiotic, and interpretive methodology has nonetheless clarified certain underlying forms of Andean social organization. Zuidema (1986) has used symbolic meaning and structure to clarify Inca history and social organization. Weismantel (1988) similarly analyzes the meaning and associations of food to elucidate relations of gender and power in a town in Ecuador. Allen (1988), writing in an interpretive rather than an explicitly symbolic framework, provides a beautiful picture of what it is like to be a member of an Andean community, as well as to work in it as an anthropologist. Urton (1981) uses symbolic analysis to help interpret Andean cosmology. Such accomplishments, however, generally do not address the issue of causation.[7] While analysis of symbolic thought may help us understand the nature of social organization, it does not explain change and social evolution.

The issue can be phrased as a question: Are we the way we are because we have thought ourselves into this predicament or because we have both consciously and unconsciously formed these structures as a result of daily encounters with the problems of existence? Is the violence that besets Peru today the result of a breakdown in social restraints caused by rapid social change, as Allen argues (1988:212–227), or is it the result of ecological and economic forces?[8] The data from Quinua strongly support the latter, materialist approach.

CULTURAL MATERIALISM AND ECONOMIC ANTHROPOLOGY

Materialist scholars have frequently treated ecology and economy as separate phenomena, with no attempt to integrate these two analytical approaches (Halperin 1989). Ecological anthropologists, often emphasizing ecological relationships at the expense of the economy (e.g., Barth 1956; Mitchell 1976b; Rappaport 1968; Thomas 1973; Winterhalder and Thomas 1978), have employed demography, ecology, technology, and subsistence economy as explanatory variables. They have frequently regarded ownership, patterns of exchange, labor relations, and other economic phenomena as dependent variables (Harris 1979:64–65). In consequence, ecological analyses sometimes read as if they are describing isolated communities, as if local communities had no ties to the larger world system. Even Julian Steward, who emphasized technoeconomic as well as techno-environmental variables (1955), ignored the role of the economy in his classic work on irrigation civilizations (1949, 1955), a lapse that distorted his own and many subsequent analyses (Mitchell 1973).

Anthropological economics, on the other hand, has tended to treat the environment only as a commodity. Many classical works on economic anthropology in general (cf. Dalton 1967; Herskovits 1952; LeClair and Schneider 1968; Sahlins 1972; Schneider 1974) and specific works on the Andes (e.g., Long and Roberts 1978; Orlove and Custred 1980) pay little attention to the ecological realities of resource availability and environmental degradation. When environment is considered, economic anthropologists have often assigned it a minor role (Long and Roberts 1984:4; Schneider 1979). They have rarely considered population dynamics, in spite of strong theoretical reasons to do so (Carneiro 1970) and in spite of the clear empirical growth of population around the world.[9]

The separation of ecology from economy distorts reality. Some of our finest works combine both analyses (Halperin and Dow 1977).

Marvin Harris's (1974) explanation of witchcraft relies on the political economy as well as ecology. The same is true for Price's (1978) refutation of Harner's (1977) overly ecological interpretation of Aztec cannibalism. Eric Wolf has similarly employed a combined ecological and economic approach throughout his work (e.g., 1959, 1982). Annis (1987) has employed an ecological and economic approach to explain the rise of Protestantism in Guatemala, reaching conclusions strikingly similar to mine. Sometimes Andeanists have also used a combined ecological and economic approach with considerable success (Bolton 1973, 1976, 1979; Brush 1977; Caballero 1981; Collins 1988; Guillet 1979; Lehmann 1982; Orlove 1977a).

Ecological analysis ties us to place, to the realities of the local environment and resources. Economic analysis not only binds us to local communities, but forces us to look at them as parts of larger systems (Chilcote and Johnson 1983; Collins 1988; de Janvry 1981; Frank 1966; Laite 1978; Meillassoux 1981; Mitchell 1987a; Orlove 1977b; Roseberry 1983; Steward 1950; Wolf 1982). Quinua is not and has never been an isolated community. Even prior to European colonialism, Quinua and other Andean communities had been incorporated into such states and empires as Huari and the Inca, in which peasants were forced to deal with nonlocal economies, elites, and governments. In the twentieth century, Quinua production has been significantly constrained by a larger Peruvian economy dominated by exports. That context itself is formed and shaped by international capital flow and demand (de Janvry 1981; Meillassoux 1981). Since the 1940s, government policy favoring exports has tended to depress local agricultural prices, fostering rural poverty and encouraging migration. Peasants have calculated the relative returns of farm and nonfarm employment, and many have decided to enter the nonfarm economy either entirely or partially.

It is unwise to regard either the economy or ecological organization as a priori the more powerful explanatory variable. Harris and Ross (1987) are correct when they assert that all societies must adapt to their ecological bases over time. Economic relations are always a part of that adaptation, however, and Harris and Ross actually utilize economic data in their specific analyses. The relative importance of one or the other variable arises from the empirical situation. Quinua's ecology constrains production and the consequent distribution of the population along the mountain slope, but it is the external economic relationships working in tandem with local ecology that have caused people to abandon their fields and to leave them uncultivated.

POPULATION PRESSURE

Population pressure, as in biological evolution, is a significant un-derlying variable, providing the dynamic force behind social change (Blankenship and Thomas 1981; Boserup 1965, 1981; Carneiro 1970, 1988; Ferroni 1980:23; Harris 1974, 1977; Harris and Ross 1987; Johnson and Earle 1987; Lewellen 1978;[10] Mitchell 1977; Price 1982; Sanders and Nichols 1988; Sanders and Price 1968; Stone, Netting, and Stone 1990; Thomas 1973). It can be initiated by population growth or (de Janvry 1981) by a squeeze on food production and dis-tribution systems. Whatever its source, population pressure forces people into creative solutions to feed themselves and their children, stimulating changes in the economy and other social spheres.

I do not wish to assert that all social change results from popula-tion pressure—witness the alterations in American residence and family patterns that have resulted from the automobile, highway construction, and cheap gasoline. Nor is population pressure only an independent variable. Population decisions are made in an ecologi-cal and economic context that encourages certain decisions over others. Nonetheless, I contend that population pressure always leads to social change and that such transformations have created the gen-eral shape of social evolution. This pressure is manifest in the costs of making a living. As population grows or resource production and distribution are constrained by outside forces, a resource does not suddenly become unavailable, but the costs of procuring it become more expensive. The actors in the system quickly perceive these rising costs and, as a result, reassess and alter their economic decisions.

Many critics of the role of population in human social evolution (e.g., Flannery 1976:225; Hayden 1981; Isbell and Schreiber 1978; Wright and Johnson 1975; see also the *Current Anthropology* com-ments on Sanders and Nichols 1988) tend to confuse population pressure with raw population growth. Population pressure common-ly results from population growth, but the two are not the same. Pop-ulation pressure is not an ecological threshold, but an ecological-economic continuum. It refers to the entire relationship between population and resource production, not simply the number of people per hectare. Other critics (cf. de Janvry 1981:142–143; Meillassoux 1981:130, and 159, note 7) view population as a dependent rather than an independent variable: "the rural poor . . . have large families because it is economically rational for them to do so" (de Janvry 1981:142). It is certainly true that people generally reproduce for mostly rational reasons, but their reproductive decisions nonetheless have population consequences that are themselves sui generis.

Systems of landownership, land use, food distribution—not just growth in numbers—condition the adequacy of people-land ratios (Lappé and Collins 1977). Economic and political conditions can even create the situation in which a society undergoing population decline nevertheless suffers significant population pressure, a description that characterizes Ireland during the nineteenth-century potato famines. English control of land and production had pushed the peasantry onto ever smaller parcels, undermining household subsistence, even though the population was declining (Harris and Ross 1987:136; Ross 1986; see also Durham 1979). Indeed, Ireland was a net exporter of food while so many of its people were starving (Harris and Ross 1987:125–138; Ross 1986). It was the colonial tenure system in this case that caused population pressure, not population growth, although the English did use an ideology of "population growth" to exculpate their own policies (Ross 1986). Environmental degradation and war have a similar impact, and the advent of Shining Path has increased the population pressures on Quinua.

Inflation and recession can also cause population pressure. When Quinuenos lose their jobs in the cities, they sometimes return home. Those who remain in the city send fewer remittances, putting further stress on the resource base of local households. Inflation has similar effects and causes migrants to reduce remittances. At the same time, when manufactured goods rise in price faster than agricultural goods, the value of cash-cropping is reduced and peasant purchases are limited.

Population growth, moreover, is important not only in terms of sheer numbers, but also in the rapidity of that growth. Rapid population growth stresses a society's ability to absorb new members.[11] A great increase in the size of the succeeding generation or a decrease in the ecological or economic capacity of the subsistence system stresses existing structures and institutional relationships. Although these stresses may lead to economic opportunity (Easterlin 1980), they also have many deleterious consequences. Rapid population decline would create similar stress.

The population structure that stems from the pattern of births, deaths, and migration further constrains productive capacity. The sex ratio (the proportion of males to females) helps determine whether or not there are sufficient laborers for a given labor regime. The age-dependency ratio, the ratio of those under age 15 and over 65 to those aged 15 to 64, determines the productive burden of the adults.

INDIVIDUAL AND SOCIAL LEVELS OF ANALYSIS

As we analyze the role of material forces in social evolution, it is necessary to distinguish between two distinct but related levels: the individual and social (cf. Brush 1977 : 19–20). The failure of scholars to make this distinction frequently clouds causal issues, especially those dealing with the importance of individual ideas versus the material conditions of life. Like mutations in biology, ideas and individual personality are always important: they provide the raw material for the process of social evolution. What needs to be explained, however, is the differential acceptance and rejection of behaviors and ideas in social systems. It is at this level—the social and evolutionary—that ecological and economic variables are important.

Societies as such never do anything.[12] The only actors are individuals who use cultural information, transmitted to them in a particular manner, and who act in their own self-interests in transmitting information to others or in behaving in a particular fashion. Focusing on people as actors forces scrutiny of peasant decisions (Barlett 1980). People decide not only what foods to produce and consume (Johnson 1980), but what other subsistence strategies to use: to cash-crop, trade, engage in commerce, migrate, send remittances, send children to school, sponsor a fiesta.

People are motivated to take particular actions not only by their material interests (Berry 1980), but also by such phenomena as ideas, beliefs, and feelings. Individuals are often driven by such sentiments as anger, sexuality, love, and desire for personal recognition, as well as by material desires. Cultural values and ideological commitment are similarly important, sometimes motivating individuals to acts of courage, even in the face of death.

People, however, do not make decisions compulsively, blindly following ideological and emotional passions. They are constrained in so doing by ecological and economic forces often beyond their control. Material forces are most important in what Steward (1955) called the "culture core," those congeries of behaviors and beliefs associated with the subsistence and (I would add) the biological system.

Sometimes ideas do not particularly affect material interests (e.g., the belief in the Trinity), but when they do, ecological and economic conditions constantly select certain behaviors over others, causing people to change in similar directions. Heroic death carries great value to many, but it still leads to extinction. Some individuals may persist in behavior at odds with their material circumstances, but most subtly alter what they do and think in response to changed material circumstances. The Roman Catholic church vigorously opposes barrier and abortifacient contraception, but most (not all) Catholics living in the United States have come to disagree with this position, believing large families are incompatible with the expenses of rearing and educating children for a technological world.

Knowledge is important, as are values. Regulation of family size demands knowledge of effective mechanisms of birth control. Conscious knowledge gives us better control over our environment, but I have no illusions that the majority will change their views on the basis of this knowledge when it runs counter to what they perceive (or unconsciously assume) to be their material interests.

In our analyses, therefore, it is necessary to differentiate between the individual origin of an idea ("mutation") and the idea's acceptance and implementation by others ("selection" and "evolution"). I do not attempt to explain the psychology of individual behavior, but rather the evolution of institutional structure. I explore, however, the impact of material constraints at the individual level and how the Peruvian ecological and economic context has favored certain responses over others, creating fundamental social change.

THE ECOLOGICAL AND ECONOMIC FORCES IN QUINUA AND AYACUCHO

The social changes in Quinua between 1966 and 1989 cannot be explained within an idealist strategy that emphasizes values, new ideas, missionaries, revolutionary agitators, or education. Most Quinuenos in 1966 liked the fiesta system, even though they were often reluctant to accept the festival posts and consequent expenses of putting them on. Nearly all were ardent Catholics, scorning Protestant believers, and happy with my gifts of photos of Quinua saints. Today most Quinuenos look back on their past religious customs with nostalgia and regret their loss.

To determine cause we must look not to ideas and symbols but to the material factors that have forced Quinuenos to change their behaviors and beliefs. Declining infant mortality has caused population to grow; in 1981 the population was growing at such a fast rate that it would double in twenty-five years if Quinuenos did not migrate. The total population in the Andean countries may have been below pre-Columbian levels until 1970 (Super 1985). It is the recent rapid growth in population and the consequent high dependency ratios that have stressed the absorptive capacity of these countries rather than the crude population per hectare. The large number of young people, moreover, creates additional stress, for they are the age group most likely to join revolutionary movements or to engage in other acts against the established order (Easterlin 1980).

In Quinua ecological constraints limit agricultural expansion as a solution to the problems of population pressure, stimulating the expansion of nonfarm work and migration. Most of the terrain is too high and cold or too low and dry for intensive cultivation. Economic constraints limit the value of farming still further. The private system of tenure that restricts access to land and water causes some land to remain uncultivated while most peasants have too little. National and international pricing and marketing policies further squeeze the peasant. Low prices for agricultural products (a process that began in the 1940s as a result of government policies) have obliged farmers to reassess the value of agricultural versus nonagricultural work. People are consequently encouraged to migrate and work harder in wage labor, petty trades, and commerce to feed their large families. These economic behaviors require capital investments (e.g., education, clothing, stock for a small store, transportation for the migrant) that stimulate further entry into the cash system. The resulting migration and nonfarm work exacerbate the problems of labor scarcity caused by high dependency ratios, further restricting the ability of the farm economy to feed the growing population.

Extensive entry into the nonfarm economy is incompatible with the *cargo* system as it existed in Quinua. This politicoreligious system was tied to agrarian production and the local system of domination. Participation in the fiesta system and peasant political organization gave peasants rights to resources (land, labor, and water), while elites used the system to obtain peasant labor. This system began to change as peasants entered the nonfarm economy and as monetary relations came increasingly to govern resource procurement for both the elite and the peasantry. Peasants who spent vast sums on fiestas were unable to provide schooling for children and capital for investments. At the same time, population growth and worsening rural-urban terms of trade encouraged the use of cash to purchase food rather than to put on fiestas.

Protestantism provides a ready-made rationale for the new social forms. Protestants had always inveighed against fiestas and the associated drinking. It was not Protestantism, however, that led to the economic changes in Quinua (the causal sequence that Max Weber had postulated for Europe). Instead, ecological and economic forces caused Quinuenos to develop an appropriate ideology. These pressures encouraged them to either modify their Catholicism or to adopt Protestantism.

The development of the Shining Path revolutionary movement must be seen as part of similar processes. The dislocation of young people in Ayacucho is palpable. As population has grown, existing ecological and economic structures have been unable to absorb the young easily. These young have studied to obtain work that is scarce or unobtainable, exacerbating their discontent. Their training has created expectations of material wealth that most will not realize. Some have entered the cocaine trade in the Ayacucho tropical forest, but the frontier lawlessness caused by that trade has only deepened social cleavages. These factors, combined with the devastating neglect of the Department of Ayacucho by the national government until recently (McClintock 1984, 1988), have created a context in which many young people have little to lose in violently opposing the established order.

Entry into the nonfarm economy has caused Quinuenos to change not only their religion, but other customs they value. Many parents bemoan the lost respect for the old found among the educated young, even though these parents worked hard to educate their own children. As Quinuenos engage in outside trade and move to Lima, they give up chewing coca leaves, in spite of the high value placed on these leaves in the sierra (Allen 1988). Coca chewing marks them as Indian, a status category that interferes with their economic prospects, so that they abandon the behavior and adopt new values (e.g., Spanish, literacy) that increase rather than limit their access to resources.

METHODOLOGICAL CONCERNS

The focus on ecology, population, and economy as the prime factors in social change centers my ethnography. This type of study necessitates long-term research in the same community, collecting data on environment, environmental adaptations, births, deaths, crops, economic demand and supply, prices, and the allocation of labor and other resources—information crucial to the study of social evolution. I did not begin my investigation of Quinua planning to study these relationships but reached this point through an evolving research design prompted by theoretical changes in anthropology and by empirical questions raised by my own data.

I started my work in Quinua in 1966. I concentrated on social organization, emphasizing data relating to stratification, the peasant political organization, and the associated fiesta system. My interest in ecology developed later, growing out of this early work, and shaped as well by the increased ecological emphasis in anthropology and in Andean studies. I returned to Quinua in the summers (May–August) of 1973, 1974, and 1980 to gather more detailed information on farming and ecological zonation, concentrating on irrigation organization.

As I was waiting to return home after my highland trips, I interviewed Quinua migrants in Lima and other areas of the coast, taking advantage of ties already established with them in Quinua. The migrant data compelled me to think more intensely of the relationships between Quinua, its migrants, and the outside world. This intellectual process was reinforced by theoretical developments in the discipline and further intensified by the explosion of the Shining Path guerrilla movement.

In 1983 I returned to Peru for four months (April–July) to work with the migrants on the coast. I focused my research on the remittances and other relationships between the migrants and the home community. I continued research in the sierra through assistants working in the community. Travel restrictions caused by the Shining Path guerrilla war prohibited my own on-site research. I returned to Lima for a year in 1987–1988, again concentrating on migrant relationships with Quinua, but continuing highland research through field assistants.

Long-term research poses certain problems. Strategies designed to study one thing are not always adequate to study another. On each trip I gathered data on economic organization, but it was not until 1974 that I began to collect systematic statistical data on the topic. Nor was I interested in Protestantism at the beginning. Rather, I wanted to know about the "authentic" religion of household ceremonies, Catholic saints, and *cargos*. I listen in exasperation to old research tapes in which I push my informant away from the topic that interested him, his displeasure with his fiesta service, to that which interested me at the time, the nature of this service. It was only in 1987 that I began to investigate Protestantism seriously.

In spite of the problems caused by changing research strategy, there is no doubt that the strengths of long-term research far outweigh its difficulties. Time has given me close personal knowledge of many Quinuenos, allowing me an entrée into their lives that has revealed intimate details of their struggles. I have witnessed many of the changes described in this book, listening as friends spoke to me of problems on one trip and confronting their solutions on later trips. These experiences have illuminated the personal dimensions of the processes at work in Quinua in greater depth than have case histories or the typical "ethnographic present" year of research. Material obtained in one field trip, moreover, has often clarified data acquired in another. Early evasions by informants about the Catholic-linked *cargo* system, for example, became clear years later after they had openly professed Protestantism. I could not have obtained these data in the one-year synchronic study typical of most anthropological research.

I was never content with my earliest understandings of Quinua, and only the interwoven strands of time, research, and theory have provided more satisfying answers. If I were to design my research looking backward, I would have collected certain types of information from the beginning, but as I did not, I am compelled to use differing types of material from differing time periods in my argument. Each strand of data, however, supports the hypothesis that Quinuenos have responded to population stress in a circumscribed environment through the expansion of nonfarm activities, which in turn has caused them to alter their religious behaviors and beliefs.

THE STRUCTURE OF THE BOOK

I explore Quinua's ecological, economic, and socioreligious evolution in the following chapters. Chapter 2 establishes the ecological limits on production in Quinua and describes Quinua's population dynamics, establishing the underlying motivation for many of the changes in the community. Chapter 3 describes the differential access to resources that constrains production. Chapter 4 analyzes how Quinuenos use their ecological and social resources to produce food. Most Quinuenos have too little land for subsistence production, encouraging their participation in the nonfarm economy.

Chapter 5 describes the economic organization of Quinua in 1966 (and earlier). Even at this time Quinuenos were not self-sufficient, so they engaged in lively exchange among themselves and with the outside world. The chapter concludes with a brief review of the outside economic forces that have constrained the Quinua economy since the 1940s, encouraging Quinuenos to enter nonfarm work. Chapter 6 describes Quinua's response to its ecological and economic pressures. Quinuenos have come to participate in wage work and the cash economy to such an extent that the current economy is very different from the one I found in 1966.

The intensification of nonfarm work has undermined traditional religious organization. Chapter 7 describes the religious system in 1966, while chapter 8 analyzes the changes that led to the decline of the *cargo* system and to the rise of Protestantism. Chapter 9 is very important to my study for it uses family history to show how individuals adjusted to the ecological and economic constraints they encountered as they coped with the large size of their families and with outside economic pressures. In chapter 10 I conclude my argument with a summary of the evidence.

My case rests on its consistency and on its ability to interpret the evidence with parsimony. The many tables interspersed throughout the text and the appendixes provide the substantiating data. For the sake of clarity I have tried to make it possible to read the exposition without referring to these tables, but they are the warp supporting my reasoning.

2.

POPULATION GROWTH AND ECOLOGICAL LIMITS

SINCE THE 1940S Quinua's population has grown very rapidly. Women with eight or ten living children are not uncommon. At least one old woman does not know the names of her grandchildren, not because she is forgetful but because she has almost fifty of them scattered throughout Peru and even four in foreign lands. Most of these children are unable to live as farmers like their parents.

Quinuenos have been unable to expand their agricultural production to accommodate this population increase. The austere beauty of Quinua is the visual expression of a harsh and severely circumscribed environment: farming is impossible in most of the Ayacucho Valley and difficult in the rest. Equatorial sunshine permits agriculture at heights greater than in most other areas of the world, but the cold at these high altitudes shortens the growing season and thus limits what can be planted. Low elevations are warmer, but their aridity makes them difficult to settle or farm. Irrigation is essential for most crops, but there is not enough water to farm the low altitudes to their full potential. Soil and climate constrain agriculture still further. Most of the soils are impossible to work in the dry season, as they are as hard as stone. The seasons alternate between wet and dry, restricting farming to a narrow band of time.

Quinuenos have responded to these ecological problems (and the economic ones described in succeeding chapters) by expanding their nonfarm economy. Faced with the choice of developing new strategies of production or starving, most Quinuenos have supplemented or replaced subsistence agriculture with permanent migration, increased cash-cropping, craft production, petty commerce, and other types of work. Others have rejected existing socioeconomic structures and have sought relief in such revolutionary movements as Shining Path.

QUINUA'S POPULATION GROWTH

The increase in Quinua's population is dramatic. In 1960 the population was increasing at an annual growth rate of 1.2 percent (table 1). This itself is a high rate of increase, with a population doubling rate of 58 years. Since that time, however, population stress has increased even more. In 1980 the annual growth rate had jumped to 2.8 percent, a doubling rate of only 25 years.

Declining mortality is the major cause of Quinua's population growth. The death rate has fallen from 18.1 deaths per thousand population in 1960 to 14.5 in 1980 (table 1). I do not have data on the specific factors causing the general mortality decline; indeed, the whole topic of Andean mortality awaits specific investigation. Nonetheless, some patterns are illuminating.

Reductions in deaths from infectious diseases have been the most important cause of declining mortality throughout Latin America (Merrick 1986:12–13). This is probably true for Quinua as well. Health care has improved over the last forty years, even if it is still woefully inadequate. Quinuenos still rely on traditional curing practices (using guinea pigs, coca leaves, and herbal remedies), but in the 1940s a few began to travel to the city of Ayacucho for occasional medical care when they had not responded to traditional techniques. Today many more travel to Ayacucho to see a physician or more commonly to buy medicines (freely available over the counter) after some self-diagnosis. I know of at least two monolingual Quechua speakers who wear corrective glasses, one of them having done so after surgery for cataracts. Quinuenos also receive medicines from migrant children and other kin on the coast and elsewhere. (I once received a prescription in the United States from my adopted mother—a Quechua-speaking peasant—requesting me to fill it and send her the medicine.) A government medical extension agent (*sanitario*) opened an office in Quinua in the early 1950s. He was the first person to give antibiotic injections. Today several traditional curers (*curanderos*) in Quinua not only cure with guinea pigs and coca leaves but also administer antibiotics.[1] The health care worker was replaced by a doctor and several nurses in 1974. Although Quinuenos complain that these practitioners are often absent from their posts, they provide more medical care than had previously been available.

Table 1. *Quinua Birth and Mortality Rates, 1940–1980*

	Births and Deaths per Thousand Population			
	1940	*1960*	*1970*	*1980*
Birth rate	12.6	30.5	41.8	42.0
Mortality rate	—	18.1	22.6	14.5
Annual growth rate (%)	—	1.2	1.9	2.8

Source: Crude births and deaths obtained from the municipal records, District of Quinua; total population derived from the nearest national census: 1940, 1961, 1972, and 1980.

The principal causes of death in the Province of Huamanga (roughly the "county" to which Quinua belongs) are respiratory and intestinal ailments (Ministerio de Salud, *Boletin de Defuncciones*, 1960–1982), data which hold true for Quinua and elsewhere (Way 1976). Infant diarrhea and consequent fluid loss are also common and are probably a major killer of the young. This diarrhea and other infections may be spread through a contaminated environment and contaminated water supplies.

Quinuenos die more frequently in the dry season. Data gathered at five-year intervals between 1955 and 1985 indicate that 247 people died in the rainy season (December through May), 361 during the dry season (June through November), an increase of almost 50 percent.[2] This large number of deaths in the dry season is surprising, since it reverses a pattern found in Nuñoa, where the abundance of food from the harvest results in fewer dry-season deaths (Way 1976). It is also a period when many people are away from the community, working as temporary migrants, so that the total population is smaller.

Quinua's higher death rate during the dry season may result from the total lack of rain in that period. Rain has two cleansing functions in Quinua: it washes away the contamination around houses and dilutes very contaminated water supplies. Although Quinuenos sweep each day, sweeping does not clean as effectively as rain. Infants and children touch what is probably very contaminated earth in the house patio, since barnyard animals roam freely there and other infants with diarrhea may have defecated there.[3]

Additionally, during the dry season, the supply of drinking water outside of the central town comes from irrigation water stored in cisterns. This supply is polluted by fecal runoff from field privies. Quinuenos contaminate the system further by bathing and washing their clothes in the irrigation canals, even on Sunday, which is the day that water is supposed to be reserved for drinking. Peasants try to bring drinking water down the canals in the night or early morning to avoid the worst dirt, but they cannot avoid all contamination. In the rainy season, the water in the cisterns is supplemented by rain, which dilutes the contamination and may result in fewer deaths. Dirty water is a frequent complaint of Quinuenos (in my investigation of the irrigation system, informants in the lower reaches of the canals would sometimes spontaneously point out the contamination to me), but they lack the resources needed to change the situation.

The highest mortality rate has been among children; 50.1 percent of the deaths between 1955 and 1985 were of children under five years of age (table 2). Children have consequently shown the most dramatic decline in mortality. In 1955 there were 241 deaths of children under five years of age for every 1000 births; this figure had plummeted to 100 in 1985 (table 3). This decline in childhood mortality is confirmed by informants: younger women have had fewer children die than older women at comparable life stages.

Table 2. *Quinua Mortality by Sex and Age: Total Deaths at Five-Year Intervals, 1955–1985* [a]

Age (years)	Male	Female	Total	%	Sex Ratio [b]
Under 1	88	76	164	26.5	1.16
1–4	77	69	146	23.6	1.12
5–9	12	9	21	3.4	1.33
10–19	10	12	22	3.6	0.83
20–29	10	10	20	3.2	1.00
30–39	5	12	17	2.7	0.42
40–49	12	8	20	3.2	1.50
50–59	16	9	25	4.0	1.78
60+	72	108	180	29.1	0.67
Age unreported	1	3	4	0.6	0.33
Total	303	316	619	99.9	0.96

Source: Municipal death records, District of Quinua.
[a] Data collected for the years 1955, 1960, 1965, 1970, 1975, 1980, and 1985.
[b] Males divided by females; the sample size is too small for reliable sex ratios between the ages of 5 and 59.

Table 3. *Childhood Mortality Rate: Deaths per 1,000 Births, District of Quinua, 1955–1985*

Age at Death	1955	1960	1965	1970	1975	1980	1985
Under 1	124	160	101	147	106	104	54
0–4 years	241	368	165	325	167	161	100

Source: Municipal records, District of Quinua.

Quinuenos have adopted ideological beliefs that help them deal with this high infant mortality; they say that the death of a child is a "happy" event because the child goes directly to heaven, bypassing this unhappy life on Earth. People dance and drink at a child's funeral, but parents nonetheless usually cry, especially for older children.

Male mortality has declined along with infant mortality. Until recently, more males died than females in nearly every age group (table 2; cf. Brush 1977: 39). I suspect this differential mortality by gender results from varied causes. Women prepare food and control its distribution and may be better nourished (Weismantel 1988: 100). Women have sometimes offered me bits of meat and told me not to tell their absent husbands about the food. My wife sitting in the kitchen with the women sometimes received better food at fiestas than I or the other men did. Men also travel, which places them at greater risk of death by accident, an important cause of Andean mortality. They also drink harder.

This gender differential in mortality has narrowed in recent years. Between 1960 and 1985, 34 percent fewer men died compared to only 4.3 percent fewer women. Greater male migration—and their increased access to cash and medical care—might partly explain this more rapid decline in male mortality. Reduced male alcohol consumption, associated with the advent of Protestantism, might be another factor.

The birth rate has increased at the same time that mortality has declined. It has jumped from 30.5 births per thousand population in 1960 to 42.0 per thousand in 1980 (table 1); there were 59.5 percent more births in 1985 than in 1960.

The increase in births results from the large number of young people rather than from increased fertility; a large childbearing cohort continues to produce large numbers of births, well after their fertility has declined, because the cohort is so large. Evidence suggests that fertility has actually declined in Quinua over the last several years. The fertility rate (the average number of births per childbearing woman) for all of the Department of Ayacucho has fallen from 7.4 in 1975 to 6.0 in 1984 and 5.8 in 1987 (Peru 1983:8; Peru 1984:52, 60; Peru 1986:13; Peru 1987:10–11), a trend that Quinuenos share. The 1987 data for Ayacucho are similar to the fertility rate of 5.62 for one Quinua hamlet in the same year.

I did not formally research birth control and pregnancy, but even in 1966 I encountered many men interested in limiting the size of their families (cf. Collins 1983). One man, unable to obtain birth control devices in the city of Ayacucho, was suspected by his neighbors (who had not known about his interest in birth control) of beating his pregnant wife to abort the fetus. Quinuenos also included several herbal abortifacients in their pharmacopeia in 1966.

Data for Nuñoa (a highland community in the Department of Puno) show that children between six and eighteen produce more food energy than they consume (Thomas 1973:16). The decline in Quinua fertility is probably a response to nonfood costs, especially in education, and to the declining value of per capita farm labor caused by increased family size. It is unlikely, however, that natality will fall to replacement levels: significant benefits accrue from migrant remittances, benefits that offset some of the costs of raising children.

The consequences of increased birth rates and declining mortality rates are graphically portrayed by the rapid increase in the ratio of births to deaths between 1955 and 1985 (table 4). In 1955, 1.75 Quinuenos were born for every one who died. This figure soared to 3.33 in 1985, a spectacular increase. These figures illustrate the great pressures newborns and their parents face. Scarce resources become even scarcer, and farmers are forced to find creative solutions to feed themselves and their families.

Table 4. *Ratio of Births to Deaths, District of Quinua, 1955–1985*

	1955	1960	1965	1970	1975	1980	1985
Births	145	163	218	231	227	249	260
Deaths	83	97	70	125	80	86	78
Ratio births/ deaths	1.75	1.68	3.11	1.85	2.84	2.90	3.33

Source: Municipal records, District of Quinua.

POPULATION STRUCTURE

Quinua's population dynamics have created a population structure with large numbers of young people and an overrepresentation of adult women compared to men. The age-dependency ratio is very high: 47.3 percent of the population was under 14 years of age in 1981 (table 5). The excess population migrates. Individuals generally leave between the ages of 15 and 25. Entire families sometimes leave together, abandoning their homes. Data on home occupancy show that the number of unoccupied houses has increased dramatically from 0.9 percent in 1961 through 6.8 percent in 1972 to 17.2 percent in 1981 (Peru 1966, 1974, 1983).

Out-migration has a number of singular consequences. It is reflected in the affective life of the people. Quinuenos and other Ayacuchanos often sing of lost lovers and family, "orphaned birds" who have left the "oppressive claws" of Ayacucho poverty. The "national anthem" of Ayacucho ("*Adiós Pueblo de Ayacucho*") laments this loss of home.

Migration has also left Quinua without enough young men, creating persistent labor shortages. Men migrate more frequently than women. Beginning with age 15 there are more females than males in the community (table 5). In 1981 there were 41 percent more women than men between the ages of 20 and 39 living in Quinua. There is a corresponding increase of males over females in the areas of the

Table 5. *Quinua Age and Sex Structure, 1981*

Age (years)	Men No.	Men %	Women No.	Women %	Total No.	Total %
0–4	477	50.5	468	49.5	945	15.9
5–9	512	50.4	503	49.6	1,015	17.1
10–14	475	55.9	374	44.1	849	14.3
15–19	264	49.7	267	50.3	531	9.0
20–24	138	42.9	183	57.1	321	5.4
25–29	114	40.0	171	60.0	285	4.8
30–34	101	43.7	130	56.3	231	3.9
35–39	104	39.4	160	60.6	264	4.5
40+	628	42.2	860	57.8	1,488	25.1
Total	2,813	47.4	3,116	52.6	5,929	100

Source: Peru 1983.

coast to which Quinuenos migrate in large numbers. The rural and working-class areas surrounding the city of Lima contained the startling ratio of 125 men to 100 women in 1961. This figure declined to 111 men to 100 women in 1981 (Maletta et al., n.d., vol. 1:48, 60), probably because at that time single men from throughout the highlands were migrating to the tropical forest *montaña* instead of the coast. The excess of adult females vis-à-vis males is a common one in the Andes, although not always as pronounced as that in Quinua (Brush 1977:38–39).

Migration and the gender imbalance in Quinua continue an ancient pattern (cf. Long and Roberts 1984:113–115; Stern 1982:38 and passim). Inca and pre-Inca peoples sent colonists (*mitimaes*) throughout their empires. The Spanish utilized a forced-labor tribute (*mita*), which caused large-scale population movements. Women commonly outnumbered men in the colonial period (Morner 1985:99). The inspection visit (*visita*) to Quinua made for Viceroy Toledo in the sixteenth century (conducted sometime between 1550 and 1575) reported 2,119 male Indians of all ages and 3,022 females, 43 percent more women than men (Cook 1975:270). What is new is the rapid population increase within a short period of time that has encouraged large numbers of people (especially men) to leave their homes and travel to the cities.

Because of outmigration Quinua has grown less rapidly than the province of Huamanga (of which Quinua and the city of Ayacucho are a part) or Peru (table 6). Between 1876 and 1981, Quinua's population increased 71 percent. Huamanga's increased 312, Peru's 531, and Lima's an astounding 3,333 percent. Quinua's total population of 6,139 in 1986 is only 19.4 percent greater than the population of 5,141 Indians reported in the sixteenth-century inspection visit of Viceroy Toledo (Cook 1975:270). This pattern is found throughout Peru. Emigrating villagers have kept local communities small in spite of high fertility rates, while the cities have grown uncontrollably.[4]

ECOLOGICAL CONSTRAINTS ON AGRICULTURAL PRODUCTION

Quinua's population has grown rapidly, but farmers have been unable to expand production to accommodate their larger families. Ecological constraints of moisture, temperature, and sunshine limit agriculture to only part of the year and to only 12.2 percent of the terrain, of which only a small proportion (the irrigated maize zone) supports dense populations. Although Quinuenos herd animals in sparse-

Table 6. Comparative Population Increase, 1876–1981

	1876	1940	1961	1972	1981	% Increase
Quinua (district)	3,478	5,649	5,348	5,522	5,929	71
Huamanga (province)	31,228	61,207	69,779	97,166	128,813	313
Ayacucho (department)	142,205	358,991	410,772	457,441	503,392	254
Lima (city)	120,994	562,885	1,632,370	2,981,292	4,154,161	3,333
Peru	2,699,945	6,207,967	9,906,746	13,538,208	17,031,221	531

Source: Peru 1878, 1966, 1974, 1983.

ly cultivated areas, animal herding supports far fewer people than does farming. Quinuenos would require new sources of water to enlarge their productive land in any significant way.

Quinua and the Ayacucho Valley experience two major seasons: a dry season (*chiraw uku*)[5] and a rainy season (*para uku*) (Rivera 1967; 1971 : 37–45; see figure 2). The rainy season generally begins in December, continues with heavy rain through February, and gradually diminishes until it ends sometime in April. Rain usually falls every day, although the amount varies from year to year. In some years old houses collapse from heavy rainfall, while in others crops fare poorly from the lack of rain.

The dry season begins in May, although light rain may still fall from time to time. Rainfall decreases gradually until July and August when there is no rain at all. It begins to rain again very lightly in September and increases in intensity until the dry season ends in November.

The seasons determine temperature as well as precipitation. The dry season, especially June and July, is the coldest period (see table 7;[6] Rivera 1967, 1971 : 30–37). Day-night temperature variation is greater than seasonal variation (Troll 1968), however, and the crucial figures for plant growth in table 7 are the minimum nighttime temperatures. Even though daytime temperatures can be quite high in the dry season, the frost that occurs at night inhibits the growth of many crops.

Altitude also influences temperature; generally, the higher the altitude, the colder the climate. Temperature decreases 0.6°C for every 100 m of altitude in the Ayacucho region (Rivera 1967, 1971). The cold temperature at high altitudes retards plant growth, so crops mature more slowly. Because the growing season (i.e., the period of frost-free nights) is short, farmers grow only the most frost-resistant crops in high regions. The warmer low altitudes favor a greater variety of crops, although the valley bottom is sometimes affected by temperature inversion. Because cold air is denser than warm air, it sometimes accumulates in the valley bottom at night. The warm air rises, warming the slopes but leaving the valley bottom cold. Nonetheless, average temperatures in the valley are much warmer than those in the upper altitudes.

High altitudes are cloudy and moist, as well as cold. High areas are characterized by low evapotranspiration potentials, although these are not as low as those proposed by Tosi (Frére et al. 1975 : 133; Knapp 1988 : 28–29, and personal communication September 14, 1989). High elevations are more moist largely because of rain. Annual precipitation in the high altitudes is nearly double that found

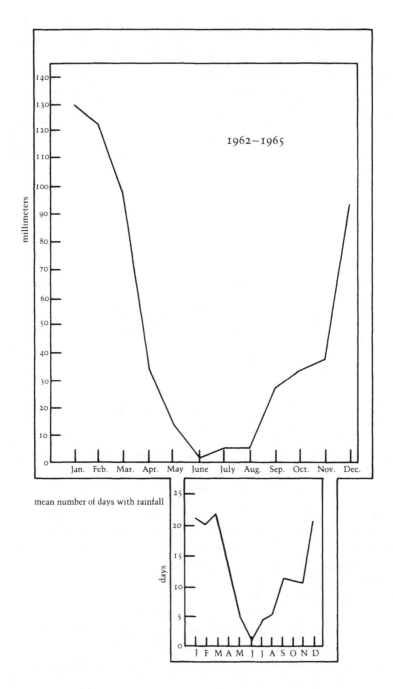

Figure 2. Mean annual rainfall in the City of Ayacucho

Table 7. *Mean Temperature in the City of Ayacucho,*
1962–1966

| Month | Degrees Centigrade | | |
	Average Temperature	Absolute Maximum	Absolute Minimum
January	15.6	27.0	7.0
February	15.2	25.4	7.0
March	14.6	25.2	6.2
April	14.9	26.3	3.4
May	14.2	25.6	2.2
June	12.4	25.0	−0.2
July	13.0	25.4	−0.5
August	14.1	26.6	1.4
September	15.0	27.1	4.3
October	16.1	27.8	4.6
November	16.6	29.6	4.7
December	16.0	28.0	5.9

Source: Rivera 1967.

lower down—500–1000 mm per year compared to 250–500 mm (Arnold 1975; Holdridge 1947; Tosi 1960; Tosi and Voertman 1964). Because of the increased rain and low evapotranspiration potentials, it is likely that soluble nutrients are leached from the soil in high altitudes, leaving fertility reduced. Further down the mountain slope, there is more sun. There are fewer clouds and these usually dissipate earlier in the day than in the upper altitudes. This augmented sunlight and heat encourage crop maturation, but the reduced moisture significantly restricts the crops that can be grown without irrigation. Quinua ceramicists also report that the soils in low altitudes have less clay than those in high ones.

THE VERTICAL ECOLOGY

The way in which Quinuenos adapt their productive activities to the altitudinal variations in temperature, moisture, and sunshine creates six vertical ecological zones (Arnold 1975; Mitchell 1976a, 1976b, 1980; see figure 3).[7] These zones are differentiated not only by vegetative characteristics but also by human behavior (Mayer 1977, 1985). They are technoenvironmental zones.[8] The zones in Quinua correspond to what Brush (1977:11) has labeled the "compressed type" of Andean vertical adaptation. They are closely spaced and

Figure 3. Quinua ecological zones

contiguous environmental zones in a steep gradient that can be traversed in a relatively short period of time.[9]

Quinuenos adapt their agropastoral production to specific ecological zones. They devote the highest zones (tundra, subalpine wet paramo, the prairie, and the moist forest) to herding. Farming is possible only in the lower portions of these high altitudes, but it is limited and supplemental to stock raising. Ecological conditions are more propitious to farming in lower altitudes, especially in the savannah and valley bottom, where stock raising is incidental to farming.

Quinua does not have glaciated peaks, and the highest ecological zone, popularly called the *puna* in Peru, is the alpine rain tundra/subalpine wet paramo (4,100 m+). Small in area, this zone consists of only the peaks that jut upward from the prairie. It is very cold, moist, and cloudy: too cold for tree growth but warm enough for the characteristic bunch grasses (*Festuca* spp., *Calamagrostis* spp.,

Stipa spp.)[10] and other low, frost-resistant vegetation. Uncultivated and uninhabited, the paramo was utilized for herding animals by inhabitants of the prairie prior to 1983. In that year the inhabitants of all zones above the savannah were forced to flee these zones in order to escape the depredation of Shining Path and the military. Therefore, the description of the paramo, prairie, and moist forest depicts the situation before 1983. (See Flannery et al. 1989 for another description of the high altitude areas above Quinua.)

The prairie (4,000–4,100 m) lies immediately below the paramo. Although still above the timberline, it is warmer, and farmers can plant bitter potatoes (*Solanum* spp.) in its upper regions. These potatoes are used only to prepare the freeze-dried potato known as *chuño*. Lower in the same zone farmers plant other potato varieties (including the white potato) and the Andean tubers known as *mashua* (*Tropaeolum tuberosum* R.&P.), *oca* (*Oxalis tuberosa* Mol.), and *olluku* (*Ullucus tuberosus* Loz.). Although relatively unknown outside of the Andes (except for the white potato), these tubers have been an important part of the Andean diet since prehistoric times. The restricted crop repertoire in this zone eliminates the possibility of significant rotation to regenerate the soil. Farmers therefore rely on long fallow periods, which vary in duration from five to seven years for every two years of cultivation, although farmers can shorten this period by applying fertilizer. The resulting large extension of fallowed fields favors animal herding—the major activity in this zone. The prairie is one of Quinua's largest areas and forms the high plain that connects Quinua to the Tambo Valley to the east.

Further down the mountain slope is the moist forest (3,400–4,000 m). Although small in area, it is warmer than the paramo and prairie and produces most of the district's tubers: potatoes, *mashua, oca,* and *olluku*. Farmers also plant such short-growth, frost-resistant crops as wheat (*Triticum* sp.), broad beans (*Vicia faba* L.), barley (*Hordeum* sp.), peas (*Pisum sativum* L.) and the *almidon* variety of quinoa (*Chenopodium quinoa* Willd.). Because the moist forest is steep and rocky with poor and shallow soils, much of it is uncultivated. The long fallow period (up to five years for every three years of cultivation) favors the growth of stunted trees, shrubs, and other underbrush.

This vegetation provides materials for basketmaking, fuel, and culinary and medicinal herbs, but at the same time it creates hazards for agricultural production by providing a habitat for birds, deer, and other predators of domesticated plants. This predation constrains farmers' choices, and they prefer not to plant barley here because the birds inhabiting the brush consume much of the grain. A eucalyptus plantation begun by the peasant community under a government forestation program in 1963 now covers much of the lower portions of the zone.

The warm and fertile savannah (2,850–3,400 m), lying below the moist forest, is Quinua's major agricultural region. It has the largest percentage of land under cultivation, much of it irrigated and cropped annually. Quinuenos plant their major staples here: maize (*Zea mays* L.), beans (*Phaseolus vulgaris* L.), squash (*Cucurbita* spp.), potatoes, wheat, barley (*Hordeum* sp.), oats (*Avena sativa* L.), quinoa, and peas.

The exceedingly dry thorn steppe (2,500–2,850 m) lies below the savannah. Very warm and sunny, this zone receives less rainfall than upper elevations, and the soil is too dry to be irrigated with water from the present irrigation system. Crops are therefore limited to those with low water needs: wheat, *hawkina* (a type of squash, *Cucurbita* sp.), peas, chick peas (*Cicer arietinum* L.), and barley. At times when the rains begin early and appear to be especially abundant, farmers will sometimes plant such water-sensitive crops as quinoa, *achita*, and maize (particularly the *uchuy morocho* variety). They do this infrequently, however, because of the risk of crop failure. They prefer to plant wheat and obtain maize or quinoa through barter or sale. Many areas of the thorn steppe are too rocky to be cultivated. The archeological site of Huari is located here, and much of the zone is covered with refuse from that site.

The lowest ecological zone is the valley bottom (ca. 2,500 m). Its natural vegetation is the same as that found in the thorn steppe, but land use differs because abundant irrigation water from the Rio Chacco permits Quinuenos to cash-crop green vegetables and fruits throughout the year. This cash-cropping, of course, is favored by close proximity to the city of Ayacucho.

Crop specialization is an important aspect of agricultural adaptation to the mountain ecology, and farmers plant different species and varieties in each altitude zone (cf. Brush 1977:80–82). Farmers choose from twenty named varieties of maize, planting most in the savannah and a few in the thorn steppe. They plant nearly fifty varieties of potatoes in the moist forest and prairie and eight varieties in lower altitudes. Most of the cultigens found in the district exhibit similar varietal specialization.

Quinua plant zonation is not simply a result of environmental constraints. Quinuenos also base the decision to plant certain foods in particular zones on such factors as the analysis of relative costs, yields, market conditions, labor availability, and cultural prefer-ences. Climate, for example, favors maize production in both the savannah and valley bottom, but Quinuenos grow most maize only in the savannah. In the valley bottom, they have abandoned maize production in favor of the more profitable cash-crop production of vegetables for the city of Ayacucho. Farmers plant maize preferen-tially in the savannah because they value maize as a food (it is in-deed an important source of energy and protein); they use the grain to make maize beer, an indispensable beverage at festive work groups and all ceremonies. Because of its nutritional and cultural importance, maize makes an ideal trade crop for foodstuffs from other altitude zones. Maize is also one of the most salable crops grown in the savannah. Moreover, because maize can be planted in only a very restricted ecological zone, farmers prefer to devote that zone to maize rather than to plant it with such crops as potatoes that can be grown elsewhere. They also consider labor demands; maize requires less labor than potatoes. Finally, irrigation in the savannah raises the altitude limit of maize production and minimizes risk, further encouraging maize production in this zone.

SETTLEMENT AND POPULATION

The productive potential of Quinua is directly related to the vertical ecology, and this potential in turn influences the distribution of people in the district. In the agricultural census of 1972, 57.6 per-cent of the terrain consisted of pasture and 23.7 percent of moun-tains and woods. Only 12.2 percent of it was classified as farmland, a figure which probably overstates its extent, since uncultivated land is often poorly defined (table 8).[11] The distribution of population

Table 8. *Quinua Land Use, 1972*

	Hectares[a]	%
Natural pasture	10,561.35	57.6
Mountains and woods	4,345.26	23.7
Farms	2,231.44	12.2
Tree plantations	20.88	0.1
Other	1,176.73	6.5
Total	18,335.66	100.1

Source: Peru 1972: 466.
[a] Figures as given in the census.

Table 9. *Settlement and Population by Ecological Zone, District of Quinua, 1961*

	Settlements		Houses	Inhabitants		Average Settlement Size
	No.	%	No.	No.	%	
Prairie	1	1.3	5	26	0.5	26
Moist forest	3	3.8	26	112	2.1	37
Savannah	55	69.6	1,165	4,482	83.8	81
Thorn steppe	8	10.1	84	316	5.9	40
Valley bottom	6	7.6	65	315	5.9	52
Unknown	6	7.6	25	97	1.8	16
Total	79	100	1,370	5,348	100	68

Source: Peru 1966: 345–347, and informant interviews.

throughout the district parallels these land-use patterns. Existing technoenvironmental adaptations favor dense settlements only in the savannah, a very small portion of the district.

The rain tundra and paramo zones are too cold for human habitation; thus the prairie is the highest inhabited zone. The limited agropastoral production of this zone (herding combined with long-fallow farming of a restricted range of crops), however, supports few people. In 1961 the prairie contained only one settlement and 26 inhabitants, or 0.5 percent of the population (table 9).[12] The moist forest is slightly more productive than the prairie, with a corresponding increase in population density. In 1961 there were three settlements with an average of 37 inhabitants each, or 2.1 percent of the district's population.

The irrigated savannah, Quinua's most productive zone, is the most densely populated. In 1961, 83.8 percent of the district's inhabitants lived here in fifty-five settlements. The average settlement size of 81 people is by far the highest in the district. This dense population is not only a product of environment, but of adroit human adaptation to the environment. Quinuenos locate savannah settlements at a border with the moist forest (cf. Brush 1977: 82) or thorn steppe. This permits simultaneous exploitation of two ecozones and thereby substantially increases carrying capacity. The location of the central town in the upper savannah near the moist forest, for example, allows the inhabitants access to tubers and pasture as well as to maize. The energy invested in irrigation, moreover, modifies the microclimate and provides water for both farming and household use.

The thorn steppe is sparsely populated because water is generally unavailable in this zone during the dry season. Only 5.9 percent of the 1961 population lived here in eight sparsely populated settlements (average size of 40), situated near the limited permanent supplies of water. The zone is exploited primarily by inhabitants of adjacent ecozones, who must bring drinking water to their fields in pots during the dry season and dig cisterns to collect rainwater in the rainy season.

The irrigated valley bottom is the secondmost densely populated ecozone (average settlement size of 52), but because the valley is narrow, the total population is small. In 1961 the valley bottom contained only six settlements and 5.9 percent of the district's population.

Quinuenos are seriously constrained by the above ecological considerations. They can do little to increase agropastoral production given their current technological and economic adaptations. A comparison of the growth in population of rural and town Quinua supports the contention that Quinuenos have been living close to the maximum population density allowed by their agropastoral adaptation. Between 1961 and 1981 the rural areas have increased only 7.6 percent, while the central town nearly doubled in size (table 10). In spite of a soaring birth rate the rural areas are unable to support a

Table 10. *Comparative Population Increase, Rural and Urban Quinua, 1876–1986*

	1876	1940	1961	1972	1981	1986	% Increase 1961– 1986
Central town	200	824	394	465	745	778	97.5
Rural hamlets	3,278	4,825	4,954	5,057	5,184	5,361	7.6
Total	3,478	5,649	5,348	5,522	5,929	6,139	14.8

Source: Peru 1878, 1948, 1966, 1974, 1983; the 1986 figures are from the *listado de establecimientos de salud*, Ministerio de Salud. I discount the 1940 figures because the figures are too high, even after one takes into account that the census combined the data for the hamlets of Lurin Sayoc and Hanan Sayoc with those for the central town; informants report a consistent increase in the size of the central town, not a decline.

significantly larger population. Although rural peasants have intensified many aspects of their nonfarm economy, they have not done
so to the same extent as the urban area, and the rural area continues
to lose proportionally more of its population to the cities. The nonfarm economy of urban Quinua has permitted a more rapid growth
in local population.

The ecological constraints found in Quinua are widespread in the
sierra. In 1972 only 5 percent of all sierra lands were cultivated and
32 percent used for pasture (Caballero 1981 : 63–64). The remaining
63 percent of the land is unutilized (and largely unutilizable) for
agropastoral production.

CONCLUSION

The ecological data from Quinua demonstrate that the population
has been pressing against limited ecological resources. Population
has been growing at a faster rate than the local ecology can sustain
without access to new water sources. Ecological limits on production are exacerbated by economic ones. Improved seed and livestock
would increase carrying capacity, but the benefits in making the improvements would not outweigh the costs in capital, labor, and
missed opportunity they entail. A few farmers have experimented
with new seeds, but only in a minor way. An expanded irrigation
system would significantly improve carrying capacity, but Quinuenos have not been able to raise the capital and labor needed to
build new dams. Worsening rural-urban terms of trade, moreover,
have encouraged Quinuenos to invest resources in nonfarm employment rather than to improve farm technology.

3.

RESOURCE OWNERSHIP
AND CONTROL

AGROPASTORAL PRODUCTION requires land, labor, water, animals, tools, seeds, and fertilizer. Peasants obtain these resources through familial bonds, inheritance, and purchase. They possess these rights unequally. Some peasants have enough productive resources to feed themselves and their families solely through farming. Most have too little land, labor or water, and they have had to engage in wage work to supplement local production for as long as they can remember.

THE FAMILIAL BASIS OF PRODUCTION

The conjugal family (the family of parents and children) is Quinua's most important social unit, the segment that owns and controls resources. Conjugal families usually reside in separate households, but many people (especially in the town) live alone, and some (especially in the hamlets) live in joint households of two or more conjugal families (table 11). When different families occupy the same household, they cultivate separate fields, store the harvest separately and generally prepare their own meals. The number of joint families, however, has declined between 1972 and 1981, one result of the economic changes in the community.

Many households are without sufficient labor to cultivate their fields. Migration has stripped the community of young men. Many Quinuenos, especially women, live alone or with an unrelated companion (cf. Brush 1977 : 32–39, 57). In a census of twenty-five households in a rural savannah hamlet in 1987 only 68 percent of them contained conjugal families (40 percent were single conjugal families and 28 percent joint family households). The remaining house-

Table 11. *Quinua Household Structure, 1972–1981*

	% of Total				
	1972			*1981*	
Household	*Town*	*Hamlets*	*Total*	*Total*	*Density[a]*
Single person[b]	37.2	13.6	15.7	19.3	1.5
Conjugal	45.5	56.9	55.9	72.4	4.7
Joint	17.3	29.5	28.4	8.3	7.6
Total household number	121	1,261	1,382	1,347	4.4

Source: Peru 1974, 1983.
[a] The number of residents divided by the number of households.
[b] The data refer to single-person households in 1972 and to nonconjugal households in 1981.

holds consisted of single persons (12 percent), grandparent-grand-child households (12 percent), and two-generation mother-daughter households (8 percent). Since the sexual division of labor is considered essential to effective agricultural production, at least 32 percent of the households are unable to field a serviceable labor force because of such adverse life circumstances as widowhood and the migration of husbands and children.

Quinuenos supplement their own household resources with those available from kinsfolk. Kinship is both patrilineal (descent through the male line) and bilateral (related to both mother's and father's kin). All kin with the same patronym form a patrilineal clan known as the *casta*. The *casta* has no corporate functions: it does not act as a body defending the rights and interests of its members. Nonetheless, people regard others with the same patronym as kin and form close ties within this group. The bilateral kin group known as the *ayllu* is more important than the *casta*. It consists of lineal (those in direct line of descent such as parents and children) and collateral relatives (those related by blood but not in a direct line, such as brothers and cousins) in one's own generation and in the first and second ascending and descending generations: siblings, siblings' children, siblings of one's parents, the children of parents' siblings, grandparents, and grandparents' siblings. More distant bilateral relatives are called *karu ayllu* (cf. Isbell 1978): lineal and collateral relatives in the third ascending and descending generations, as well as descendants of grandparents' siblings. People rarely reckon kinship beyond the second generation, which is the basis of the distinction between *ayllu* and *karu ayllu*. *Karu ayllu* are relatives whose exact relationship to the speaker is unknown.

Kin collaborate frequently with one another, providing access to such important resources as labor, housing, and political support and influence. Ties to one's natal family and the natal family of one's parents are very strong. A farmer calls upon his neighboring patrikin to work in his fields. A woman calls on her sisters to cook and serve food during a fiesta. A man expects his daughter's husband to assist him at a fiesta. A family sends a child to live with a kinsperson in Lima. A leader in a communal dispute expects his kin to support him. A household knows that kin will come to celebrate fiestas and lifepassage events and to bury and mourn a dead member. In spite of myths of egalitarianism ("brothers help one another"), many of these ties are exploitative. The rich employ kin ties to obtain clients, and the poor to get patrons.

Male cooperation is facilitated by Quinua's rules of marriage residence. A newly married couple is expected to live in the household of the man's parents for a few months, after which they build their own house on land provided by the man's father. This virilocal residence creates a group of nearby male relatives who help one another in irrigation and most agricultural tasks. As agricultural production has declined in importance, the incidence of virilocal residence has declined as well. In 1967, 74 percent of the families (26 of 35) in one savannah hamlet shared a patronym with one or more families in the hamlet, one measure of virilocal residence.[1] In 1987 only 65 percent of the households in another savannah hamlet shared a patronym (36 of 55). As farm work has declined in importance relative to migration and other nonfarm work, the economic forces favoring virilocal residence have also declined.

Quinuenos do not accept kin ties passively, but actively create ritual kin through godparenthood (*padrinazgo*), an important institution throughout Latin America (Mintz and Wolf 1950). In Quinua people are asked to become godparents by sponsoring a variety of events in a person's life: baptism, first haircut, first communion, confirmation, and marriage. In addition, people sometimes select godparents for adoptions, funerals, and even such minor events as opening up an earth oven or blessing a new car or house. But Quinuenos consider such ties less important than those established in the usual fashion.

Except for marriage the important tie is not that between godparents and child but that between the godparents and the parents.

The godfather (*padrino*) and godmother (*madrina*) of a child become the *compadre* and *comadre* (or coparents), respectively, of the child's parents. The object of the parents in asking someone to sponsor their child is to obtain these *compadre* ties. Compadres become in effect ritual kin with all the attendant obligations of kinship. Like kin compadres are expected to respect and help one another, making themselves available for counsel, work, patronage, and protection.

In marriage the relationship between godparent and child is more significant than that between godparent and parent. Marriage godparents are charged with helping ensure that the marriage is a good one. They counsel the married pair and in the past even punished the party at fault in a marital dispute, whipping the wrongdoer just as a parent whips a disobedient child. Godparents are also expected to help their godchildren in dealing with the police and other authorities, as well as providing whatever other material help they can. The married pair reciprocate with respect and labor. It is the rare godchild who will not work on his godparent's fields during the festive work group (the *minka*), held at times in which labor is very scarce.

Often considered reciprocal and benevolent, godparenthood like kinship is an institution deeply embedded in the system of social stratification (see also Fioravanti-Molinié 1982:225–226; Muratorio 1980; Rasnake 1988:44; Sanchez 1982:182–183; Weismantel 1988:71, 82–83, 179). Quinuenos usually use godparenthood to obtain access to some material or social benefit. Peasants select godparents from among the rich and powerful who can provide work and political protection. The peasant, however, is careful to select a godparent who is not too rich, for overbearing godparents may ask their compadres or godchildren to even wash their clothes. Rich people establish godparent ties to poor people in order to obtain labor and political support. It is difficult for a compadre or godchild to refuse requests to work or to help celebrate a fiesta. Coastal migrants use *compadrazgo* in the same way. They obtain laborers to cultivate their Quinua fields and servants and workers for coastal projects.

Ties of kinship and ritual kinship are always overlain with sentiment and etiquette, even when most opportunistic. Quinuenos must not appear self-interested. They are expected to do things freely (*de voluntad*) and not for a reward. Proper behavior among kin and fictive kin is supported supernaturally: people who commit incest or who behave disrespectfully toward parents and other important kin and ritual kin are punished with hail or some other supernatural sanction. Nonsupernatural sanctions are also used. People gossip about those who ignore their kin ties. They pressure kin to attend fiestas, forcing them into a public acknowledgment of the kin relationships. At these fiestas people drink in a dyadic chain of drinking and counterdrinking that is impossible to escape and forces people to interact with one another whether they want to or not. Nonetheless, people do use kinship and ritual kinship to further personal ends, and they walk a delicate line between the two goals.

SYSTEM OF LAND TENURE

Until 1973 farmers acquired land by means of three systems of tenure: communal, private, and hacienda. In the moist forest, prairie, and paramo, land tenure was and is communal, belonging to the formally recognized peasant community.[2] Ideally, Quinuenos obtain unused communal land by petitioning the president of the community. He determines if the land is truly unused and not simply in fallow. He assigns the use rights, giving preference to those who have participated extensively in the *cargo* system. Actual practice, however, is much more complex. Powerful townspeople have sometimes taken communal land without asking the president. Although a farmer cannot sell his use rights, he can transmit them to his children through inheritance. Once a farmer has use rights, he continues to maintain them and only forfeits them if he or his family stops farming the land. One man, for example, was cultivating about one-half hectare of communal land that he traced to his paternal grandfather. This man was childless, but in 1974 his stepdaughter had begun to farm the land in order to ensure that she would inherit it. In consequence, little good communal land lies idle. Most large tracts of unsown land are either in fallow or too poor for intensive cultivation (cf. Caballero 1981 : 353).

In the savannah most land is owned privately, primarily by small owners. Until recently, the savannah also contained lands associated with particular saints (*cofradía* lands). These church-owned lands were cultivated by the organizers (*mayordomos*) of the fiestas. Most of these fields were small and of poor quality. The archbishop sold the last one and a half hectares in 1987 for a miserable $12.50,[3] but the peasant community bought them back for the central school (*nucleo escolar*) to use as an experimental agricultural field.

Until the agrarian reform, which began to affect Quinua in 1973, haciendas owned most of the valley bottom land, much of the thorn steppe, and a few sections of the lower savannah, but only small extensions of land in other zones. Hacienda peons received cultivation rights, grazing rights, or water from the hacienda in return for cultivating the fields of the hacienda or caring for its animals. The number of peons resident on the haciendas had declined steadily from 15.5 percent of Quinua's population in 1876 to 3.7 percent in 1961 (Peru 1878, 1948, 1966). Before the agrarian reform in 1972, most of the owners of the eight large and six small haciendas lived in the central town of Quinua or in the city of Ayacucho.

At the time of the agrarian reform, many hacienda peons lived in the independent community, maintaining only a peripheral relationship with the hacienda. They were in fact independent peasants who used the hacienda to supplement production from privately owned fields (Skar 1982:80). The agrarian reform created cooperatives out of the remaining haciendas. The fields were subsequently divided among the former peons; in 1981 there were two such cooperatives, with a total of 177 inhabitants (Peru 1983).

LAND OWNERSHIP AND USUFRUCT

Children inherit from each parent separately. The inheritance is frequently given while the parents are still living, in a formal land division known as the *chacra partición*. At this event the parents divide their lands and household goods among the children. Sometimes parents do not distribute their land because they fear their children will not provide for them adequately in old age; in such cases the parents may retain ownership rights and only assign children use rights. Some unfortunate old people are said by informants to have been abandoned by their children after the *chacra partición*, forcing the parents to live off the charity of siblings.

Ideally all children inherit equally, although preference in inheritance of the home is given to the youngest (the *nuñopaqhua*), who is expected to care for his or her parents in their old age. Actual practice, however, varies significantly from this ideal. If the youngest child is unwilling or unable to remain in Quinua, some other sibling may inherit the home, perhaps an unmarried sister who has had a child. The operative principle is that parents transmit the home and best lands to the child who remains to care for them. Increasingly, however, the home is torn down after the death of the parents, and the materials (adobe bricks, roof tiles, etc.) are divided equally by the children. Parents may also give favorite children more inheritance or other children less because they have had more expenses with them. They sometimes favor daughters over sons in order to provide them with resources independent of their husbands.

Farmers supplement inherited land through a variety of mechanisms, often cultivating the land of migrants. Many migrants pay someone directly to cultivate their lands; an equally large number, however, leave their lands to be bought or cultivated by others. When lands are sold, Quinuenos expect the owner to offer them first to the sibling who owns adjacent land, after that to other siblings or kin, then to neighboring nonkin, and only then to someone else.

Land changes hands frequently, and many people buy lands far from their hamlets of birth. In one savannah hamlet in 1987, 34.6 percent of the inhabitants counted had bought the majority of their lands, while an additional 15.4 percent had purchased some of them, even though they had inherited the majority of their holdings (table 12). Land prices vary depending on quality and location. Irrigated land and land near the central town is the most expensive. In 1974 four *yugadas* of unirrigated savannah land about forty-five minutes from the central town sold for $187 (or $360 per hectare). In the same year, a prime irrigated *yugada* adjacent to the central town sold for $327 (or $2,523 per hectare). Houses in the central town are similarly dear. In 1967 two choice houses in the central town sold for $720 and $1,200, respectively.

Migrants have often complained to me that Quinua land prices are so paltry that they hold on to their land rather than sell it. The above data suggest that the reluctance to sell is probably based on other considerations. These land and house prices are considerable by both local and migrant standards. (In 1987 in Lima one middle-class extended family fed ten adults for less than $100 per month.) Any reluctance to sell may be more the result of factors other than low prices (unclear title, desire for a Quinua base, difficulty of arranging a sale).

Peasants sometimes rent lands for a direct cash outlay (*arriendo* or *alquilay*). Land rents are relatively cheap. In 1974, one-eighth hec-

Table 12. *Origin of Land Owned in a Rural Savannah Hamlet: Quinua, 1987*

	No. of Respondents	% of Total
Nearly all inherited	10	38.5
Nearly all purchased	9	34.6
Equally inherited and purchased	4	15.4
Obtained from spouse	2	7.7
No data	1	3.8
Total	26	100.0

Source: 1987 census by research assistant.

tare (one *yugada*) of good terrain rented for $11.70 (or $93.60 per
hectare) for the agricultural season, and a poor plot rented for $2.34
(or $18.72 per hectare); the daily agricultural wage was $0.75. At
times land is used as collateral for an interest-free loan (*prenda*). Use
of the field is retained by the lender until the money is returned; the
cultivation rights are considered sufficient interest.[4] Peasants also
pay rent in labor by working for a large landowner who gives cultivation rights in return.

More farmers obtain fields through sharecropping (*muhu puray* or
a medias) than through rental. In the ideal scheme, the owner provides the land and the sharecropper provides the seed. All other monetary costs (fertilizer, insecticide, hired labor) are shared equally.
The sharecropper does the work and the yield is divided in half. The
owner of the field, however, usually works alongside the sharecropper in the harvest: he fears he will not get his complete portion of
the produce if he is not there to protect his interests. In actuality,
sharecropping takes variant forms; farmers negotiate the labor, monetary inputs, and returns, using the ideal scheme as a model.

Many Quinuenos acquire usufruct rights in return for caring for
another's field or house (a practice known as *tiapakuq*). Since the
owner makes no contribution to crop production, this is not sharecropping; the person who plants the field is under no obligation to
give its owner any of the harvest, although he usually gives something, especially if the owner visits the household of the cultivator.
Parents frequently continue to cultivate the fields they have distributed to their children as inheritance and only give the children
gifts from the harvest. Migrants often leave their lands in the care
of kin and receive portions of the harvest as gifts when they visit
Quinua.

Townspeople sometimes acquire land by force. They take communal lands without asking the president or accept privately owned
property as bribes from litigants in disputes. At least one person had
amassed a considerable amount of land in this latter fashion, although his descendants subsequently lost it in one way or another.

Men also obtain usufruct rights through marriage, although the
way in which this is done must be handled with some delicacy. Husbands and wives retain the property they have brought to the marriage separately, regardless of the number of years they have been
married. People insult a man who lives off his wife's fields directly,
calling him male daughter-in-law (*machu llumchuy*). Men try to
avoid these insults by buying lands in addition to those of their
wives. Nonetheless, some men will not cultivate their wives' fields
directly, although they do help their children cultivate them. In this

way the men are able to cultivate all the fields jointly as a conjugal family enterprise without losing the good opinion of their fellows.

It is difficult to get precise data on Quinua landownership. Peasants are suspicious of questions about land, fearing that the information may be used against them in a land dispute or that it might be used to charge taxes (cf. Collins 1988:98). In 1973 tensions about property were so high that in one case an informant who knew me well abruptly refused either to answer more questions or to continue serving as informant even though we had only been talking about the distribution of irrigation water. Almost all land titles, moreover, are suspect. Quinuenos rarely register title transfers to correspond to the demands of Peruvian law, relying instead on the extralegal registering of land sales (when they register them at all) with the justices of the peace. Titles are also often imprecise. Two well-to-do families, for example, have a single title to their adjacent fields. The common grandfather of the male head of both families is listed as the owner, even though he never occupied either farm. In other cases, peasants were cultivating the lands of migrant siblings as if those lands were their own.

A further difficulty is that Quinuenos (and indeed most Quechua-speaking peasants) measure land in terms of *yugadas*. A *yugada*[5] consists of the quantity of land that can be plowed in one day. A *yugada* varies in size depending on the terrain, but Quinuenos estimate there are 4 *yugadas* to 1 hectare, an approximation that is incorrect but which has probably been used in national censuses and by researchers.[6] Actual measurements of six fields in Quinua's savannah (ranging from 1 to 3 *yugadas* each), however, produced an average of 0.1294 hectares per *yugada*.[7] My figures, therefore, assume that there are 7.7 *yugadas* to a hectare.

I use a variety of sources to estimate ownership: Informant reports about themselves, informant estimates about their neighbors, the 1972 Peruvian agricultural census, and a 1977 report by a Quinua official.[8] The various sources of information coincide in suggesting that most Quinua families own or control 2–4 *yugadas* of farmland, about 0.25–0.50 hectare.

Land is distributed unevenly. A small minority have no lands, but most such people migrate to the Coast or the tropical forest *montaña*. Only a few of the landless remain in Quinua, working as peons in return for land or food. Some work for a single patron, often an older widow. Such peons are sometimes promised land on the patron's death, although they do not always receive it. The 1977 government report (Peru 1977a) states that 2 percent of the registered peasant community members (*comuneros*) (30 of 1,730) are landless, a percentage that informants consider very low. The number of land-less (or people unable to cultivate their lands) has increased since 1983, as many former residents of the prairie and moist forest aban-doned their lands when they fled from the guerrilla war.

The vast majority of Quinuenos have some land, although not al-ways privately owned. Even though the 1972 agricultural census records that 54.2 percent of the households (agropastoral units)[9] owned most of their property (table 13), I suspect that the figures re-flect control of land as well as ownership. It is very likely, moreover, that more land is sharecropped than the 2.7 percent reported by the same census; Brush (1977:88) found that 43 percent of the land in Uchucmarca was sharecropped.

The census suggests that the mean size of household landholdings is 0.85 hectares (table 14),[10] although further extrapolation of the census provides a mean size of 0.59 hectares.[11] These figures include both farm and pastoral land. Farmland in the census constitutes only 17.4 percent of the total land devoted to farms and pastures (table 8). Applying this proportion to the mean of 0.59 hectares indicates that

Table 13. *Form of Land Tenancy in Quinua, 1972*[a]

	Households	
	% of Total	Mean Hectares Controlled[b]
Privately owned		
With legal title	41.9	2.11
Without title	2.7	1.57
More than 50% privately owned	9.6	2.73
Subtotal	54.2	2.19
Undeclared	29.1	0.23
Other mixed tenures	10.9	2.61
Rented or sharecropped	2.7	2.21
Agrarian reform cooperatives	2.2	23.69
Obtained from peasant community	0.8	1.12
Total number	1,570	3,335.66

Source: Peru 1972.

[a] The peasant community's 15,000 hectares have been excluded from these calcula-tions; the censual category of agropastoral units has been translated as households (see text for caveats concerning the agricultural census).

[b] The figures provided by the census.

Table 14. *Landownership in District of Quinua, 1972*

Type of Ownership	No.	Censual	Calculated[a]	Hectares per APU[b]
		Agropastoral Units (APU)		
		Total Hectares		
Individual households	1,566	2,551.66	1,325.54	0.85
Cooperative	2	5.50	2.86	1.43
Peasant community	1	15,000.00	7,792.21	7,792.21
Society of persons	1	776.00	403.11	403.11
Undeclared	1	2.50	1.30	1.30
Total	1,571	18,335.66	9,525.02	6.06

Source: Peru 1972.
[a] The censual figure multiplied by 4 and divided by 7.7 (see note 10).
[b] Calculated hectares divided by number of agropastoral units.

Quinua households on the average own or control 0.10 hectares of farmland, about 0.5 *yugada*.

This figure is probably much too low. Quinuenos are unlikely to have given correct information about ownership to census takers, a touchy topic at best. One must be careful in using Peru's 1972 agricultural census. People had been very fearful of it; many lied about the true state of affairs. People indicated to me in 1973 that many others (not themselves!) hid their animals and produce when the census takers came in 1972.

Nonetheless, Quinuenos do gossip about one another. They report that most families in the savannah own around 2 *yugadas,* about 0.25 hectare. This figure coincides with the 1977 government report that claims that most *comuneros* possess two parcels of land, probably 2 *yugadas* or less (Peru 1977a). I accept the Quinuenos's suggested mode but prefer to give it a range of 0.25–0.50 hectare of farmland because some households farm 4 *yugadas*. Peasants in Quinua with 1.5 hectares (12 *yugadas*) are considered prosperous. A very few have as much as 8 hectares (60 *yugadas*), and still fewer were large landowners with haciendas, but this was before the agrarian reform. Farm holdings, therefore, are truly minuscule for most people.

The data from Quinua are consistent with data from most other areas of Ayacucho and the highlands: 18.2 percent of the agropastoral units in the Province of Huamanga and 17.6 percent throughout the Department of Ayacucho are smaller than 0.5 hectare (Maletta et al. n.d., vol. 3 : 25). In Matapuquio in nearby Andahuaylas, the families in one barrio (Hanay) owned an average of 0.40 hectares (0.25 irrigated and 0.15 nonirrigated); in the other barrio (Uray), they owned 0.27 hectares (0.16 irrigated and 0.11 nonirrigated) (Skar 1982 : 260–261, 279). In Matahuasi, a prosperous village in the Mantaro Valley with a crop mix similar to Quinua's, 73 percent of the population owns under a hectare (Long and Roberts 1984 : 170–171). For the altiplano, Collins (1988 : 100) has obtained higher figures for a different agropastoral mix, but in the same area Dew (1969 : 57) reports an even lower figure of 0.22 hectares of land owned per family, and two other studies give figures of 0.3 and 1.1 hectares (CIDA 1966 : 128–129). The Yura who inhabit an exceedingly arid area of the Bolivian sierra possess 0.5 – 2.0 hectares, with a mode of 1.0 hectare (Rasnake 1988 : 33). In Puquio-Pampon in Huánuco, Burchard (1974 : 245) found that 25 percent of the families had less than 0.26 hectares, while an additional 59 percent had 0.31–0.73 hectares. (These figures are obtained by multiplying Burchard's hectares by 4 and dividing by 7.7; see note 10.) Brush (1977 : 86) obtains considerably larger landholding in the District of Uchucmarca in the Department of Cajamarca: 1.58 hectares per household. Brush recognizes the relatively favorable tenure pattern in Uchucmarca compared to other communities (ibid. : 35 – 36). The larger size of Uchucmarca landholdings appears to be the result of an anomalous recent opening of new land.

Gross figures on landownership from one area to the next, of course, are not truly comparable since they represent differing methodological problems in obtaining the data, as well as differing environments and subsistence systems. Nonetheless, the data from other areas are generally consistent with the data from Quinua: most highland peasants have inadequate land to live from agropastoral production alone (Long and Roberts 1984 : 171). Indeed, one Peruvian economist believes this problem of tenure is more severe for Peru than for all areas of Latin America other than Colombia (Caballero 1981 : 61–62).

ANIMAL OWNERSHIP

Nearly all Quinuenos are farmers, but most of them supplement their agricultural production with animal husbandry.[12] Animals produce wool, hides, and milk (usually not drunk, but made into cheese) and are beasts of burden. Llamas, horses, mules, and burros carry cargo and, except for the llama, thresh the grain. Cattle dung is an important fuel, and all animals fertilize agricultural fields (Winterhalder, Larsen, and Thomas 1974). Plow oxen (called a *par de yuntas*) are especially advantageous. Their owner uses them not only to plow his own fields, but he employs them as a business, plowing the fields of others in return for labor, pasture, or money (cf. Brush 1977:92–93). Sheep, cattle, chickens, and pigs are sources of food, but Quinuenos generally sell the food rather than consume it themselves. Animals perform too many services, and their flesh is too valuable merely to be eaten.

The type of herding that people engage in is significantly influenced by ecological zone. Before the guerrilla war accelerated in 1983, most herding was in the higher altitudes (4,000+ m), and especially the prairie (Flannery et al. 1989). Inhabitants of this zone were primarily pastoralists, herding their own animals and those of the agriculturalists of lower zones. Llamas, sheep, horses, and cattle—the most common animals in this zone—grazed in the large uncultivated areas.

Farmers in the upper savannah also have a great variety of animals: cattle, sheep, goats, horses, mules, and burros. Prior to the guerrilla war in 1983, they maintained large herds in this zone through transhumance, sending their sheep and cattle to high altitude pastures in August. The animals remained there during the rainy-season crop cycle, tended by residents of these higher zones, and returned to the savannah at the beginning of the harvest on May 3. Savannah farmers also kept a few horses, burros, and cattle with them, grazing the animals in rocky and moist areas in the savannah and in the nearby moist forest. In July they might graze their animals on stalks of barley. Grown as the second crop in the dry-season cycle, the barley is ready when little other forage is available.

In the thorn steppe, people herd great numbers of goats and a few sheep, cattle, and burros. Exceedingly rocky and dry, much of this zone is either uncultivated or left in fallow. These same ecological conditions limit water and forage during the dry season, so that herding is not as important as in the prairie.

Inhabitants of the lower savannah and valley bottom herd fewer animals than those in the prairie, upper savannah, and thorn steppe. The lower savannah is too dry to grow forage; the irrigated valley bottom can grow forage, but it is too unprofitable. The distance of both zones prohibits transhumance to the prairie. The inhabitants of these zones graze their few sheep, goats, and cattle in the poor terrain and rocky ravines of the thorn steppe.

Farmers below the moist forest also keep such barnyard animals as guinea pigs, pigs, chickens, ducks, and turkeys. In the higher zones, they only raise pigs.

Like data on landownership, specific data on animal ownership are difficult to obtain. Nonetheless, most savannah landowners have at least one burro, several goats and sheep, and a few cattle. Everyone also raises at least two pigs and as many guinea pigs and chickens as possible. Data from the 1972 agricultural census significantly understate the number of animals owned, but even so, 43.7 percent of the households are reported as having a mean of 3 head of cattle and 58.2 percent with a mean of 4.2 chickens (table 15).

Animal ownership depends on wealth and household labor. One wealthy farmer in the midsavannah in 1974, who dedicated himself mostly to farming and only incidentally to stock raising, generally kept: 1 horse, 2–3 burros, 3–5 cows, 3–5 oxen, 50–60 sheep, 30–40 goats, 6–10 pigs, 20–30 chickens, 20–40 guinea pigs, 20–30 ducks, 3–4 turkeys (but mainly for status value and decoration), and 2 oxen for plowing. Because of lack of pasture and time to herd them, another prosperous savannah family had fewer animals, keeping only 1 burro and 3 cows, in addition to barnyard animals. The differences are in part a result of the number of children available to herd. The first farmer had six sons and four daughters. The second had only

Table 15. *Animal Ownership, District of Quinua, 1972*

Animals	% of Households	Mean Head per Household
Stock		
Cattle	43.7	3.0
Sheep	29.8	8.4
Goats	27.1	7.9
Burros	25.8	1.8
Horses	1.7	2.1
Llamas	1.1	10.7
Mules	1.0	1.8
Alpacas	0.3	4.5
Barnyard		
Chickens	58.2	4.2
Pigs	40.2	2.0
Guinea pigs	28.8	5.0
Ducks	2.7	3.0
Turkeys	1.5	2.4
Rabbits	0.5	3.6

Source: Peru 1972; households are agropastoral units; total number of agropastoral units is 1,571.

three sons (one a toddler) and two resident teenage daughters. One cannot herd without labor. A poor family might have only one or two pigs, a few chickens, and some guinea pigs. A cow or even a burro would be out of reach economically. They not only lack the capital to obtain breeding stock but often lack sufficient labor and pasture for larger animals.[13]

WATER

Agricultural production, as life itself, depends on water. Water in Quinua and other Andean communities is scarce and rationed. Its scarcity limits production even more than does that of land. The savannah is fed by a series of small irrigation systems. They have only enough water for a single irrigation turn during the rainy-season planting (*hatun tarpuy*) but that water permits high-altitude maize cultivation (Mitchell 1976a). There is insufficient water to either irrigate crops in time of sustained drought or to plant a dry-season crop (*michka*) in more than a few fields in the upper reaches of the irrigation system.

In recent memory, water has never been distributed equally. Until 1966 when a national water law was applied to Quinua, haciendas received significant preference. In the Hanan Sayoc irrigation network, one hacienda took all the water every Saturday. In Lurin Sayoc haciendas received the water on Mondays and Tuesdays, while in the Suso network haciendas had the water every day but Sunday. Peasants were often forced to buy water from the haciendas with money or labor (Mitchell n.d.).

Except for days that had been reserved for haciendas, water is distributed on a first-come, first-served basis during most of the year. During the crucial rainy-season planting (September–December), however, peasants respond to the great demand for water by implementing a formal system of irrigation turns known as the *patacha*, although they still reserve Sunday for the first-come–first-served distribution of drinking water. In 1966 water for agriculture cost $0.75 a day in Hanan Sayoc but was free in Lurin Sayoc. Peasants from both barrios sometimes buy a neighbor's excess water with a bottle or half bottle of cane alcohol (*aguardiente*).

Previously, people who participated in the system of festival posts and the peasant political organization (the *cargo* system) had special rights to water. Quinuenos often fought (and still fight) over water, sometimes exchanging blows. In such fights, they support their competing water claims with assertions about their communal service, especially participation in the *cargos* and work on irrigation corvées. Since the decline of the *cargo* system, Quinuenos legitimize water rights largely through their work on the irrigation system. A list of irrigation workers is kept for this purpose. People who have worked on cleaning the system are those who have rights to water, although powerful townspeople are often able to get water even though they have not participated as they should.

LABOR

Scarce and difficult to obtain (Caballero 1981:124–136; Collins 1988; Maltby 1980), labor determines—after water—what, when, and if farmers can plant. A farmer will not plant a crop if he does not have sufficient labor to do so. Many limit their potato planting because of such constraints.[14] Farmers must often supplement household labor by labor arrangements with kin, affines, and ritual kin, as well as by purchase. Even the poor use hired labor from time to time. At times of labor scarcity large landowners initiate festive labor groups, supplementing pay with abundant and special foods, as well as maize beer (*chicha*) and cane alcohol (*aguardiente* or *trago*).

Cultural rules govern the allocation of household and other labor, although Quinuenos tend to be flexible about these rules, ignoring them if they must (cf. Allen 1988:78; Collins 1983; Painter 1984). Women manage the family purse, working hard to fill it. All women have some sort of cash work, whether selling animal products or marketing produce. They also run many of the local stores. Men used to be the long-distance traders, but since the advent of truck transportation, women make such trips as well. Men remain the truck drivers and the owners and managers of most of the larger stores.

A woman spins and dyes the yarn, while men weave it into ponchos, shawls, and blankets. Women, however, weave small articles, such as belts, swaddling cloths, and the ties for pants legs. They are able to weave such small pieces on a portable back-strap loom while they are pasturing the animals. In ceramics, men fabricate and fire the pots, while both women and men paint them. The designs, however, are patrilineally inherited (when they are inherited and not new), and wives adjust their painting styles to those of their husbands.

Although women work hard in agriculture, men do the heaviest work. They plow, turn the ground with the foot plow, hoe, irrigate, cultivate crops, and do the most strenuous labor in the harvest. Only men work in wage labor, the festive work group, or the labor corvée. As men migrate or work at wage labor, women often have to work harder (cf. Weismantel 1988 : 176–177). Ceramicists often make pots during the harvest season, leaving the harvest to their wives. As one informant put it, "If we don't make ceramics, how will we get money to buy coca and food?" Women are consequently hard pressed to complete their agricultural work, although some women work at male tasks to fill the gap.

Women may do the least strenuous agricultural labor, but they work longer hours than men. Women as well as men sow, fertilize, weed, and harvest. Although women do not work in agriculture for wages, they do so for payment in kind. Women also dry and store the harvest, prepare and serve meals, and oversee the larder, making sure that it lasts the entire year. They tend the animals, although children often herd and men do so occasionally. Women wash clothes and clean house. They care for children, starting as very young girls when they attend to their younger siblings. A woman's hands are rarely idle. Even when walking she carries her child and other load in a shawl on her back, which frees her hands for spinning wool into yarn.

Young children guard crops against animals. They also do such light tasks as husking maize, removing the grain from quinoa stalks by rubbing them against rocks, or pinching the flowers from potato plants to increase production. Children begin to work on these light tasks when they are five or six. Girls graduate to many adult tasks around ten, and boys assume the heavier male tasks around fifteen. Before 1960 most children worked on the farm throughout the year, but since then they have been less available during the school year, April through December.

NONHOUSEHOLD LABOR

Nonhousehold labor is needed during periods of peak labor demand. I do not have data on the amount of such labor used in Quinua, but 35.9 percent of the agricultural enterprises (unidades agrícolas) in the sierra that are smaller than two hectares supplement household labor with temporary workers (Caballero 1981 : 121). The percentage is even higher in other studies (Cotlear 1988 : 234) and in Quinua— where nearly everyone needs an occasional worker or so. This demand for laborers in Quinua has become even greater in recent years as male entry into the nonfarm economy has limited the number of men available for farm work.

Nonhousehold labor recruitment is difficult. The simplest and preferred form of labor is wage labor (jornal), in which the farmer pays a day laborer (called a peon) a wage and provides him with coca leaves, cigarettes, and lunch (Skar 1982 : 215–216). In 1966 day laborers were paid $0.56 per day, a figure consistent with the $0.46 that a worker received in Uchucmarca in 1971 (Brush 1977:106). In 1973 a laborer in Quinua got about the same amount as he did in 1966 ($0.58), but by 1980 his wage had inflated to $1.11. In 1987 a peon was earning even more: $1.88 if the owner provided the hoe to work with as well as lunch, coca, and cigarettes; $2.19 if the worker brought his own hoe but still received the extras; and $3.12 if the worker brought his own hoe and received no extras. Not only demand but the cost of other goods and services determines these wages. In 1987 a guinea pig cost $1.88, while a meal of chicken soup was $0.98. A wage laborer will not work for the equivalent of two bowls of soup. This inflation of agricultural wages and food prices, of course, is another measure of the increasing monetization of the Quinua economy.

Quinua agricultural wages, as those throughout the highlands, are nonetheless low compared to wages on the coast even today (cf. Caballero 1981:171–172). The low productivity of sierra agriculture certainly limits farm salaries. At the same time, the labor market is affected by noncapitalist mechanisms of labor recruitment. If labor prices go too high, a family will work harder itself or use the non-cash mechanisms of recruitment known as *ayni* and *yanapay* to recruit labor.

Ayni is a form of balanced reciprocity used to obtain services and goods (cf. Allen 1988:92–94; Brown 1987; Brush 1977:104–105; Guillet 1980; Mayer 1974; Skar 1982:213–214). Kinsfolk, neighbors, and ritual kin exchange labor on a day-for-day basis. A man might work in his neighbor's fields for a day, but the neighbor must reciprocate the service at some future date. Quinuenos also share beasts of burden in *ayni* or in exchange for work. They use *ayni* to care for one another's houses, fields, and animals during absences. Kin sometimes supply in *ayni* the coca leaves, cigarettes, and alcohol used by peons during a festive work group. *Ayni* is also used in nonwork contexts. During fiestas, for example, a person may bring a case of beer in *ayni*, in which case the beer is supposed to be returned doubled (although the exchange is often only an equal one) when the giver has a fiesta.

In 1966 wealthy Quinuenos rarely employed *ayni* to recruit labor because of its low prestige and the requirement of returning the labor. Farmers are reluctant to commit themselves to a future labor demand that is likely to take place when they need to work in their own fields. The wealthy used reciprocal labor with kin, but only as an affirmation of the kin tie. The poor used, and use, reciprocal labor more frequently, especially during the cultivation of crops when there is a shortage of laborers, but even the poor prefer other mechanisms because of the inconvenience of the obligation to return the labor (cf. Brush 1977: 105–106). The return labor also competes with nonagricultural work, a distinct disadvantage as Quinuenos have entered the cash economy. In 1988 farmers worked in agricultural *ayni* even less frequently than previously, although everyone still employs it to distribute goods, care for houses and animals, and obtain animals in exchange for work.

Ayni is a contractual and balanced relationship, unlike the system of generalized reciprocity called *yanapay* (or *yanapakuy*). In the system of balanced reciprocity the work request is specific as is the date set for the labor return. In generalized reciprocity people help one another freely without any specific expectation of return (Skar 1982: 212–213). People may arrange the same task, such as helping a neighbor build a house, as either balanced or generalized reciprocity, depending on the understanding involved.

Quinuenos exchange goods and services in generalized reciprocity frequently. A person often brings a gift of agricultural produce when visiting kin. People also help one another plant a sick neighbor's fields, kill an animal, open a grave for a burial, cut firewood for a fiesta, and cook and serve fiesta meals. They imbed the reciprocity in social relationships. Affines (in-laws) frequently provide help in generalized reciprocity. A man will act as host, for example, at a ceremony involving his wife's parents; a woman will work with her sisters-in-law to help cook the food for the fiesta of her husband's parents.

Workers demand payment in kind during the harvests of maize, wheat, and potatoes because the cash value of the produce is slightly more than the daily wage, a pattern also found in Uchucmarca (Brush 1977: 107–108). In 1987 men earned from 15 to 20 kilos of potatoes for a day's labor (with a market value of $2.81–$3.75), while women received somewhat less. The workers also take the best portions of the harvest (called *huanlla*) and leave some of the crop unharvested to return later to harvest it themselves, a practice the owner of the field discourages. Landowners dislike payment in kind because it costs more than wage labor; however, they must use it to get the necessary laborers. Some women go from field to field during the potato harvest, looking for this readily available work.

Landowners generally employ festive work groups (the *minka*) to get ten or more male adult laborers (Skar 1982: 216). They provide the men and their wives—women who are not working in the fields—music (*qarahui*), abundant alcohol, coca leaves, cigarettes, and excellent food. They also pay the laborers the daily wage or slightly less; but some workers (especially kin) work in reciprocal labor (*ayni*), and others work for payment in kind. The festive work group is much more expensive for the landowner than other forms of labor.[15] On one festive work group to cultivate maize in January 1967, workers were paid $0.38–$0.56 for the day depending on their work. The owner of the field estimated the cost of the additional cane alcohol, maize beer, coca leaves, cigarettes, and food as more than doubling the total labor cost to $1.12 per person. Few people employ the festive work group because few have the large extension of terrain that requires it.

The Andean literature has focused on the festive characteristics of this work group (Erasmus 1956) rather than on its economic function (Orlove 1980). In Quinua landowners employ the agricultural festive work group to recruit laborers during the second cultivation of maize (*sara kutipa*) and potatoes (*papa qutuy*) and for the harvest and threshing of wheat, times when everyone is busy and labor is scarce. While they enjoy the festivity, and obtain prestige from sponsoring the *minka*, landowners employ it primarily for economic reasons: laborers are reluctant to work for those who do not provide such amenities.

The festive work group has nonetheless declined in recent years. In 1988 peasants were willing to work without the festive work group, but only when the landowner provided other important services in addition to pay. Because currently peasants have greater cash incomes than in 1966, they are no longer as attracted by the special foods, but are enticed by the influence of the powerful. Large landowners who provide crisis help to their regular workers (e.g., resolving political and police problems, helping supply work for children) are able to obtain agricultural laborers without the festive work group (Mallon 1983:152).

We must be careful to distinguish the festive work group from the system of corvée labor known as the *faena* (also called *huajina* or *fajina*). The polity organizes corvée labor to build and repair irrigation canals, roads, bridges, and public buildings.[16] This labor is the tax obligation of the conjugal family, not the household, and each family must contribute a male worker or pay a fine. The family may send a member of the conjugal unit to the work, often a younger son, or a peon hired as a replacement. Certain townspeople, however, avoid both corvée work and the fine because they are involved in communal responsibilities. Someone who works on organizing a project will not have to work on the labor corvée.

People are expected to work on only those projects that benefit them. A person, for example, will work in repairing only the roads in a hamlet where he has property. Nonetheless, the notion of "benefit" is unclear and peasants often have to work on central town projects that they regard as useless to them. In such cases the drum and flute that summon the people to work on the assigned morning may be answered with few hands, a pattern that has increased in recent years.

Corvée labor consists of invariable projects that occur every year, and variable ones, which political authorities initiate periodically. Quinuenos still do invariable corvée labor, but in recent years they no longer use it to repair roads and bridges (table 16). In 1966 families contributed seven to nine days of invariable corvée labor, but in 1988 they contributed only four to six. Variable corvée labor has nearly disappeared. In 1966 labor corvées still built and repaired public buildings (schools, municipal buildings, communal hall, church and chapels), spaces (plaza, streets) and utilities (irrigation system). Quinuenos no longer work in the labor corvée for the same reasons that they no longer participate enthusiastically in the fiesta system: having entered the cash economy more and more, they avoid drains on income and unpaid work that gives few return benefits.

Agricultural laborers work about six hours a day, three in the morning and three in the afternoon. They work for ninety-minute periods separated by half-hour coca breaks. They take about an hour and a half for lunch. The use of coca leaves in the Andes is of consid-

Table 16. *Invariable Corvée Labor, District of Quinua, 1966 and 1988*

	Number of Days	
	1966	*1988*
Irrigation canals[a]	1–2	1–2
Irrigation reservoir[a]	1	1
School building and repair	1–2	1–2
Cemetery maintenance	1	1
Roads and bridges		
In central town	1	0
In hamlets	2	0
Total	7–9	4–6

Source: Informant data and personal observation.
[a] Nonusers of the irrigation system do not have to work on it.

erable importance (Allen 1988) and appears to be an adaptation to a situation in which calories are scarce.[17] When the work is very heavy, however, the coca and lunch breaks are shortened to gain time.

CAPITAL

Peasants need capital to buy land, fertilizer, seeds, and labor. Although they avoid cash payments as much as possible, they are often and increasingly forced to use money. This money is usually scarce (Brown 1987; Guillet 1980; Mallon 1983:62 and passim). During the dry season in 1974, one prosperous peasant family spent an average of $4.84 a week on production, 27 percent of all their expenses (the daily agricultural wage was $0.70) (see table 24). Production expenses would have been even higher at other times of the year. In the Cuzco region, Gonzales (1987:93) has found that annual production expenses varied from 14.5 percent ($37.00) to 30.3 percent ($63.00) of all monetary expenses in the five communities he studied.

Previously, Quinuenos fertilized with local animal dung, but many farmers had too few animals for their needs and had to purchase dung from large animal herders or bird guano from the coastal islands. In the early 1960s they began to supplement natural fertilizers with chemical ones. Quinuenos apply chemical fertilizers and insecticides widely today. They purchase them from the Ministry of Agriculture in Quinua or Ayacucho. The ministry maintains a storeroom in Quinua that is administered by someone nominated by the community who receives a percentage of the sales.

Farmers also need money for seed. Although everyone stores seed, they often do not store enough and must buy supplemental seed from specialists. They previously bought such seed in the neighboring town of Huamanguilla but do so today in the city of Ayacucho.

Since most people do not own a plow and animals, they have to obtain them through rental or labor exchange. Plows and plow animals are scarce. Only 33.9 percent of the households interviewed in the agricultural census of 1972 said they owned them (Peru 1972; cf. Brush 1977:92–93; Rasnake 1988:33). The lack of a plow is a significant impediment to agricultural production. In 1974 farmers paid $1.18 per day for a plow, the animals to draw it, and the labor of the owner. They also must provide lunch, coca leaves, and cigarettes to the owner and fodder to the animals. Farmers plow about one-eighth hectare a day. Since they sometimes have to plow a field twice, they may have had to pay as much as $2.35 to plow a one-eighth hectare of land in 1974, not counting the extras, an amount more than three times the cost of a day laborer ($0.70). The costs have increased somewhat over the years. In 1987 plow rental cost $6.25. It would cost a farmer $12.50 to plow his one-eighth hectare twice, an amount that is four times the daily agricultural wage of $3.12.

To avoid these cash expenses, farmers frequently give pasture in return for a day's plowing. The amount of pasture needed for a day's plowing depends on its quality. They also exchange labor for plowing. A peasant sometimes receives a plow and animals on loan from a large landowner, keeping them as his own, in return for plowing the owner's fields.

Farmers must transport produce from the fields to their homes. They do so with their own burros or with those rented from neighbors with cash or in reciprocal exchange. The feed and care of these burros, as well as the rental, are additional production expenses. Farmers also incur marketing costs. In the past they transported their produce long distances on burros, but in 1988 they paid for truck transportation.

In 1966 farmers also needed capital for participation in the system of religious and political *cargos* (discussed in chapter 7). Participation in the *cargo* system was an additional capital expense that allowed Quinuenos access to productive resources, especially water, labor, and communal land.

CONCLUSIONS

Most Quinuenos have insufficient land, water, labor, and capital for self-subsistence. Like the ecological constraints described in chapter 2, the unequal distribution of productive resources encourages peasants to intensify cash-producing activities. Farmers with too little land or water for self-sustenance must secure food. Some work as day agricultural laborers; others specialize in crafts or petty sales. Many migrate, at times using the money earned through migration to purchase land in Quinua. This migration in turn produces labor scarcity, propelling rich peasants and even poor ones to employ various strategies to secure workers. Many of these strategies require additional capital, creating further pressures on peasants to intensify nonagricultural production or to migrate. The poor are most affected by scarcity of land and cash, the rich by scarcity of labor and water. Although Quinuenos are affected differently by these economic limits on production, everyone is affected by one or another scarcity to some extent.

4.

AGRICULTURAL PRODUCTION AND FOOD CONSUMPTION

IN EARLIER chapters we have considered the resources available to Quinuenos: environmental (climate and the vertical ecosystem), social (ties of kin and fictive kin), and economic (access to land, animals, water, labor, and capital). Quinuenos use these resources to produce food. In this chapter we shall consider how savannah residents go about agricultural production, still the primary occupation of most of the population.

AGRICULTURAL FIELDS

Farmers utilize both outfields and infields. Called *chacras*, outfields are located away from the home and planted in the rainy-season cycle. Although they are often irrigated, *chacras* are generally cultivated less intensively than are infields. Infields are irrigated plots located close to home that are heavily fertilized with animal dung. They are always enclosed by walls of adobe or spiny plants to keep out the foraging animals that have been brought down from the pastures in the dry season. Near the central town, some of the infields are terraced with walls of stone or maguey, which has such a dense root system that it serves as a retaining wall (Mitchell 1987c).

The vast majority of fields in the savannah and valley bottom are irrigated outfields. Farmers sow savannah fields with maize, potatoes, barley, wheat, and peas. In the valley bottom they plant vegetables. In all other ecozones they must make do with unirrigated outfields, in which they grow wheat, barley, quinoa, peas, broad beans, and potatoes.

Although generally encircled by fences of trees, maguey, cactus, broom plant, or piles of stone, outfields are never completely enclosed. To prevent animals eating the crops, savannah farmers send their large herds to the high-altitude grasslands prior to sowing. They carefully watch the animals that remain, although the animals sometimes enter fields, destroying crops and creating disputes among neighbors.

Infields are used for maize, kitchen gardens, fruit orchards, and the dry-season crop. Farmers plant their best maize in permanent maize infields (known as *maizales* or *sara chacra*) next to the home. They avoid crop rotation in these fields by staking animals in them during the dry season and adding animal dung and bird guano by hand during the growing season. The irrigation system may also add fertile silt to these and all irrigated fields, providing phosphorus and other nutrients (Knapp 1987). Quinuenos also use the permanent maize fields as privies, thereby fertilizing them with human waste. In recent years farmers have come to supplement natural fertilizers with manufactured ones.

Many farmers maintain an irrigated infield as a kitchen garden (*huerta*) to grow *coles*, chili peppers, carrots, parsley, herbs, onions, broad beans, flowers, fruits, and at lower altitudes, tomatoes. They sometimes also plant them with small amounts of maize or potatoes. Kitchen gardens, however, are a luxury because they require frequent irrigation and take land out of cereal production.

A few wealthy people have an infield (also known as *huerta*) devoted exclusively to fruit trees, especially peaches, apples, *nispero*, *guinda*, *lucuma*, lemons, and oranges, but this is rare. Farmers generally cultivate fruit trees on the borders of outfields or in kitchen gardens, rather than in a special orchard.

In the upper savannah, close to the beginning of the irrigation system, some farmers maintain large infields (*solares*) to plant dry-season crops. In the lower savannah only a few of the rich and powerful command the necessary water and labor to maintain such fields far from the head irrigation intake.

In the agricultural census of 1972, irrigated fields (both infields and outfields) totaled 479.18 hectares, a figure that comprises 41.3 percent of all farmland (table 17).[1] Since all farmland is only 12.2 percent of all Quinua terrain (see table 8), irrigated infields are a minute proportion of all Quinua land.

THE AGRICULTURAL CYCLE

Quinua has two agricultural cycles: *hatun tarpuy* and *michka* (see also Brush 1977; Urton 1981 : 23–32). The term *hatun tarpuy* literally translates as "great planting," but because it takes place during

Table 17. *Distribution of Irrigated, Nonirrigated, and Fallow Farmland in Quinua, 1972*

	Percentage		
	Irrigated	Nonirrigated	Total
Under cultivation	81.3	76.8	78.6
In fallow			
Less than one year	2.4	4.7	3.8
More than one year	16.3	18.5	17.6
Total hectares			
Censual amount	922.44	1,309.00	2,231.44
Calculated amount[a]	479.19	680.00	1,159.19
Percentage of total	41.3	58.7	100.0

Source: Peru 1972: 480.
[a] Censual hectares multiplied by 4 divided by 7.7 (see chapter 3, note 10).

the rainy season, I have glossed it as "rainy-season cycle." Farmers produce most of the districts foodstuffs in this agricultural cycle, which exists in all cultivated ecological zones. The sowing lasts from September to December, and the harvest from April to July (Mitchell 1976a, 1976b, and 1980; see appendix 3).

Quinuenos use the term *michka* to refer to any crop planted out of its normal season (cf. Fujii and Tomoeda 1981 : 44). I have glossed the term as "dry-season cycle" because it is usually planted during the dry season, from August through September, a few weeks before the main planting (see appendix 4 for the calendar of major work in the dry-season cycle). Farmers plant the dry-season cycle in infields. They generally employ it for cash-cropping because it is harvested from December through February, when the shortage of fresh food results in high prices in urban markets. They plant potatoes preferentially, especially the quick-maturing *chawcha* variety, which yields the best monetary return. Farmers also grow green maize frequently in this crop cycle and sometimes plant peas, barley, wheat, and green vegetables. Farmers not only obtain cash but they minimize risk with a dry-season planting, since it provides them an additional opportunity for agricultural success. They are also able to distribute their agricultural work load more efficiently when they cultivate the two cycles (Mitchell 1980).

Quinuenos sometimes employ the dry-season planting for crop rotation and for double-cropping. In the valley bottom they almost always plant the dry season crop as part of a regime of double-cropping. In that zone, two crops a year are the rule rather than the exception. Farmers double-crop less frequently in the savannah, although in February they sometimes plant a second crop of barley, wheat, or peas after the harvest of the first crop of potatoes. They may stagger this second planting to produce a steady supply of crops for sale in Ayacucho. They also use the barley for animal fodder, as it is harvested in July and August when there is little other animal food available.

Despite its advantages, very few farmers plant the dry-season cycle because its heavy labor investment competes with temporary migration for work. The dry-season cycle requires walled infields, heavy fertilization, and constant surveillance against bird predation. Farmers must also irrigate dry-season crops, a major investment of labor. Moreover, few crops can physically tolerate the nighttime frosts. Since temporary work on the cotton plantations and highway construction brings a greater return than cash-cropping, farmers are reluctant to remain in Quinua to plant the dry-season cycle. It is only in the water-rich valley bottom where Quinuenos are heavily involved in the cash-cropping of green vegetables that farmers characteristically plant this cycle.

CROPPING METHODS AND SOIL FERTILITY

Crop yield depends on careful management practices to maintain soil fertility. Before the 1960s, farmers fertilized their fields with animal dung and bird guano. Since that time they have increasingly replaced these natural fertilizers with chemical ones, especially in potato cultivation. Fertilizer is scarce and expensive, so that farmers also employ crop interplanting, rotation, and fallowing. Interplanting different species in the same field mimics the natural ecosystem, increasing fertility and reducing risk. Legumes, such as peas, return nitrogen to the soil when interplanted or rotated with maize. Rotation and fallowing improve crop sanitation by inhibiting the spread of disease and pests. Such forage crops as barley, wheat, and alfalfa used at the end of a rotation cycle bring animals and their dung to the field. Interplanting also limits water and soil runoff because most interplanted crops are sown in rows that crosscut the main crop.

Because there is a great variety of cultigens in the savannah and valley bottom, farmers are able to interplant and rotate extensively in these zones. These practices combined with fertilization facilitate year-round cropping.

In the savannah and valley bottom, farmers divide the main crop with rows of interplanted crops, known as *mellgas* (often pro-

nounced *millga*), sown one and a half to two meters apart. Quinuenos use these interplanted rows to delineate the work zone of
each laborer during crop cultivation. They are unaware that the
mellga provides them the additional benefits of crop interplanting,
but that ignorance does not make this function any less important.
Farmers almost always plant maize with *mellgas* (*sara mellga*), separating the maize with rows of peas, broad beans, quinoa, or barley,
and less frequently beans, squash, wheat, or *kayhua*. They prefer to
plant rapidly maturing crops in the *mellga* to have fresh food before
the main harvest. They generally plant broad beans (*haba mellga*) in
a similar fashion.

In another form of interplanting, farmers crosscut a maize field
with additional rows (*siqi*) of quinoa or barley. They plant the rows
at right angles to the maize rows. In a kitchen garden or newly
opened field they may also sow maize intermixed randomly with the
same crops used in the *mellga*, a practice called *chapu tarpuy*.

The *tabla*, an interplanted row similar to the *mellga* but spaced
further apart, is a cropping method that farmers use primarily in tuber cultivation (potatoes, *mashua*, *oca*, and *olluku*). They divide the
tuber field into work zones by sowing rows of quinoa, oats, green
peas, barley, or broad beans about ten meters apart.

Quinuenos supplement crop interplanting with rotation, especially in the savannah, which has the requisite variety of crops (cf.
Urton 1981:32–35). Unlike other farmers of the Andes, Quinuenos
do not employ a sectoral fallowing system in which the community
regulates the period of fallow (Orlove and Godoy 1986). Quinuenos
make decisions to fallow individually (or in consultation with
neighbors) on the basis of personal needs. Farmers rotate all fields
other than permanent maize fields whenever possible. They favor
the rotation of potatoes with maize, in either a two-year or three-
year sequence. Most people divide a field between potatoes and interplanted maize, switching the crops in each half annually. Those
with sufficient fields sometimes sow a third year of barley or wheat
after the maize. Farmers with infields frequently rotate them between dry-season and rainy-season plantings, creating more complex schemes. They may sow dry-season potatoes in August, harvest
them in February, and then plant barley or wheat. They harvest
this crop in September and immediately plant the field with rainy-
season maize that they harvest in June. They begin the rotation
cycle again in August. Some farmers extend the rotation to four
years by growing rainy-season wheat between the maize and potatoes. Most farmers, however, have too few fields to achieve such

complex rotations and are restricted to the two-year rotation of potatoes with interplanted maize.

The moist forest, prairie, and thorn steppe have too few crops for significant interplanting or rotation and fields must be fallowed.[2] There are no simple rules for fallowing: the duration depends on the amount and type of land and the ability to fertilize and work it. Marginal land is fallowed before good land. Land is also rested when farmers run out of seed or labor. Migrants may even leave irrigated savannah fields unsown for lack of labor. In the agricultural census of 1972, 17.6 percent of the cultivated fields had lain fallow for more than a year (see table 17). Since farmers try to cultivate irrigated fields annually, it is probable that the 16.3 percent of irrigated fields in fallow resulted from reasons other than crop rotation. I suspect that most of the irrigated fields in fallow belong to migrants and that the percentage of unsown fields may be even higher today.

In the moist forest and prairie, Quinuenos rest their fields after a sequence of rotation. In the lower moist forest a common rotation and fallow pattern is (1) potatoes; (2) *mashua, oca,* or *olluku;* (3) wheat; (4) one to five years of fallow. Quinuenos also rotate potatoes with barley, broad beans, quinoa, and wheat. In higher areas of the moist forest and prairie where only tubers can grow, they will rotate the potatoes with *mashua, oca,* or *olluku,* followed by five to seven years of fallow. In still higher zones, where only bitter potatoes are grown and no crop rotation is possible, land lies fallow for six to seven years for every year of cultivation.

Fields also need fallowing in the thorn steppe, since the soil and climate there do not permit elaborate rotation. Farmers often plant wheat two years in a row, followed by peas or chick peas. Depending on the amount and quality of land they own, they may rest the land for the next two to three years, a period important in storing water for the subsequent crop. People with few fields, however, leave them fallow only if they run out of seed.

AGRICULTURAL LABOR REQUIREMENTS

Farming produces energy (food), but that production of course takes work. Potatoes and maize are Quinua's two most important crops. Potatoes yield more kilos per hectare than do maize, but they need significantly more labor (see appendixes 5–7 for a more complete exposition of the data).[3] In the most common case (the field prepared with a single plowing), the production of one *yugada*[4] of rainy-season potatoes requires 44 labor person-days (the number of total

Table 18. *Labor Requirements of Potatoes and Maize, Rainy-Season Crop Cycle (Hatun Tarpuy), Upper Savannah*[a]

	Days[b]	Men	Women	Men or Women	Total Laborers	Person-Days[b] per Yugada	per Hectare
Potatoes (*ruyaq sisa* variety)							
Irrigation	4.75–6.25	4	0	3–4	7–8	6.00	38
Plowing (two)	2.00	4	0	0	4	4.00	31
Seed potato curing	0.25	1	0	0	1	0.25	2
Sowing with hoe	1.00	4	0	1–2	5–6	6.00	46
Crop cultivation (two)	1.50	9	0	0–3	9–12	8.25	64
Harvest	1.75–3.00	5–9	4	0	9–13	8.00	62
Storage	7.00–11.00	1	6–9	0	7–10	11.25	87
Total	18.25–25.00	28–32	10–13	4–9	42–54	43.75	330
Maize (*almidon* variety)							
Irrigation	4.75–6.25	4	0	3–4	7–8	6.00	38
Fertilizing field	0.25	1	0	0	1	0.25	2
Plowing (one)	1.00	2	0	0	2	2.00	15
Sowing (with plow)	1.00	1	0	1	2	2.00	15
Crop cultivation (two)	3.00	5–6	0	0–1	5–7	6.00	46
Harvest	2.00–3.00	4–5	4–5	0	8–10	7.75	60
Storage	25.00–30.00	4–5	4–7	4	12–16	7.00	54
Total	37.00–44.50	21–24	8–12	8–10	37–46	31.00	230

Source: Informant interviews and observation; data largely reflect the experience of one informant.

[a] Time spent in the preparation of *chuño* or guarding the drying *cocopa* or *chochoca* is not included.

[b] Calculated by adding the figures in appendixes 6 and 7; the person-days per hectare are derived from those per *yugada* multiplied by 7.7 (and ⌐⌐est whole number), except for ⌐⌐⌐ation, where ⌐⌐ ⌐⌐intenance labor of the system is the same regardless of size of terrain.

days of human labor) compared to only 31 for maize (table 18). Potato production, therefore, requires 42 percent more labor than maize. Although cash-cropping potatoes is financially rewarding, the heavy labor demand competes with labor required in subsistence production and other economic activities. Potato farming requires more men than does maize farming, so that the male labor scarcity caused by migration limits its utility still further.

AGRICULTURAL PRODUCTION

It is difficult to measure agricultural production without supervised weighing of seeds and yields in the field. Unable to do this because of informant reluctance and constraints of time, I have employed the agricultural census of 1972 and informant data to arrive at estimates. I am aware of the problems in using informant data and the even greater ones in relying on a government census, but I am less concerned with reporting absolute figures than answering the question: Do Quinua households have enough land for subsistence? Both sources demonstrate that the answer is no. Most farmers have too little land to provide themselves and their families with sufficient food. These data contribute to our understanding of why farmers migrate and why they engage in so many nonfarm economic activities.

According to the 1972 agricultural census, maize, wheat, and barley are the most important crops, followed by peas, potatoes, and broad beans (Peru 1972). Maize is the premier crop in the census: 60 percent of the households reported planting maize in 1972, but only 8 percent reported planting potatoes. Although the census is correct in naming these crops as the most important ones in Quinua, the production figures are inaccurate. Since nearly every household in the savannah produces maize and since many households outside the savannah have maize fields in this zone, the census figure reporting only 60 percent of the households producing maize is much too low. More households also produce potatoes than the 8 percent indicated by the census. Most savannah families plant potatoes, even if in smaller quantities than maize. Low production figures are to be expected in a census feared by peasants as a preliminary to land seizure or taxation. The peasants, incidentally, were correct in their suspicions, as only one year after the census the Velasco government introduced a land reform program in Quinua attempting to alter local tenure patterns (Mitchell 1987c).

Informants report higher yields per hectare than those found in the census. In a good irrigated *yugada* (0.1294 hectare) in the upper savannah, one small Quinua producer (who farmed a total of two

Table 19. *Common Agricultural Yields from One Yugada, District of Quinua (Figures in Kilograms)*

	Gross Yield	Seed Weight	Net Yield	Consumable Yield	
				Range	Median
Potatoes	1,000–2,000	100–200	800–1,900	680–1,615	1,150
Maize	450–750	20–30	430–720	365–610	490
Potato–maize ratio	2.2–2.7	5.0–6.7	1.9–2.6	2.0–2.8	2.3

Source: One informant's experience obtained through interviews; the figures are rounded (see text).

Table 20. *Maize and Potatoes: Comparative Gross Production (Kilograms per Hectare)*

	Quinua		Uchucmarca	All Peru		South America	World
	Mitchell	Census		Census	Other		
Potatoes	8,855	1,659	2,693	2,407	5,500	9,853	13,852
Maize	3,773	421	609	800	1,727	1,925	3,345
Potato–maize ratio	2.3	3.9	4.4	3.0	3.2	5.1	4.1

Source: The figures in Quinua (Mitchell) are the medians of the gross yield in table 19 multiplied by 7.7; Quinua (Census) data are the actual figures reported in Peru 1972; Uchucmarca is from Brush 1977:174; "All Peru (Census)" data are from Peru 1972; "All Peru (Other)" data for potatoes are from the *Potato Atlas* of the International Potato Center 1978; all other data are from the FAO *Production Yearbook* for 1978–1981.

plots of a *yugada* each that he alternated between maize and potatoes) estimated in 1974 that his potato yields (planting the *ruyaq sisa* variety) ranged between 1,000 and 2,000 kilos per *yugada* (table 19). He used between 100 and 200 kilos of seed potatoes, and his costs of production in the 1973–1974 rainy-season cycle were $46.80 for seed potatoes, fertilizer, insecticide, and laborers. He sold 500 kilos of his crop for $0.12 the kilo giving him a gross return of $58.50, which more than met his costs. The rest of the crop he kept for home consumption.

His maize yields (planting the *almidon* variety) were much less, ranging between 500 and 800 kilos of husked and dried ears per *yugada* using 20 to 30 kilos of seed.[5] The kernels make up .933 of the combined dried cob and kernel weight,[6] giving us a net range for the kernel weight of 450 to 750 kilos (with figures rounded to the nearest 25 kilos) (table 19). His production costs in 1974 were $23.40, which he met by selling 200 kilos at $0.12 the kilo. He kept the rest of the maize and the crops planted in the *mellga* for home consumption.

Other informants say this farmer's experiences are common ones[7] and can be used to estimate regular maize and potato yields. A *yugada* of good land in good years yields between 1,000 and 2,000 kilos of potatoes and between 450 and 750 kilos of maize, a ratio of 2.2–2.7 to 1 (table 19). This is close to the ratio throughout Peru of 3.0 kilos of potatoes to 1 kilo of maize (Caballero 1981:185).[8] Nevertheless, these production figures for Quinua are very high compared to the rest of Peru. If a hectare contains 7.7 *yugadas*, a Quinua hectare yields a median of 8,855 kilos of potatoes and 3,773 kilos of maize (table 20). The per hectare production for all Peru, however, is only 5,500 kilos for potatoes and 1,727 kilos for maize (table 20).

If my figures on production err on the high side, of course, the Quinua peasant has even more difficulty in feeding his family than my analysis below indicates.[9]

Gross production figures, of course, do not tell us how much of the crop is available for consumption. Although Quinuenos buy seed, many obtain seed from the prior harvest. If we subtract seed weights from the figures for Quinua, we get a net yield per *yugada* of between 800 to 1,900 kilos of potatoes and between 430 and 720 kilos of maize (table 19). These figures, however, do not account for postharvest food losses, which have been calculated at 15 percent of production for developing countries (National Research Council 1978). Applying this 15 percent figure provides a consumable yield for a *yugada* of between 680 and 1,615 kilos of potatoes (or a median of 1,150 kilos) and 365 and 610 kilos of maize (median of 490 kilos) (figures rounded to nearest 5 kilos).

The data clearly show that potatoes outproduce maize on the basis of weight. This is important to Quinuenos who think in terms of weight and prices. If we compare maize and potatoes on the basis of their caloric and protein values rather than gross weight, however, maize actually yields more food value than potatoes even though it yields less in weight (INCAP-ICNND 1961; Gebhardt 1988). Potatoes are 77.9 percent water and yield 790 calories and 28 grams of protein per kilogram. Maize is only 10.6 percent water and yields a much higher 3,610 calories and 94 grams of protein per kilogram (INCAP-ICNND 1961). In Quinua, a *yugada* of maize provides nearly twice the consumable calories and almost one and a half times the consumable protein of a *yugada* of potatoes (see table 21). Maize provides Quinuenos with more of their necessary calories and protein than do potatoes, in spite of gross weight differences.[10] I suggest that this nutritional importance is the reason why maize carries such ceremonial importance in the Andes and why people invest so much labor in building and maintaining irrigated maize zones.

Raw figures on agricultural production can be deceptive, as land quality varies with ecological zone, soil, and the availability of water. Fertilizer, labor, crop rotation, fallowing, seed, disease, and drought are other important variables. In some years agricultural production will be high, while in others a farmer may not even get back the seeds he has planted. In the 1988–1989 agricultural year the rains were delayed and then appeared in terrible force, destroying

Table 21. *Comparative Food Value of Maize and Potatoes: Consumable Yields from One* Yugada, *Upper Savannah,* Quinua

	Net Median Yield		
	Weight[a] (Kilograms)	Calories[b]	Protein[c] (Grams)
Dried maize	490	1,768,900	46,060
Potatoes	1,150	908,500	32,200
Maize–potato ratio	0.43	1.95	1.43

Source: INCAP-ICNND 1961 and informant data.

[a]Median net consumable yield (see table 19).

[b]Calculated by multiplying the production in weight by 3,610 calories per kilogram for maize and 790 calories per kilogram for potatoes (INCAP-ICNND 1961).

[c]Calculated by multiplying the production in weight by 94 grams per kilogram for maize and 28 grams per kilogram for potatoes (INCAP-ICNND 1961).

much of the crop, so that Quinuenos report that they only harvested about 200 kilos each of maize and potatoes per *yugada*, a much diminished crop. For these reasons, we cannot use the figures on yields as fixed amounts. Nonetheless, they are measures of the relative productivity of Quinua's two most important crops, and when combined with data on food consumption, they suggest the minimum amount of land necessary to feed a single person through subsistence farming in good agricultural years.

HOUSEHOLD FOOD CONSUMPTION AND LAND REQUIREMENTS

Quinuenos eat differently depending on location and social class (see also Cavero 1953:23–24).[11] Townspeople awaken before dawn around 6:00 A.M. and eat a breakfast of rolls (made with bleached wheat flour) and a hot drink made of herbs, milk with chocolate, or a very thin oatmeal (*quaker*) around 7:00. At noon they eat lunch, the principal meal, which begins with a hearty soup. The most common soups are maize soup, barley soup, wheat soup, and seven seeds soup (milled barley, maize, wheat, peas, chick peas, broad beans, and quinoa). Women generally add small amounts of lard, mutton, beef, potatoes, greens, or noodles to the main ingredient. Maize soup for six adults, for example, might contain one kilo of milled maize, one-half kilo of potatoes, a bunch of wild mustard called *llullu* (*Brassica campestres*), half a bunch of fresh oregano, an ounce of lard, an onion, and two ounces of salt, as well as the water. The soup is followed by a main course of rice or noodles with small amounts of mutton. A soup is served for dinner around 5:00 P.M. Quinuenos go to sleep just after nightfall around 7:00.

Peasants in the savannah awaken and retire for the night around the same time as townspeople, but they eat very differently. They usually begin breakfast with hot water mixed with sugar and *machka* (toasted and milled maize, *achita*, wheat, or chick peas). A short while later, they generally have a second course of soup that they call lunch (*almuerzo*). They eat a similar soup for dinner. These soups are like those of the townspeople, except they are made with animal fat and rarely with meat. Midday lunch (called *dusiy*) is a minor meal, since women are not home to cook and everyone is generally working in the fields. Peasants usually eat a dry lunch of hominy (*mote*), parched maize, boiled potatoes, and chili sauce, or perhaps some food made out of wheat, quinoa, or peas. If they are at home, they may reheat the morning soup for lunch. Heavy agricultural labor, however, requires a substantial lunch, usually a hearty wheat soup. In the 1950s the peasant diet began to incorporate more sugar, rice, and noodles, so that today some peasants eat meals that approximate those of the townspeople.

All meals other than the townspeople's breakfast are served with a condiment of chopped or crushed chili peppers mixed with water, chopped chives, and salt. Diners season their own food with this condiment at the table.

Maize and potatoes are the preeminent foods in the savannah area of Quinua. They are both added to soups and prepared as main courses. A common bowl filled with boiled potatoes and another of hominy is generally placed on the table at most savannah meals. Ubiquitous in all but the high-altitude areas where maize is not produced, hominy (dried maize kernels boiled in water) is a major form in which maize is eaten. This pattern differs from areas in southern Peru where maize is consumed primarily in the form of beer (Fujii and Tomoeda 1981 : 45; Yamamoto 1981 : 105). The diners serve themselves. They pick out kernels of hominy, remove the fibrous base, and eat the remainder. From the other bowl they select potatoes, which they peel, dip in chili sauce, and eat. They discard the peels, leaving them on the table or throwing them on the floor for the chickens and guinea pigs. In the high-altitude grazing and potato-growing regions, people eat less maize and more potatoes (Flannery et al. 1989).

Except for the peasant lunch, when the woman is unable to cook, food is freshly prepared at all meals. Women never save food from one day to the next, but feed any leftovers to the pigs.

Peasants and townspeople also eat differently depending on the time of year. At fiestas celebrants eat more meat and other special foods than at other times of year. They also drink maize beer at these celebrations, as well as during festive agricultural work groups. This beer is a source of calories and nutrition and should not be dismissed as mere intoxicant (cf. Fujii and Tomoeda 1981:45, 65; Yamamoto 1981 : 105).

The availability of fresh food diminishes after the harvest, as does the total quantity of food consumed (cf. Allen 1988 : 137; Gonzales 1987 : 58–60).[12] In January and February many Quinuenos supplement their agricultural produce with a wild mustard called *yuyo* or *llullu*, which grows on the border of puna springs and lakes. Many people have to migrate in March to obtain cash to buy food as well as other things. In one study reported by Schaedel (1967, Table 5), people in the community of Chacán consumed daily 1,593 calories and 37 grams of protein per capita in June right after the harvest, but only 1,340 calories and 34 grams of protein a day in December, a de-

Table 22. *Adult Food Consumption for One Quinua Family, Upper Savannah, 6/28/74–8/3/74*

Daily per Capita Consumption in Kilos

Grains, Tubers, Vegetables		Fruits	
Potatoes	.553	*Molle* berries	.052
Maize	.517	Apples	.005
Squash	.491		
Wheat	.176	Prepared Foods	
Mashua	.154	Bread	.036
Onions	.127	Noodles	.013
Oca	.079	Oil (liters)	.013
Lentils	.053	Wheat flour	.002
Quinoa	.048	Herbs	
Carrots	.036	Parsley	.052
Broad beans	.035	Oregano	.041
Peas	.035	Coriander	.007
Olluku	.031	Yerba buena	.007
Chickpeas	.023	*Paycco*	.004
Barley	.022	*Torongil*	.002
Beans	.009	*Moña*	.002
Machka	.009	*Huakatay*	<.001
Oats	.009		
Yuyu	.005	Condiments	
Peanuts	.004	Salt	.026
Meat, Fish, Poultry		Sugar	.015
Fish	.018	Chocolate	.009
Bacon	.010	Chili peppers	.006
Meat	.009	Vanilla	.006
Animal fats	.003	Achiote	<.001
Tripe	.001	Various spices	<.001
Milk, Cheese, Eggs			
Milk (liters)	.020		
Eggs	.005		
Cheese	.004		

Source: Diary of field assistant.

cline of 16 percent and 8 percent, respectively. This reduction is considerable when one considers the marginal caloric and protein intake even at the harvest time.

A field assistant recorded the food consumption of his family for two months in 1973 (table 22). The family were wealthy peasants who lived in the savannah near the central town. The head of household had lived on the coast for sixteen years, raising money to buy land, while his wife and children had remained in Quinua. At the time of the data gathering, he had been residing permanently in Quinua for four years and was cultivating one hectare (eight *yugadas*) of good irrigated savannah land, one-half hectare (four *yugadas*) of moderately good nonirrigated savannah land, and one-half hectare (four *yugadas*) of poor nonirrigated land in the thorn steppe. The household consisted of the male head (age 53), his wife (in her 40s), their three sons (age 23, 9, and 2), and two daughters (age 10 and 12). A third daughter was living in Lima. In my data on per capita consumption, I exclude the 2-year-old but include the children 9, 10, and 12 years of age. The per capita figures therefore underestimate adult consumption considerably.

Food consumption, of course, differs with economic level, and it is likely that this family consumed more than most poor families. Average annual per capita consumption in the Cuzco region is certainly less (Gonzales 1987:99). My data, moreover, were collected during the harvest, which is a period of general abundance. The consumption of squash, green maize, and some of the tubers, such as *mashua*, is especially high at this time of year, while that of wheat and other dried and storable grains is lower. Nonetheless, several interesting patterns characteristic of Quinua cuisine emerge from the data.

This family and most Quinuenos obtain their protein in plant form. They rarely eat animal products and fish. Most Quinuenos use large quantities of salt, and this family consumed more salt than sugar. During the period of data collection, they consumed mostly local products, obtaining only a few prepared foods and condiments from outside Quinua. Even though fairly wealthy, they ate few noodles and no rice. It is likely that data collected well after the harvest in March and April would include more such prepared foods.

Potatoes and maize, closely followed by squash, were the major items in their diet during this period right after the harvest. They ate 0.517 kg of maize and 0.553 kg of potatoes per day per person, consumption figures strikingly close to independent estimates of moderately well-off informants who say that a peasant adult usually consumes around 0.5 kg of maize and 0.5 kg of potatoes per day.[13] The figure on potato consumption is also close to Ferroni's calculation that in the central and southern highlands people eat on average 0.494 kg of potatoes daily (1980, Tables 6.9 and 6.10).[14] These data allow us to estimate that, if the food is available, Quinuenos would consume around 182 kg of maize and 182 kg of potatoes per person per year. Of course, if the food is unavailable, as it is for many Quinuenos, people eat less.

Combining the estimate above for Quinuenos' optimal food consumption (182 kg of maize and 182 kg of potatoes consumed per capita per year) with that for median agricultural production (490 kg of consumable maize and 1,150 kg of potatoes produced per *yugada* each year) suggests that one person requires 0.371 *yugada* in a good year for maize consumption (182 kg/490 kg) and 0.158 *yugada* for potatoes (182 kg/1,150 kg). Everyone therefore requires at least 0.529 *yugada* for just their optimal maize and potato requirements. In poor years, however, when production is much less, people require more land or have to reduce their food consumption.

If we project their food consumption pattern over the year, this family also consumed 64.24 kg of wheat, 56.21 kg of *mashua*, and 46.35 kg of onions per capita per year (table 22). Quinuenos produce 281 kg, 375 kg, and 449 kg (consumable yield) of these foods, respectively, per *yugada* per year. (See appendix 8 for a discussion of the methodology used to extrapolate production figures from the 1972 agricultural census.) These figures suggest that a savannah adult requires at least 0.229 *yugada* for optimal wheat consumption, 0.150 *yugada* for *mashua*, and 0.103 *yugada* for onions. Adding these figures to those for potatoes and maize indicates that it takes at least 1.011 *yugada* to provision an adult with these five staples. An adult would, of course, need additional land for squash (also consumed in large quantities), as well as for all other foods: *oca*, lentils, quinoa, carrots, broad beans, peas, *olluku*, chick peas, barley, beans, *machka*, and oats.

These data support the conclusion that Quinuenos living in the savannah require *at least* 1 *yugada* of land per capita in *good* years. Since my production figures are high compared to most other studies (and since I have not included some important foods in my calculations), it is probable that savannah residents need even more land per person. Those living in the thorn steppe and high-altitude areas, where resource production is low, require still more.

The average household in 1981 had 4.4 occupants, and the average conjugal family had 4.7 (table 11). Many households, of course, were much larger. The 112 joint families averaged 7.6 people. If the average family of 4 or 5 persons owns 1 *yugada* (twice the mean suggested by the agricultural census), they can barely feed 1 adult, and the others must do without. If they own 2 *yugadas* (the mode proposed by most informants), they can hardly feed 2 adults in good agricultural years, and they certainly cannot feed any children. If they own 4 *yugadas* (the upper limit of my modal range of 2–4 *yugadas*), they can feed at least some of the children as well as the adults. However, this family would be unable to cash-crop in a significant way to provide its cash needs for seeds, fertilizer, labor, coca leaves, alcohol, medicine, school supplies, and so on. They would have no food for ceremonial expenditures and would be unable to supply themselves with food in poor years. Families with one-half hectare (4 *yugadas*) could possibly live on their own production in good years, but life would be bland and precarious. Since my data on agricultural production appear to be high, however, the situation is probably more difficult for the Quinua family than these figures indicate.[15]

The production and consumption data show that many Quinuenos are unable to grow enough food to feed themselves on their own farms (cf. Flannery et al. 1989:76). Many informants report that even in good years they only produce enough maize, wheat, and potatoes to last about half a year, after which they must either reduce consumption or revert to the market to purchase food. In poor years, their situation is much worse. These findings are supported by departmentwide information showing that during 1971–1979 Ayacucho only produced an average of 130 kg of potatoes and 50–52 kg of maize per capita per year (Jurado 1983, as cited in Degregori 1986:202). The situation is even worse than indicated, of course, because some of this produce is sold outside rather than consumed within the department. Indeed, Ferroni calculates that 63 percent of all sierra families have insufficient land to support themselves from their own agricultural production (1980:155).

The above production figures also suggest why farmers cash-crop potatoes more frequently than maize. The weight yield is better, and they often command the highest price per weight of any crop in urban markets. The heavy labor demand of potatoes, however, militates against cash-cropping potatoes in a major way. Most peasants are able to plant only small amounts because of limited labor. Farmers consequently turn to nonfarm cash-producing activities to supplement agricultural production. During the last forty years, as population has increased and the Peruvian economy has become less favorable for rural agriculture, the problems have become more difficult for the Quinueno, forcing more and more peasants off the farm and into the cash economy.

5.

THE STRUCTURE OF
ECONOMIC EXCHANGE,
1966–1974

ALTHOUGH QUINUA is largely an agricultural community, for as long as they can remember, its people have been unable to support themselves solely from their own fields. Farmers must struggle to obtain agricultural resources, clothing, schooling, medicines, coca leaves, and such things of pleasure as musical instruments. In 1967 a peasant spent about $0.19 a day for coca leaves, one-third the daily agricultural wage of $0.56. Quinuenos, therefore, have always tried to earn cash. The present chapter focuses on the Quinua economy as it existed in 1966–1974 and earlier. The chapter concludes with a discussion of the macroeconomic events that began to constrain Quinua production after the 1940s and that helped initiate the changes in the Quinua economy discussed in chapter 6.

INTERZONAL TRADE

Even though they strive for self-sufficiency, most Peruvian peasants are unable to provision themselves from their own fields (Figueroa 1984). The majority of Quinua peasants do not have enough land to supply their families with essential foods, while any expansion of terrain is restricted by local ecology. Even large landowners suffer production deficits because of natural factors (e.g., rain, insects, disease) and labor shortages. Farmers not only need the products of ecozones in which they have no fields (cf. Caballero 1981:54) but also goods not produced locally, such as coca leaves and salt.

All peasant households employ various strategies to produce a surplus of ecologically favored crops and animal products to barter for those from other zones. People of the valley bottom offer fruits and vegetables; those from the thorn steppe *molle* berries and prickly pear; those from the savannah maize and potatoes; and (before 1983) those from the moist forest and higher zones tubers, meat, and wool. People within the same ecological zone also exchange agricultural products, and a family in the savannah may use its excess wheat to obtain maize from a neighbor.

Quinuenos also exchange crafts and services for food. The poor exchange their labor for payment in kind during crop cultivation and especially during the harvest to supplement their own production. Before the 1960s ceramics were produced primarily to barter for food, although in 1966 cash sales had already become important. In 1967 a ceramicist earned half a sack of potatoes (about 25 kilos) in exchange for one vessel known as a *porongo* (cf. Arnold 1972).

Until 1983 pastoralists cared for the animals of savannah farmers, receiving cash, produce, or labor in return. In 1980 farmers paid the herders $0.37 per season (August to April) for the care of each cow and $0.18 for each sheep (the daily agricultural wage was $1.11). The cash payment was supplemented with gifts of maize beer, coca leaves, cigarettes, brandy and a large plate of cooked chicken, guinea pig, and potatoes—known as the *derecho*. The owners also gave additional gifts of maize and other food and drink throughout the year, when they made periodic visits to oversee the care of their animals and to ensure they were given any offspring. Peasants sometimes contributed labor to the pastoralist in lieu of or to supplement cash payments; they would help cultivate potatoes and help build and repair animal corrals.

Residents of all zones use eggs, cheese, and (to a lesser extent) agricultural products to obtain such imported products as coca leaves, sugar, rice, and noodles from town shopkeepers. People with access to cash and urban centers purchase coca leaves and manufactured goods (clothing, soap, matches, agricultural tools, rice, bread, sugar, noodles) to exchange for foods from more rural areas. Crop theft, especially of potatoes and maize, is also common and must be viewed as another strategy for supplementing agricultural production.

Many people travel during the harvest season to different eco-zones for trade. Before 1983 they would, for example, bring potatoes, dried meat, and wool from the higher altitudes to exchange for maize grown in lower altitudes. They made the trip in June and July, when the maize was drying in the sun before storage. It is always cheaper to go directly to the farmer to barter, especially during the harvest, than to barter in the market. Sellers are motivated to give a cheaper price at home because of the time saved by not having to take goods to the market and also because of the company and help in the field generally provided by the trader.

In 1967 I accompanied one woman from the central town on such a trade trip. This woman was a monolingual Quechua-speaker who had been born in the rural savannah but had moved to the town after her marriage. She took three burros loaded with coca leaves, sugar, rice, and bread to the hamlet of Ñahuinpuquio, some four hours away in the prairie. There she visited three fields, chatting with the owners and helping them harvest. She was known to them because she traveled there every May to trade, and they also visited her when they came to the central town. After a decent interval, she produced her goods in exchange for *oca, mashua, olluku,* and broad beans. Her rate of exchange was very favorable. For only $0.20 in trade goods, she obtained a sack (about 50 kilos) of *oca, mashua, olluku,* and broad beans that would have cost $0.94 in the Quinua market. We were not alone in our trade but encountered other traders from other areas of Quinua, each bringing trade goods or local produce for barter.

The agricultural tribute assigned to the priest must also be considered a form of trade, albeit an involuntary one. Until 1980 the priest received a portion of everybody's harvest known as the *primicia.* All landowners contributed the same amount of produce to the priest regardless of property size. The poor, therefore, paid relatively more than the rich. The priest divided his rights into regional sectors and sold them to rich townspeople. The buyers traveled with hired laborers to harvest their sections, but peasants rushed to complete their harvest before the buyers arrived in order to pay as little as possible. The quantity of food was considerable. The harvest of the Hanan Sayoc *primicia* took from two to four weeks.

THE SUNDAY MARKET

A market is held in the central town every Sunday morning (see Appleby 1976a; Bromley 1976, 1981; and Orlove 1986 for other descriptions of Andean markets). Some outside merchants specialize in going from market to market with specialty goods: coca leaves, clothing, shoes, pots and pans, other manufactured household goods, medicines, and such specialty foods as fish. Others come to purchase local produce for home consumption or to bulk it for resale. Local food vendors sell prepared foods. The heart of the market, however, is the exchange of local produce, which accounts for most market volume (cf. Bromley 1981). The market in Quinua specializes in maize and vegetables, while neighboring communities specialize in meat, potatoes, and other high-altitude products.

Quinuenos hold the market in the street in front of the church. Peasant women pay a fee to the municipality ($0.02 in 1967, or $0.05

in 1974) for a place in which to exchange agricultural produce. They heap the produce in small piles on shawls on the ground in front of them. Rich peasants may bring their produce to the market throughout the year, while smaller landholders generally do so only in the months immediately after the harvest. The poorest have no surplus for barter and usually only bring prickly pear in the months of January through March.

The Sunday market is an exciting event. Peasants arrive in the central town at dawn to buy and sell produce. The streets are filled with people and the cantinas do a thriving business in sales of cane alcohol and maize beer. Political authorities take advantage of the market to hold political reunions (*asambleas*) and make public announcements. In the past the peasant political leaders also gathered near the marketplace to receive orders from the town authorities.

Buyers and sellers establish personal relationships, and regular vendors and clients call one another *caseras* (cf. Orlove 1986:93). The seller favors regular clients by selling or bartering better-quality goods at a slight discount, providing credit, and giving an extra quantity (*yapa*), similar to a baker's dozen. The buyer is loyal in dealing with the same *casera* and no other.

The majority of exchanges in the market were by barter (*trueque*) in 1966, although townswomen always tried to use cash. They were ashamed to barter because it signified lack of money. Cash sale is also easier, as people do not have to search for a coincidence of interests—that is, two people wanting to exchange what each desires. Peasants preferred barter, however, because money was in short supply, whereas produce was not. They bartered for potatoes, grains, vegetables, fruits, and coca leaves but generally paid cash for rice, sugar, noodles, bread, soap, and fertilizer. As we shall see in chapter 6, cash sales became more common in 1988.

Cash prices were (and are) determined by demand and the calculation of production and distribution costs. Peasants are well aware of the monetary costs involved in the production and transport of their crop. They always try to recover at least those costs, although they do not consciously factor in the cost of their own labor. Demand is also important. Women are very reluctant to return home with leftover produce and will discount its monetary and exchange value when demand is slack.

The municipality takes an active role in controlling the market prices of vegetables from the valley bottom and other imported goods. Women often complain in secret to the municipal police when a price is too high, and the seller may be fined. The municipality, however, does not control prices of potatoes, maize, or other foods produced in the savannah.

Women set barter values according to the quality of the goods and demand. They assign the exchange value through discussion, using the cash value of their goods as a rough guide (cf. Orlove 1986:94). Cash and barter values are only roughly equivalent, however. Interzonal trade affects barter values but has less influence on cash prices. If a woman can get one volume of potatoes for an equal volume of prickly pear by traveling to the potato producer, barter demand is affected; but since the people who pay cash do not travel to barter, cash demand is unaffected. In addition, women sometimes alter their cash price—but not their barter price—in response to cash needs. When they do so, they are treating cash as a commodity, a good like any other to be acquired when the need arises.

Circumstances often force small producers to barter rather than to sell their goods for cash. It is more difficult to sell in small rather than large quantities; the cash price is also significantly less, while the unit transport cost is higher. The large producer, on the other hand, gets a better cash price than the small producer, and her unit costs are less.

Large producers are usually able to obtain advantageous rates of exchange in barter as well as cash transactions. The relative advantages of the large vis-à-vis the small producer is illustrated by the experience of one large producer who sells the majority of her produce but always keeps some for exchange, which she uses to considerable advantage. In 1988 she gave one sack of potatoes (about 50 kilos) in return for one sack of barley (about 70 kilos) from a small producer who had come to her home to make the exchange. In the market, the sack of potatoes would have cost about $0.16 the kilo, while the barley would have cost $0.25 the kilo. The large producer was ahead by 60 percent. To get a better price, the small producer would have had to travel to Ayacucho, losing a day in the journey, paying for the trip and food, risking the unknown, and gambling on making a sale at a good price. By bartering in Quinua, she avoids these costs and risks and is offered friendship, and food if she arrives during mealtime. She also maintains a personal relationship with the large producer, which might be of advantage at some future date—to secure such benefits as work, political help, or godparenthood ties.[1]

SOCIOCEREMONIAL EXCHANGE

Peasants also exchange produce and wealth in socioceremonial exchanges. The giving and receiving of food and drink are important social acts that are used to initiate and maintain social relationships. Such gifts cannot be refused without causing ill will—creating significant problems for the researcher, as well as for Quinuenos. I have been drunk or overfed more times than I care to recount! Quinuenos often exchange food informally, using the food to create and affirm social bonds. Someone visiting a friend, *compadre*, or relative may bring a small gift of bread or produce, which is reciprocated in some way by the recipient. A person cultivating another's land often remits a portion of the harvest to the owner.

Quinuenos use a formal gift known as the *derecho* or *huallpa qui* to establish a contract. A person who accepts this plate of chicken (*huallpa*), guinea pig (*qui*), and refried potatoes after the donor has made a specific request has accepted a contract, an acceptance as binding in public opinion as a signature. The organizer (*mayordomo*) of a fiesta secures fellow workers (*cargo* holders) by giving them this food. Parents seek out godparents for their children in the same way. In a general context, without a specific request, chicken and guinea pig are a way of saying "thank you," and the quantity given is frequently less than when the presentation is part of a contract. In this case the gift is known simply as *huallpa qui*, not as *derecho*.

Gifts of maize beer, brandy, cigarettes, and coca leaves commonly accompany work groups. Food and alcohol are also distributed during public and private fiestas. Public fiestas are associated with the *cargo* system discussed in chapter 7. Private fiestas center on life-passage events, especially birthdays, baptisms, first haircuts, and marriages. People use private fiestas to maintain their standing in the community and thereby initiate and maintain important personal relationships. They also, of course, enjoy the drinking and dancing at these social affairs for their own sake.

Ostensibly reciprocal, these exchanges of food and drink often tend to foster and sustain relations of inequality. Large landowners, the rich, and powerful Quinuenos give these goods to peasants working in their fields or on public work projects. The wealthy also distribute prodigious quantities of food at fiestas, and it is at such times that peasants eat meat and other specialty foods.

LONG-DISTANCE TRADE

In addition to exchange within the community, Quinuenos trade with other areas of Peru, using both barter and cash. They exchange food locally, getting meat from the neighboring community of Vinchos and potatoes from Huamanguilla. They get manufactured goods from the cities of Ayacucho, Lima, and Huancayo. From the warm valleys in the North, they obtain fruit, chilies, and avocados. From the high altitudes in the South, they get cloth and animals. From the East they get salt and such tropical forest *montaña* products as fruit, chilies, and coca leaves. Eastern Peru also provides them with such high-altitude products as tubers, wool, hides, cloth, broad beans, freeze-dried *oca* (*kaya*), freeze-dried *olluku* (*chullqi*), and freeze-dried potatoes (*chuño*). From western Peru they get salt and additional high-altitude products: freeze-dried tubers, wool, hides, and cloth.

Some traders come to Quinua, their llamas and burros burdened with goods, displaying their wares from house to house. The arrival of traders from Huancavelica bringing high-altitude products in exchange for maize is an annual event around harvest time (May through August). Other traders and merchants come to the Sunday market. Some travel to Quinua during the harvest, arranging to buy produce in bulk. In addition, some Quinuenos travel throughout Peru to trade and to sell hats, food, and whatever else will bring an income. In one hamlet in 1987, 24 percent of the heads of households often traveled away from Quinua on overnight buying or sales trips. Another 20 percent made regular day trips (usually for business purposes) to the city of Ayacucho. At the present time traders travel by truck; formerly they did so by mule train. (See Burchard 1974 for a description of the economic advantages of Andean trade.)

Trade between Quinua and the outside, as well as within the community itself, is facilitated by an extensive system of foot and animal roads. Since the construction of Peru's highway system, Quinuenos have allowed some of these foot roads to deteriorate, but the major ones are still in good condition. They connect Quinua with the tropical forest *montaña* to the east and the coastal plain to the west, as well as with other Andean valleys, such as Cuzco and Mantaro.

CASH INCOME

Within living memory, peasants have always cash-cropped a small portion of the total harvest (cf. Brush 1977:114–115; Caballero

1981 : 285). The major cash crops are vegetables from the valley bottom (carrots, lettuce, onions), maize from the savannah (especially green maize), and potatoes from the prairie, savannah, thorn steppe, and valley bottom. Farmers also sow peas, onions, lentils, wheat, barley, and broad beans for cash sale. The dry-season cycle is almost always a cash crop of potatoes, as they are ready for sale in February, three months before the main harvest, and bring high prices. In 1974 they received $0.14 per kilo for dry-season potatoes but only $0.07 for those from the main harvest. Some informants devoted their potato land to dry-season production, selling all the yield and buying potatoes for home consumption when prices declined. In effect, they doubled their potato production with this strategy. Not everyone can do this, however, because of insufficient labor or water.

In addition to cash-cropping, all Quinua families produce a variety of additional incomes. They rarely consume their animals or animal products but sell the eggs, cheese, wool, animal fat, and animals. In 1967 they sold their eggs to town stores for $0.03 each, and the store resold them for $0.04 each. They also sell or barter natural products like firewood, prickly pears, and *molle* berries. They sell these goods to stores in the town or to buyers who come to the Sunday market. This produce eventually reaches the city of Ayacucho.

Quinuenos also manufacture various goods, work at assorted trades, and engage in petty commerce to obtain cash and goods through barter. Artisans have produced ceramics, roof tiles, adobe bricks, cloth, ponchos, blankets, sweaters, hats, mandolins, guitars, and wooden spoons for many years. Guitar makers routinely took their instruments to the Sunday fair in Huancayo to sell or trade. In 1966 Quinuenos made bread sporadically for the Sunday fair and special breads shaped like babies or horses for All Saints Day. Every hamlet has carpenters, masons (for house construction), blacksmiths (for the repair of agricultural tools), and cooks who help prepare food at fiestas. Specialists (called *perritos*) assess the value of a field to be sold; others (*tasaq*) appraise the damages an animal has made to someone's field. Less common, but frequent enough, are musicians, tailors, shoemakers, barbers, herders, mule drivers, beekeepers, curers, and witches, as well as such rare specialists as the person who decorates the floats and altars during fiestas. A very few families also have paid servants.

In addition, Quinua employs such professional workers as the postmaster, police, priest, health care workers, municipal secretary, and schoolteachers. Most of these professionals come from outside Quinua, although some of them have married Quinuenos.

Some rich townspeople lend money at interest (as high as 60 percent annually in the 1960s). Other townspeople use their political position to obtain work on government projects. The mayor of the town, for example, earned $2.49 per day in 1967 as the watchman for the construction of a dam in Hanan Sayoc. The authorities are also able to use their influence to obtain bribes. One mayor was placed in jail in the 1970s because he sold (or so some claimed) false identity documents.

Even before 1966 many Quinuenos engaged in some sort of commerce. Alcohol has always been important and provided income to those who prepare or sell it. A few small stores existed in 1966. The proliferation of these stores is discussed in chapter 6, along with other activities that have increased in importance: ceramic manufacture, highway work, food sales to travelers, and the collecting of cochineal and other natural products. Migration and migrant remittances have been an important source of household income since at least the turn of the century. The increased importance of such migration over time is also discussed in chapter 6.

Table 23 illustrates the partial 1974 income of the head of household and his wife in a prosperous peasant family, the same one whose food consumption is described in chapter 4. The data only record monetary income obtained through cash sales and do not include the value of the food they consume or barter. This family obtained 65.4 percent of its monetary income from agriculture, 15.3 percent from pastoral activities, and 17.5 percent from petty commerce, the majority of this from the wife's lively business of prepar-

Table 23. *Household Monetary Income for One Family during 38 Days in Dry Season, 6/28/74–8/3/74*

| | Weekly Income | | |
	Soles	US $[a]	% of Total
Source of Income			
Agriculture	335.45	7.85	65.4
Animals/animal products	78.28	1.83	15.3
Petty commerce	89.71	2.10	17.5
Unknown	9.21	0.22	1.8
Total weekly income	512.66	12.00	100.0

Source: Diary of research assistant.

[a] US dollars are the equivalent of the earnings in soles.

Table 24. *Household Monetary Expenses for One Family during 38 Days in Dry Season, 6/28/74–8/3/74*

	Weekly Expenses		
	Soles	*US $[a]*	*% of Total*
Type of Expense			
Consumption			
Food	362.99	8.49	47.8
Household	85.29	2.00	11.2
Personal	44.67	1.05	5.9
Medicine	59.13	1.38	7.8
Subtotal	552.08	12.92	72.7
Production	206.96	4.84	27.3
Total	759.04	17.76	100.0

Source: Diary of research assistant.
[a] US dollars are the equivalent of the amount in soles.

ing and selling curds. These data do not include ancillary income in the conjugal family that may have been factored into the couple's economic decisions. A daughter living in Lima may have been sending the family remittances of money and manufactured goods from time to time, and a son receiving an income as my research assistant may have also provided his parents with at least the expectation of his contributions. Elsewhere in the sierra, peasant families typically obtain 25–40 percent of their monetary income from local and nonlocal wages (Caballero 1981:220; Figueroa 1984:49).

Table 24 summarizes partial 1974 monetary expenses of the same Quinua family. Nearly 50 percent of the family's expenditures were spent on food, in spite of the fact that this family owns more land than most people (one hectare of good irrigated savannah land, one-half hectare of moderately good nonirrigated savannah land, and one-half hectare of poor nonirrigated land in the thorn steppe).[2] The fact that the data were gathered during the harvest may have influenced food purchases: the family may have been buying foods for storage, a strategy that their wealth would have allowed. They certainly bought more meat than they consumed. The family devoted 27.3 percent of its budget to agricultural production and nearly 8 percent to medicines, a relatively high percentage common in the budgets of those Peruvians who can afford them.

Although covering a period of only five and a half weeks, these budget data demonstrate the close linkage of peasants to the cash economy. In this five-week period expenses were $31.30 greater than income (the daily agricultural wage was $0.70). Since the data were collected during the harvest, when agricultural income is high but production and food expenses low, this family would have an even more difficult time balancing its budget during the rest of the year. Such budget figures prompt people to migrate and to intensify cash-producing activities.

Although prosperous, the family is not unusual in its cash activities, although poorer peasants would have sold fewer crops. Moreover, this family has not always been prosperous. The head of household had lived on the coast for much of his life because he could not make ends meet on the basis of Quinua income alone. The family used this extra-local income to buy their lands. The parents are uneducated and speak poor Spanish, but their children have all been educated and one became an important townsman in the mid-1970s, after these data were collected.

Other studies by economists suggest that monetary income, as opposed to subsistence production, represents more than 50 percent of all peasant income (de Janvry 1981:242–246; Gonzales 1987:25–26, 85–91) and even as much as 65–80 percent (Caballero 1981: 228). One survey of the southern sierra in the late 1970s, for example, demonstrated that the peasants studied obtained half of their income from monetary sources (Figueroa 1984:48–49, 129–130). Cash-cropping accounted for 14 percent of total monetary income, the sale of livestock 23 percent, commerce and artisan sales 23 percent, local wages 23 percent, and migrant wages 17 percent. They spent most of this income on food, as in Quinua, with their expenses distributed as follows: production was 6.8 percent of total monetary expenditures, investment in tools and animals 4.6 percent, food 45.4 percent, nondurable goods 12.8 percent, clothing 14.4 percent, education 3.8 percent, and other expenses 12.2 percent (Figueroa 1984: 49–51).[3] Additional evidence from Cuzco, moreover, indicates that poor people obtain most of their income from the sale of their labor, while the rich obtain it from the sale of agropastoral produce (Gonzales 1987:88–89). If the above data are correct—and I believe they are—subsistence production and barter represent a much smaller part of peasant production than had been previously thought.

THE NATIONAL ECONOMY AND LOCAL PRODUCTION[4]

It is clear that Quinuenos and other highland peasants are not self-sufficient but produce goods for outside markets (Caballero 1981:

205–235). Changes in these markets exert profound constraints on peasant production.

Peru's national economy has been export driven since the guano boom in the mid–nineteenth century. Exports have varied over time, but the major ones are agricultural (sugar, cotton, and to a lesser extent, coffee), pastoral (sheep and alpaca wool), and extractive (copper, silver, gold, lead, zinc, guano, fish products, and in the past, petroleum). In recent years, coca has become a new if illegal export.

Quinua has participated in the booms and busts of the export economy. Nonlocal and nonagricultural wages are generally higher than local and agricultural wages (Gonzales 1987:112). In the last century Quinua sent migrants to work on the coastal guano islands. The guano boom ended in the 1870s, but some Quinua migrants were still working in guano production in the early 1900s. In this century Quinuenos have worked largely in coastal cotton production. They did so, with varying interruptions, until the decline of cotton production in the 1960s (Reid 1985:25–27; Matos Mar 1984: 28–31; Morner 1985:163–187; Thorp and Bertram 1978:23–144).

Prior to the 1940s, Quinua's economy was more or less in equilibrium with population and demand. Peasants made up for the deficits in local production through trade and temporary migration to work on cotton plantations. This strategy became less successful in the 1940s, a period when Peru began to take its modern shape (Caballero 1981:313–332; Matos Mar 1984:32–34). At this time population began its explosive growth, not only in Quinua but throughout Peru, pushing peasants against their local ecological limits. They migrated in increasing numbers from the highlands to the coast, causing the rapid growth of Lima and other cities (Matos Mar 1984:43–47, 72–73). Some of these migrants became part of a new urban class of workers, merchants, and entrepreneurs. Many, however, remained poor, taking whatever odd jobs they could in order to survive. This poverty was often better than that in the highlands, where even casual labor was unavailable.

During this same period, the Peruvian government began to control food prices and to support cheap food imports and capitalist food production on the coast to supplement low urban wages. In consequence, the calories and proteins supplied by wheat and rice have become cheaper than those supplied by traditional foods, especially potatoes (Ferroni 1980:50). These subsidy policies have dampened farm production, depressed rural employment, and pushed people out of local communities into the wage economy. The resulting domestic food shortages have further encouraged food imports (Appleby 1982; Collins 1988:20–21; de Janvry 1981; Ferroni 1980; Franklin et al. 1985; Long and Roberts 1984:60–63; Thorp and Bertram 1978; see Meillassoux 1981 for a description of similar processes elsewhere in the world).

Increased population and the declining profitability of agriculture created a rural crisis. Many peasants turned to entrepreneurial activities and wage work; they continued to farm but in a more supplemental way than previously. Quinuenos have always engaged in nonfarm activities, but they did so with increasing vigor with every new assault on their ability to feed themselves and their children. In the 1960s the development of synthetic fabrics reduced international demand for cotton, eliminating the most important source of traditional wage labor and thereby greatly encouraging the search for nonfarm work. The Velasco land reform in the 1970s completed the transition, as the newly formed cotton cooperatives lost the capital needed to hire temporary laborers (cf. de Janvry 1981:138, 212–213).

Urban food prices continued to be kept artificially low throughout the 1960s and 1970s, and rural-urban terms of trade became increasingly unfavorable for sierra producers (de Janvry 1981:240). Sierra peasants sell maize, potatoes, barley, wheat, beef, mutton, and milk in order to buy rice, cooking oil, fats, noodles, sugar, beer, cane alcohol, soda, textiles, school supplies, detergents, soaps, candles, kerosene, plastics, and salt from the coast (Caballero 1981:212). Between 1961 and 1972 the value of these sierra products dropped by 15.2 percent in comparison to the price of the commercial goods (ibid.). Since income from wages and the sale of artisan and pastoral products has not declined as rapidly as has that from agricultural products (Gonzales 1987:110), peasants have been encouraged to devote more and more labor to nonagricultural activities. Food production has consequently stagnated, and per capita production has actually declined (Thorp and Bertram 1978:315).

Peru has been in a profound economic depression since the 1970s, characterized by low prices for primary products, declining agricultural production, declining real wages, a large balance-of-payments deficit, a soaring public debt service, and high inflation. In 1972 wheat imports were 22 percent higher than in 1968 (Dobyns and Doughty 1976:262), and the debt service consumed 23 percent of all export earnings in 1975 (Reid 1985:66).

The problems have worsened in the 1980s. The gross economic product (controlled for inflation) was stagnant in Peru generally and declined in Ayacucho by 12.3 percent between 1979 and 1985 (table

Table 25. *Gross Economic Product in Ayacucho, Lima, and Peru,*
1979–1985

	In Thousands of Intis		
	1979	1985	% Change
Ayacucho (department)	27,767	24,356	−12.3
Lima	1,543,470	1,555,592	0.8
All Peru	3,490,135	3,526,240	1.0

Source: Peru 1987: 25–26.
[a] Value of the inti adjusted for inflation since 1979.

25). Because of population growth, per capita production has declined even more. In 1985 per capita income in Peru was at 1965 levels (*New York Times*, June 12, 1989). In 1989 inflation was more
than 3,000 percent (*Peru Económico* 1990, vol. 13, no. 2). Food prices
have risen faster than wages. Demand has fallen, factories have
closed or laid off workers, and there has been a "growing struggle for
poor families to cover their minimal food needs" (Riding 1989:42).
Malnutrition has become widespread (*New York Times*, June 12,
1989); per capita wheat consumption has fallen precipitously: from
65 kg in 1987 to 39 kg in 1989 (*Lima Times*, no. 734, September 8,
1989). Cocaine production has become the one boom amid economic chaos (Kawell 1989; Matos Mar 1984:55–56).
  Quinua and its migrants have felt the effects of this crisis. Although rural areas are protected somewhat from urban inflation and
poverty (Gonzales 1987:103, 106–107), Quinua migrants have lost
work, consequently sending fewer remittances to their homes in
Quinua. Migrant families who were once well-off are less so today,
and some would return to Quinua were it not for the guerrilla war.
At least one entrepreneur in Lima in mid-1989 has had to dismiss
most of his work force (composed largely of recent Quinua migrants), retreating into household production. Per capita production
in Quinua has also suffered. The ceramic industry and many other
nonfarm occupations have become saturated with people looking for
work. Studies in Cuzco have shown that peasants there are eating
less sugar, rice, milk, cheese, and meat in response to the inflationary spiral (Gonzales 1987:141). They have retreated to eating the agricultural products grown on their fields. Since many peasants have
insufficient land to do this well, the data suggest that they are hun-
grier today than they were in the past.
  In all my years working in Peru, I have had few informants or

friends say to me, either spontaneously or in response to a question, that life is better now, that things have improved this year over last. Instead, both farmers and migrants express a very pessimistic view of life: the crops are poorer, prices of necessities are higher, goods are more scarce, getting by is more difficult. The only exceptions are some of the richer townspeople, the ones who have succeeded admirably in the new economic order. But they tend to point to the town's progress—the stores, the lights, the electricity, the plaza, the monument—not their own.

The general pessimism is expressed in Ayacucho music: people sing of the claws of ironic poverty, of friends and family lost to migration, as well as of unrequited love. When drunk, people often cry and speak of their poverty and their misery, sometimes erupting in violence and rage (cf. Allen 1988:210–213). I have heard many people say that the death of a child is a good thing, that the child goes directly to the angels and thereby escapes the misery found on this earth.

I used to think that this pessimism was a cultural artifact predisposing people to see life in negative rather than positive terms. I now believe this interpretation erroneous. Andean pessimism is a realistic appraisal of their demographic, ecological, and economic history and status. Things may be better for some, but they are not for most, and everyone suffers the stress of increasing ecological and economic pressures. These pressures have not only led to economic changes (discussed in the next chapter) but have created fertile ground for the growth of Shining Path.

6.

THE DYNAMICS OF
ECONOMIC CHANGE

ALTHOUGH QUINUENOS have always been articulated with the cash economy, they are much more so today. Responding to population growth, ecological constraints, and the diminishing value of farm production during the last forty years, they have come to rely increasingly on commerce and wage labor to supplement subsistence farm production, a phenomenon found throughout the Department of Ayacucho (Degregori 1986:63–64). Many more Quinuenos obtained significant income in 1989 from ceramic manufacture, commerce, trucking, cash-cropping, highway food selling, and migration than they did in 1966.[1] Reliance on commerce has led to additional pressures for cash to pay for transport, education, and appropriate clothing. Symbols of new statuses have become important, and some people buy such things as infant rubber pants and commercial rather than maize beer.

Except for the teachers and a few others, most people still farm. Even the largest shopkeepers farm to provision their households and to cash-crop. Many migrants raise crops on Quinua land, trucking the food to their homes in Lima or elsewhere. Farming, however, has declined in importance as Quinuenos have become increasingly involved in the nonfarm economy. A man who earns enough income from ceramic manufacture to buy several bicycles, radios, record players, and supplemental food is still a farmer, but his farmwork no longer has the central importance it once had. The same is true for the poorer Quinueno who must work harder at cash-producing activities to buy food, school supplies for his children, and his daily supply of coca leaves (cf. Ferroni 1980:18).

The state has created the infrastructure for these economic developments, providing roads, schools, and work. This state presence, however, is not an independent variable, but is itself a product of Peru's growing population and the economic integration of the nation. Local communities throughout the country suffer ecological and economic pressures similar to those in Quinua. They clamor for roads and schools, sometimes constructing the roads themselves to facilitate market access (Appleby 1976b). The government has also responded to the export sector by building roads and railroads to facilitate mining and wool extraction. The growing population and improved transportation have encouraged the development of internal markets. The city of Ayacucho grew dramatically after the reopening of the University of Huamanga in 1959 and the expansion of state agencies in the city in the 1960s (Degregori 1986:46), providing Quinua with a larger market for its agricultural production.

ECONOMIC CHANGES: 1966–1988

In 1966 Quinua looked like a sleepy backwater: dirt streets, few stores, humble housing, little traffic, and neither potable water nor electricity. Although many people owned portable radios, only a small number could afford record players, bicycles, or sewing machines. The economic changes since then have been profound and dramatic (table 26). Twenty-two years later the central town boasts electricity and potable water (inaugurated in December 1966) and telephone service (inaugurated in 1987). The plaza is paved, stores are abundant, and many houses have stucco fronts and sport television antennas.

Local nonfarm work has increased. There are at least four times as many highway food sellers and ten times more ceramicists today than in 1966. Daily passenger service by sixteen small passenger trucks or buses (colectivos) is a world away from the virtual absence of transportation two decades ago. In a census of twenty-five households in a rural savannah hamlet (some twenty minutes on foot from the central town) in 1987, 40 percent of the households received the majority of their income through nonagricultural work: long-distance trade (16 percent), migrant work (16 percent), white-collar work (4 percent), and store ownership (4 percent). An additional 48 percent received supplemental income through craft production (28 percent) and petty sales (20 percent), while only 12 percent of the households reported no nonagricultural work.

The increase in male employment is illustrated in table 27, which summarizes data contained in municipal marriage and birth records and therefore reflects the self-perceptions of the participants and judgments made by the municipal authorities. Both sets of records

Table 26. *Economic Changes, District of Quinua, 1966–1988*

	Year	
	1966	*1988*
Patterns of Production		
Stores (*tiendas*)		
Large and well stocked	2	8
Medium	0	8
Small and poorly stocked	6	22
Commercial ceramicists	<50	>500[a]
Highway food sellers		
Number of sellers	10–15	40–80
Days per week	2 half days	7 full days
Transportation		
Small trucks (*camionetas*)	0	21
Large trucks (*camiones*)[b]	10	5
Private cars	0	4
Highway traffic	Slight	Heavy
Quinua-Ayacucho *colectivos*[c]	0	16
Sunday Market		
Size	Small	Large
Exchange	Barter	Increased cash sale
Types of goods	Agricultural	Agricultural and manufactured
Provenance of customers	Quinua	Quinua and Ayacucho
Cash-cropping	Some	More
Bread production	Sporadic	Daily
Patterns of Consumption		
Two-story houses	8	29
Electricity	—	Central town
Televisions	—	Central town
Potable water	—	Central town
Asphalted streets	None	Central town
Highway	Dirt	Asphalt
Consumption of rice, noodles, and sugar	Central town	Town and hamlets

Source: Informant data and personal observation.

[a] The figure of 500 ceramicists is a very rough estimate.

[b] The 1988 figure includes 4 gasoline trucks in the valley bottom.

[c] The 16 small passenger trucks (known as *micros* or *colectivos*) are also included in the number for small-truck ownership.

Table 27. *Male Employment, District of Quinua: Percentage of Farm and Nonfarm Workers, 1955–1985*

	1955	1960	1965	1970	1975	1980	1985	Total
Birth Records								
Farm work	83.6	85.0	87.5	80.5	81.8	69.9	63.5	77.7
Nonfarm work	16.4	15.0	12.5	19.5	18.2	30.1	36.5	22.3
Number	146	160	216	231	203	249	260	1,465
Marriage Records								
Farm work	75.9	62.1	79.3	76.7	69.2	—	—	72.7
Nonfarm work	24.1	37.9	20.7	23.3	30.8	—	—	27.3
Number	29	29	29	30	26	—	—	143

Source: Municipal records, District of Quinua.

demonstrate the importance of nonagricultural work: 22.3 percent
of the men in the birth records and 27.3 percent in the marriage ones
had nonfarm occupations. The birth data show a clear trend toward
the increasing importance of nonfarm work, from 16.4 percent in
1955 to 36.5 percent in 1985. This trend is also reflected in the marriage data, although less clearly: nonfarm workers increased from
24.1 percent in 1955 to 30.8 percent in 1975.[2] Since almost everyone
has some sort of part-time work to raise cash, these data underestimate the number of occupations in Quinua.

Quinuenos are cash-cropping more today than previously, a process of intensification that commenced in the mid-1940s (cf. Allen
1988 : 30; Cotlear 1988). In 1966 peasants still produced primarily for
home consumption, but a great many also produced potatoes for
cash sale. Although still essentially subsistence producers, almost
all farmers in 1988 devoted a larger portion of their crop to cash sale.
In 1966 they took their crop to Ayacucho or Tambo, but at the present time, they sell much of their surplus production to highway food
vendors or to dealers in the Sunday market.

Potatoes are still the preferred cash crop, but other crops are sold
as well. Quinuenos have substituted cash sales for many interzonal
barter exchanges. They prefer, for example, to sell maize or wheat in
Ayacucho and to use the money to buy potatoes rather than barter
for them. Most farmers in the valley bottom have replaced subsistence crops with the cash-cropping of vegetables, a process that had
been well underway in 1966. In higher altitudes wheat and barley
have replaced the less commercial achita (Chenopodium pallidi-
culae) and quinoa.[3]

This increase in cash-cropping is not unique to Quinua: peasants
throughout the sierra are replacing subsistence crops, such as quinoa, broad beans, and cañihua, for cash ones, especially maize and
potatoes (Caballero 1981 : 182; Cotlear 1988; Gonzales 1987 : 156).
The declining rural-urban terms of trade have fostered this increase.
Peasants must produce more cash crops to simply maintain their
standard of living (cf. Ferroni 1980 : 21).[4] Peasants consequently shift
production depending on market conditions. In the 1950s Quinuenos reduced their wheat acreage dramatically in response to the
collapsed market for the grain. In the 1970s they began to grow
lentils because of high prices; in 1974 lentils sold for $0.70 the kilo
while maize only sold for $0.19 and barley for $0.16. In Quinua, as in
Cuzco, rich peasants have increased their cash-cropping more than
poor peasants; the poor have insufficient land to do so (Gonzales
1987 : 156).

Peasants first planted eucalyptus trees as a cash crop in the 1940s.

Before that time eucalyptus trees were used occasionally to provide fuel and building materials. The number of trees was limited because peasants feared the trees would impoverish the soil (which they do) and because there was no market for them. A returned migrant (a chief on the highway construction crew) began to plant stands of eucalyptus on infertile soils. Other Quinuenos followed his example, slowly at first but with quickening intensity. It takes ten years for a tree to produce, but many Quinuenos now own private eucalyptus stands, and a communal plantation, begun under government auspices in 1963, covers much of the moist forest. Eucalyptus trees are sold to Quinuenos for fuel and house posts and to outsiders for utility poles, mine supports, and bridge materials. These trees are significant sources of revenue for many farmers. A large tree was worth $64.00 in 1967, and posts used for electric utility poles sold for $31.00 each in 1987.

Peasants have harvested cochineal, dried insects collected from the nopal cactus, for some time in Quinua. People sometimes camp out under a tree during the dry season to harvest the cochineal as well as the associated prickly pears. Responding to a developing market in the early 1970s Quinuenos increased production. In 1973 they sold the cochineal for $1.40–$1.64 a pound. Since a peasant can collect a pound in about two hours, the return was very lucrative compared to the daily agricultural wage of $0.58. They continue to harvest cochineal today. Taking advantage of a market which began in the 1960s, peasants also collect and sell *tara*, a plant used in tanning (Rivera 1971:158–159). *Tara* production in Ayacucho is one of the highest in Peru, and in 1988 the government began to build a processing plant for the city.

Changes in the Sunday market reflect the underlying economic shifts. In 1966 the market consisted primarily of Quinuenos exchanging their surplus agricultural produce, with only a few outsiders or purveyors of manufactured goods. The market grew in size after 1974 when the newly paved highway increased its accessibility to the growing population of Ayacucho. The market in 1988 was considerably larger, contained more diverse goods, and lasted later into the day. Quinua is not alone in such market growth. The 27 markets found in the Department of Puno in 1900, for example, had grown to 118 in the 1970s, the greatest growth having taken place since 1940 (Appleby 1976a; see also Bromley 1976).

In 1988 the Quinua market was supplied with manufactured goods—agricultural tools, household utensils, matches, candles, clothing, yarn, ropes, dyes, spices, chili peppers, sugar, rice, noodles, and alcoholic drinks—by merchants from Quinua, Ayacucho, Huancayo, and elsewhere. The majority of transactions in the market are still by barter, but there are more cash sales than in 1966. Wholesalers come from Ayacucho to buy eggs. Since 1974, many individual Ayacuchanos have come for their weekly produce. As in 1966, women still come from the valley bottom to sell and barter vegetables and to purchase produce in quantity, especially maize and potatoes, acting as the major wholesalers of these products.[5] In 1988, however, sellers insist on cash sales by standard weights rather than barter; they believe they get a better rate of exchange with cash.

Other agricultural changes illustrate the increasing importance of cash relationships. Although Quinuenos have always needed cash for fertilizer and labor, they became more deeply embedded in the cash economy in the 1960s when some began to borrow money from the Agrarian Bank to purchase chemical fertilizers and insecticides. Such loans were restricted in number, however, by a bank rule limiting loans to people with four hectares or more of land. Peasants and townspeople were also reluctant to assume increased risk. Loss of a potato crop because of drought or disease is common. The need to pay back the agricultural loan after such a loss made the risk intolerable to many farmers.

In 1972 the government opened an agricultural office in the district. Although the extension agent only helped people with large acreage, he encouraged them to use insecticides and chemical fertilizers, and their example inspired others. In 1977 a Quinua political authority estimated that 990 people had bought fertilizer, 2,000 had purchased insecticides, and 50 had borrowed from the Agrarian Bank (Peru 1977a).[6] In 1988 chemical insecticides and fertilizers were commonly used, and a great many more people had taken out agricultural loans (some say nearly everyone). As a measure to combat the guerrilla war, these loans have been interest-free in Ayacucho since 1986.

A few townspeople spoke to me in 1966 of their dreams of using tractors, but none had yet used them. In 1988, some of them were plowing their fields with tractors. Tractors are substitutes for scarce human labor. Unlike animal traction, moreover, tractors can be used without irrigation, allowing people to plow whenever they want, and thereby easing the demand for labor at the sowing. Renting for $7.81 an hour, these tractors are placing townspeople still more firmly in the cash economy. They (and most Quinuenos) are dependent on harvests and market forces in ways that would not have been contemplated in 1966.

Some agricultural changes are a direct result of the growing population. The central town has nearly doubled in size since 1961, while the hamlets have grown by 7.6 percent (see table 10). This growth has placed a serious strain on water resources. Since the irrigation system provides both agricultural and drinking water, increased human and animal consumption has reduced the water available for cultivation. In 1987 diminished water flow caused the rainy-season sowing to be delayed by two weeks in Hanan Sayoc.

The guerrilla war has exacerbated the problems of population growth. Fleeing the relatively unsafe high-altitude areas, peasants have settled in the more secure central town, creating additional strains on water resources. At the same time, the civil disorder has caused a disproportionate number of young people to leave, as they are the group most likely to be harmed by the violence. This has increased the shortage of agricultural laborers, and at least one family is importing laborers from Ayacucho to work on its fields.

Economic life has quickened not only in agriculture but generally. Older Quinuenos remember that a few townspeople always had small, poorly stocked stores selling alcohol, salt, and noodles. They had to go to the neighboring town of Huamanguilla to make major purchases. This pattern changed in 1952 when an educated peasant opened the first large, well-stocked store in Quinua. His business prospered, but he had to leave it for lack of capital in 1960. In 1966, six small stores sold coca leaves, cane alcohol, beer, soda, bread, noodles, crackers, some ceramics, and other odds and ends. Two well-stocked stores carried such additional products as sugar, rice, canned goods, clothing, toys, cooking oil, kerosene, watches, and specialty potatoes in quantity. By 1988 the number and quality of the stores had risen dramatically. There are now at least twenty-two small and poorly stocked stores that sell alcohol, coca leaves, and a few other goods; eight medium-size stores that sell in addition to the above a small variety of noodles, rice, crackers, canned tuna fish, kerosene and soda pop; and eight well-stocked ones that sell the above goods in larger quantities and that also sell some dry goods (clothing, sandals) and sundries.

Women of the central town and countryside (known as *controlistas* or *vivanderas*) have sold food on the highway for many years. Before 1950 a few women sold maize beer, food, and forage to mule drivers and people in an occasional truck on Saturdays and Sundays. The number of food sellers expanded along with increased truck traffic in the 1950s; ten to fifteen women sold food in the plaza for half a day on Saturdays and Sundays, but expanded to all day during major fiestas. In 1967 they earned $0.14 for a plate of soup. By

1987 the changes were again dramatic. In 1987 a meal of chicken soup had inflated to $0.95. About forty women regularly sell food all day, every day of the week, in a special locale constructed in 1974. Forty more peddle food occasionally, and their children rush the trucks and cars to hawk soft drinks and candy. Travelers witness similar developments at truck and bus stops throughout the Andes.

As peasants have entered the cash economy, household craft production has declined, a phenomenon documented for the altiplano by Collins (1988 : 146). In the altiplano scarcity of labor has meant less available for household craft production. This shortage has caused people to purchase what they formerly produced and forced peasants ever more firmly into the cash economy. Today Quinuenos buy more manufactured goods of all sorts (e.g., metal spoons and plates, manufactured clothing, kerosene for fuel) than they did previously.

These manufactured products have become symbols of success in the new economic order. Bottled beer will sometimes be served as the first or second round of drinks, to be replaced by the cheaper maize beer and cane alcohol as the party goes on. Whenever I am in Peru, people always ask me about prices in the United States compared to those in Peru. The desire for such consumer goods as radios and phonographs is widespread. Peasants often use records at fiestas rather than locally produced music. The owners of radios and phonographs sometimes transform these symbols into hard cash by renting them out to others.

MIGRATION

Migration has been one of Quinua's most important mechanisms to supplement local resource production. In the first half of the twentieth century most migration was temporary, although some Quinuenos remained permanently on the coast. Men went in search of wage work in the cotton harvest, often leaving wives and children behind to cultivate the fields. They generally left in late February through April, a period of low work demand in Quinua (after crop cultivation and before the harvest) but in time for the cotton harvest on the coast. It is also a time when food from Quinua's harvest is running out and people need to purchase food as well as seeds and fertilizer for the next sowing. Many Quinuenos have also worked for the Ministry of Transport on highway construction and repair, a form of temporary migration begun in 1924 when some villagers worked to extend the highway eastward from the community. In the 1940s at least forty Quinuenos worked on highways throughout the

Ayacucho region. Since the late 1950s their number has increased to some two hundred men.

Most households relied (and still rely) on remittances from this and other temporary migration (cf. Caballero 1981:161–163; Collins 1988; Cotlear 1988; Mallon 1983:247–267; Painter 1981, 1984). In 1967 peasants could earn $1.40 a day in the cotton harvest, and a careful person could return with $40.00 to $80.00. Highway work is not considered very lucrative, but highway wages are higher than those earned in local agricultural labor. In 1973 an agricultural laborer earned $0.59 per day—but only $0.47 if the farmer also provided coca leaves, cigarettes, and tools. A laborer on the highway was paid nearly double—$1.10 per day. He, of course, had greater expenses than the person who remained in Quinua.

Families use the money from temporary migration and remittances from permanent migrants not only to pay for food and agricultural production but to buy personal and household necessities and amenities: clothing, kerosene, metal forks and spoons. Many have used the money to buy land or the trade goods used in some commercial venture. In the past, many migrated to earn money to sponsor a fiesta or some other *cargo*. Today people still migrate to get the money for a wedding or other life-passage event.

The number of migrants has increased dramatically since 1940, as peasants have responded to population growth and the ecological and economic constraints on rural production, a pattern found throughout the central Andes (Caballero 1981:147–172; Collins 1988; Figueroa 1984; Weismantel 1988:30, 176–177). Increased numbers of migrants, moreover, remain on the coast than did previously. In genealogical data collected in 1966, only 34.6 percent of one informant's kin were living outside Quinua, the town where they had been born. In 1987 more than 50 percent of the people born in Quinua lived elsewhere. In one rural hamlet 61.8 percent of male children over 19 and 55.4 percent of all children over that age had migrated, primarily to Lima and Ayacucho (table 28). This percentage of migrants is higher than that of their parents; only 36 percent of the parents have had extended migration experience (greater than a year) away from Quinua, a percentage close to that of my 1966 genealogical data.

In spite of the large numbers of migrants, Quinua appears to have fewer migrants than other areas of the sierra. In one survey, it was estimated that 75 percent of the children in the late 1970s migrated permanently (Figueroa 1984:77), whereas only 55.4 percent of Quinua children over 19 had left in 1987 (table 28). The greater number of Quinuenos remaining at home may result from the presence

Table 28. *Location of Children of Parents in a Rural*
Savannah Hamlet, 1987

| | % Living in | | | | | Total Number |
	Quinua	Ayacucho	Lima	Montaña	Other	
Male						
Over 19	38.2	25.5	32.7	1.8	1.8	55
Under 19	100.0	—	—	—	—	6
Total	44.3	23.0	29.5	1.6	1.6	61
Female						
Over 19	54.1	18.9	21.6	2.7	2.7	37
Under 19	87.5	12.5	—	—	—	8
Total	60.0	17.8	17.8	2.2	2.2	45
Male and Female						
Over 19	44.6	22.8	28.3	2.2	2.2	92
Under 19	92.9	7.1	—	—	—	14
Total	50.9	20.8	24.5	1.9	1.9	106

Source: Census of 25 households (of which 4 had no children) made by a research assistant.

of substantial economic alternatives, especially ceramic manufacture and commerce resulting from the highway and proximity to the city of Ayacucho, rather than from reduced pressures.

First-generation migrants generally maintain active ties with Quinua (see Altamirano 1984a, 1984b, 1988). The ties are so strong that it would be incorrect to say that Quinua is only a highland community. Rather, it is the highland base of an extended familial and economic network. Several migrants' clubs on the coast provide moral and occasional economic and political assistance to the highland district. Some migrants are active political officials in Quinua. The man responsible for registering Quinua as a native community in 1940, for example, lived on the coast. He raised his family there, although he served as head of the Quinua community (*personero*) for more than twenty years. He visited Quinua periodically to arrange political matters and attend to his fields.

Male migrants, especially highway workers and those living in Ayacucho, often have wives and children in Quinua to which they return frequently. Fewer men on the coast maintain families in Quinua, but 4.4 percent of a sample of coastal migrants have conjugal family in Quinua.[7] Many migrants return to Quinua for extended stays (see Altamirano 1985); 44.3 percent of the migrants on the coast had returned to live in Quinua for periods of a year or more, and most had remained there for more than two years. Many others have returned to Quinua permanently, sometimes after having retired from coastal employment.

Quinua is an important source of food for migrants. 41.6 percent of migrants interviewed on the coast received at least 50 kilos of produce from Quinua annually (usually potatoes, maize, dried meat, cheese, peas, or quinoa). Most Quinuenos residing in Ayacucho and 34.2 percent of the migrants on the coast obtain this food through active participation in the cultivation of their fields. They travel to Quinua just before the sowing in September, often using the patronal fiesta to the Virgin of Cocharcas as a pretext but in fact contracting for laborers or arranging for sharecropping. They usually return again in May during the harvest (cf. Allen 1988:36; Collins 1988). Some 41 percent of Quinua migrants on the coast also receive produce by means of gifts known as *encomiendas*. It is nearly impossible for someone to travel to the coast or the tropical forest without bringing such gifts, no matter how small, to his or her relatives as well as to the relatives of kinsfolk and friends.

I do not have numerical data on the remittances received in Quinua, but 38.8 percent of the coastal migrants interviewed claimed to send significant remittances (money, medicine, clothing, candles, rice, and noodles) to relatives there. If we assume that this percentage means that at least one quarter of Quinua households receive remittances (a not unreasonable figure that allows for exaggeration), we can see that the economic impact on the community is considerable.

A number of migrants also use Quinua as a source of cheap and reliable labor. Some are labor recruiters (*enganchadores*), contracting for temporary agricultural workers. Others go to Quinua to get laborers for their own projects. In 1988 about twenty Lima workshops produced ceramics using imported Quinua artisans. Migrants prefer Quinua servants but have been unable to get them in recent years, as young women prefer to work in businesses in Quinua rather than as servants on the coast. The fact that they are able to do so—while their mothers were not—is another measure of the economic changes in the community.

Individuals, of course, migrate for a variety of reasons, including the attractions of city life. It is useful, however, to distinguish between the individual and social level of analysis. At the social level the question is not individual motivation but why so many Quinuenos are constrained to migrate at the times they do. Such proximate causes of migration as marital difficulties are always underlain by Quinua's ecological and economic reality: insufficient land and income for the growing population. Nearly all the migrants interviewed on the coast recognized economic factors as being the most important reason they migrated, even when they spoke of other considerations. Ayacucho is one of the poorest departments in Peru. It also has one of the highest rates of migration, exceeded in 1972 only by the departments of Apurímac and Huancavelica (Caballero 1981 : 141).

Quinuenos, of course, are not only pushed out of the local community but are attracted by the relative benefits of the points of destination. Until recently the coast attracted Quinuenos with its (a) easy entry by means of cotton work; (b) relatively diversified employment and high wages (Caballero 1981 : 170–172); (c) increased possibilities of social mobility; (d) improved health care; and (e) better education. These benefits are seen as outweighing such negative realities as (a) anonymity; (b) crime; (c) cultural prejudices against people from the highlands; (d) loss of family, friends, and culture; and (e) noise, dirt, and squalor.

Migration has increased Quinua's access to cash, but at the same time, it has created a seeming paradox: by fostering migration, population pressure has created labor shortages and the abandonment of agricultural fields. There are too few men for many agricultural tasks. It is very difficult to obtain workers, which produces additional stress on household production and encourages more migration.

Caballero (1981 : 163) has suggested that migration has not been a significant source of capital accumulation in the sierra but is important more as a mechanism to maintain peasant reproduction. As their farm incomes have declined, peasants have migrated in order to sustain their peasant way of life. Caballero (1981 : 333–367) is correct when he emphasizes the limits of capitalist penetration of the peasant economy—the majority of peasants still focus on home production and use cash employment to continue living as peasants. Many Quinuenos, however, migrate not just for consumption but to obtain capital to buy store stock, trucks, and education. Those are important changes in production. Even those who focus on migration to purchase food have set in motion forces that have altered the traditional way of life.

CERAMIC MANUFACTURE

As far back as my informants can remember, most Quinua houses have had ornamental ceramic churches or some other ceramic adornment placed on the roof during the last day of the house construction. The origin of this custom is placed in myth. A diviner (pongo) by the name of Miguel Lunasco is said to have been sent by the mountain god (*tayta urqu*) to a waterfall in Huamangura ravine and to two lakes (*yana qucha* and *tuktu qucha*) in the puna, where he would have drowned but for the miraculous intervention of the Virgin. He returned repeatedly to bathe in the water, each time inspired by the mountain god with new designs for roof pots: churches, bulls, tropical forest Indians (known as *chunchus*), musicians, dogs, deer, and *vicuña*. He also returned with designs for ceremonial pots: some used to make offerings to the mountain god, others used to provide gifts to musicians and other helpers during fiestas, and still others used to serve maize beer at fiestas.

These pots were the beginning of the ceramic industry, but until recently they were made only on a contractual basis by a few individuals. Before 1960, ten ceramicists were located in only one region of the district.[8] They generally produced plates for common household use, although they also made a few churches and other special pots. They bartered these ceramics for food and sometimes traveled to distant communities in times of scarcity to trade for maize and other products. Occasional pieces were sold to shops in town or Ayacucho. They used the cash they received to purchase food, coca leaves, and other goods.

In the late 1940s a few Quinua townspeople and a family of Ayacucho merchants began the first significant commercial trade in ceramics. Churches, bulls, and crosses were exchanged for rice, noodles, and sugar. As the ceramicists became more knowledgeable about the demand for their work, they insisted on receiving cash, which provided a better return. At first sold only during Peruvian Independence Day, these ceramics were gradually displayed regularly in shops in Quinua, Ayacucho, and beginning in 1947, in Lima. (They were bought by anthropologists in the Campo de Marte in Lima as early as 1949, according to Richard Adams, personal communication, May 1990.) A few ceramicists began to earn significant cash incomes. One family of Ayacucho merchants displayed the pots at many of the Lima artisan fairs, thereby spreading knowledge of the craft and creating demand for production. In the early 1960s a North American owner of an artisan shop located in Miraflores, a wealthy and fashionable section of Lima, began to contract for ceramics and suggest new shapes. At the same time, a Quinua townsman set up a ceramic shop in Vitarte, an old working-class and industrial suburb of Lima. He brought six ceramicists to work in the shop and transported the paint and clay by truck from Quinua. Two Peace Corps volunteers worked with the ceramicists in Quinua briefly in the early 1960s, but they had difficulties with some members of the community and had to leave.

A ceramicist painting the new design of a candelabra, 1966.

Many Quinuenos took up the craft to meet the demand. The first ceramic school, teaching a one-year curriculum, was established in 1965. In 1966, thirty students were enrolled, many of them recruited personally by the teachers who went door-to-door through the community. The central school began teaching ceramics in 1967, and an additional artisan school that teaches ceramics, among other crafts, was established in 1974. Fewer than fifty potters plied their trade in 1966. Today there are hundreds who produce an ever-growing variety of shapes for tourist and export consumption.

One consequence of the commercialization of ceramics and the increase in the number of ceramicists has been a constant pressure to change designs to maintain sales, as the market for particular designs becomes saturated. Quinuenos produce many more shapes today than they did in 1966, and few people make the household churches that were the start of the whole phenomenon. Similar forces appear responsible for a decline in the economic value of craft production in the Cuzco area (Gonzales 1987: 127).

It would be difficult to overestimate the effect of the ceramic industry on the local economy. Although ceramics sell in retail for much more money than the artisans receive, the earnings of ceramicists have been nonetheless stupendous by local standards. In March 1967 one informant estimated that ceramicists earned around $160.00 per year. Even by 1967, most transactions in the market involving ceramics were for cash, although some exchange for potatoes or coca still took place. Ceramicists also hired occasional workers to paint the pots. Today, the vast majority of ceramic sales are for cash. Quinua ceramics are sold in nearly every artisan shop in Ayacucho and Lima and are shipped to the United States, Europe, and Japan. I have seen them in the United States in museum shops, department stores, and even street fairs. A household industry, it is a major source of income for producers and exporters. Townspeople participated very early on as intermediary exporters. In 1988 a number of ceramicists themselves owned trucks and transported their work directly to Lima, while others were involved in export to foreign countries. At least one cooperative has been formed, uniting fifteen households to market their production.[9]

Once insulted as Indians and considered of low social status, ceramicists have reversed their social position through their wealth and outside prestige. Some have moved from the countryside to become respected townsmen. A man who subsequently became mayor of the district (his father had been mayor of the peasant political organization) told me in 1974: "We are not [insulted now] because little by little people have come to understand what ceramic [production] is. . . . Previously we were ashamed, but not now." Even some townspeople, who once disdained ceramic production, now make ceramics, although the majority of them are involved in sales and distribution rather than manufacture.

THE INFRASTRUCTURE

The state has provided the infrastructure for many of these economic developments in the form of roads, schools, jobs, and technical assistance. Even excluding the large increase in the police force, a response to the Shining Path guerrilla movement, the number of permanent government functionaries in Quinua is today more than four times greater than in 1966 (see table 29).[10] Some of them (e.g., the agricultural extension agents) have been directly involved in fostering economic change. Taken together, this group also constitutes an increased cash market. In 1966, for example, the health care worker earned about $92.00 per month. Although he complained

Table 29. *Noneducational Government Resources, District of Quinua*

	1966	1988
Ministerial Employees		
Post office	1	1
Telephone, water, and electricity	0	3
Transport	0	4–5
Development (CORPA)	0	3
Medical post-hospital[a]	1	5
Agriculture	0[b]	1–2
Police	4	25–30
Museum	0	1
Municipal Employees		
Guardian of monument	0	1
Secretary	1	1
Plumber	0	1
Electrician	0	1
Municipal police	0	2
Street cleaners	0	2
Total	7	51–58

Source: Informant data and personal observation.

[a] The medical post and medical extension agent were replaced in 1974 by a two-room hospital with one physician, two residents, and two nurses.

[b] An agricultural extension agent made occasional visits in 1966.

it was too little, it was very high by peasant standards, and he spent much of the cash in Quinua on rent, food, alcohol, and miscellaneous items. The growth in the number of such incomes has increased the local market significantly. (It must be pointed out that government employees often have trouble being paid on time and their pay is sometimes several months in arrears.)

The state has had an active part in the expansion of education, reacting to forceful demand on the part of parents, who regard schooling and the ability to speak Spanish as the entrée into the national social system. In 1966 the majority of the adult population was illiterate and spoke only Quechua, but the process of creating the current literate and bilingual population (speaking Quechua at home and Spanish to outsiders) was well under way.

In 1936 (and even earlier), a girls' school and a boys' school stood in the central town, and two coeducational schools were located in the hamlets. Each of the schools had one teacher who taught only through the second grade. Any student wishing more education had to live in Ayacucho or elsewhere. Many did so, at great expense to their families, which had to pay for their room and board.

School attendance accelerated in the 1940s, and in 1953 Quinuenos built a central school (*nucleo escolar*) covering all primary grades. From that time on they have constructed many new schools. Peasants contributed free labor, and the state supplied building materials and teachers. In 1987 ten primary schools, a secondary school, three nursery schools, and two artisan schools employed seventy-seven teachers and served 2,171 students. Not only are most young people literate, but the large number of teachers increases the cash market in Quinua, even though most commute from Ayacucho (see table 30). Many stores are located around the central school to serve the teachers and students.

The distribution of literacy by age demonstrates that the great impetus in literacy began around 1945 (see table 31). Only 28 percent of rural men and 3 percent of rural women 40 years old or older in 1981 were literate. The figures were 89 percent and 83 percent, respectively, for their children ages 10 to 14. The percentage of literate townspeople has always been high, but the percentage of their children who are literate is even higher. Only 46 percent of townspeople over 40 were literate in 1981 compared to 90 percent of their children 10 to 14.

Schooling entails considerable costs. Parents must buy supplies for their students and forgo their labor. Clothing is an added cost. Children of even the richest families ordinarily dress in ragged clothing until they enter school. Once they enter school, however,

Table 30. Numbers of Students and Teachers, District of Quinua, 1986

Schools	Central Town		Hamlets		Total	
	Students	Teachers	Students	Teachers	Students	Teachers
Nursery	57	2	63	2	120	4
Primary	623	17	925	28	1,548	45
Secondary	192	11	0	0	192	11
Technical	39	6	0	0	39	6
Ceramic[a]	22	2	0	0	22	2
Other	31	2	219	7	250	9
Total	964	40	1,207	37	2,171	77

Source: Peru, Ministerio de Educación 1986; Resumen Estadistico de Supervivencia, al junio de 1986; Ministerio de Educación, Oficina de Presupuesto y Planificacción Educativa, Dirección de Estadística.
[a]This ceramic school is run by the Ministry of Industry and Tourism, rather than by the Ministry of Education.

Table 31. Literacy by Age and Location, District of Quinua, 1981

% Literate in Each Age Group

Age (years)	Central Town			Hamlets			District		
	Men	Women	Total	Men	Women	Total	Men	Women	Total
5–9	56	39	46	39	36	38	41	38	39
10–14	88	90	90	89	83	87	90	84	87
15–19	100	97	98	94	73	84	95	76	86
20–24	96	87	91	89	53	69	91	59	73
25–29	90	45	67	85	37	55	86	39	58
30–34	100	53	76	77	22	46	81	27	51
35–39	88	28	62	71	15	36	75	17	40
40+	78	18	46	28	3	14	32	4	16

Source: Peru 1983.

Schoolchildren standing in front of their father's new truck, 1967.

they are pressured to buy uniforms or to at least conform to a more urban dress code. In 1966 the school placed great emphasis on each student carrying a clean handkerchief. It was not important that it ever be used (its use, of course, would dirty the handkerchief) but that it be produced on demand at the school.[11] Before the central school and secondary school were built in Quinua, moreover, parents had to pay to send their children to Ayacucho.

Such costs must be considered capital investments that improve a family's potential for wealth and power. One young man from a rural area just outside the central town, for example, was paying $1.88 a month rent to attend high school in Ayacucho in 1966. This was a considerable sum, difficult to raise by his family. The daily agricultural wage at the time was $0.38. In addition, he had expenses for clothes, food, transportation, school supplies, and incidentals. When he graduated in 1974, however, he was able to use his high school degree to get an important bureaucratic post. His family's investment in education has been returned severalfold.

Other Quinuenos, however, have not had any significant economic return on their investment in education. One young man born in Quinua worked as a carpenter in Lima to attend the university there. He finished the university but was unable to get decent work in Peru. He then emigrated illegally to the United States, where he works at odd jobs and in construction. Other young men have been unable to raise the capital for their education and have had to end their schooling early.

Quinuenos began to send children to school at the same time that they were migrating and expanding market activities. Spanish and literacy minimized their chance of being exploited in these markets and improved the prospects of children in securing work. Special effort was (and is) often placed on educating an older child, who is then expected to educate his younger siblings, although many parents complain that not all such children fulfill that obligation.

THE HIGHWAY SYSTEM

Quinua's modern road system began in 1924 with the construction of the central highway, a dirt road connecting the cities of Ayacucho and Huancayo, built to commemorate the 100th anniversary of the Battle of Ayacucho. This highway runs through the valley bottom, but a feeder road to the battlefield built at the same time connected the central town to the highway and thereby the cities of Ayacucho, Huancayo, and Lima. The national government extended this feeder road to the next valley east (Tambo) in the 1930s and to the tropical forest *montaña* in the 1950s and early 1960s. Widened and asphalted as far as Quinua in 1974, in commemoration of the 150th anniversary of the battle, this road is today the major link between Ayacucho and the tropical forest. The government built an additional road through Huari in 1974, which connected Quinua to the archeological ruins and the town of Pacaycasa.

Traffic increased gradually. In the late 1940s only an occasional truck passed through the town. In 1966 even the city of Ayacucho had so few cars that one could walk in the streets with impunity. Traffic was moderate on the central highway, but very few trucks used the feeder road through Quinua. Four or five trucks passed through Quinua on Mondays, traveling to a market in the tropical forest that was held on Tuesdays. These trucks returned to Ayacucho and passed through Quinua on Wednesdays. Five to ten additional trucks and a bus traveled eastward to fairs in Tambo and San Miguel on Saturdays, returning on Sundays. Occasionally, ministry or private cars came through the town. Usually after a long wait, Quinuenos climbed into the back of a truck, rarely into the more expensive cab, taking their produce to one of the markets or to Ayacucho. In 1966 many peasants still traveled to the city on foot (about three hours downhill to Ayacucho and four hours to return). If they had cargo, it was carried on burros.

In 1951 the same individual who opened the first large store in Quinua was the first to buy a large truck to haul goods. Several other men followed suit in subsequent years and used the trucks to carry produce and other goods to Huancayo, Cuzco, and Lima. Today only one such truck remains, and it is not used often. Four gasoline trucks operate in the valley bottom to provision the gasoline stations along the busy central highway; other trucks did not prove to be profitable, and Quinuenos were forced to sell them or to move with their trucks to Ayacucho.

A townsman established the first regular passenger transportation (a light truck) between Quinua and Ayacucho in 1967. He obtained the downpayment for the truck from savings (kept in a bank account) derived from his government salary, his wife's store, and cash-cropping. He paid off the rest of the truck in monthly installments obtained from the truck's earnings. This profitable service was quickly supplemented by others. Traffic was still light as late as 1973 but increased significantly after the highway was paved in 1974. Occasional taxis began to arrive with tourists. Cars and small buses (*micros*) crowded the city of Ayacucho by that time as well. A small bus began to run between Quinua and Ayacucho in 1976. The service was discontinued in 1983 because of increased competition from small trucks and the insecurity caused by guerrilla activity.

Today people no longer have to wait long to get transportation to wherever they want to go. Several market fairs in different locations of the tropical forest now attract truck traffic throughout the week, and many people ride in private trucks, cars, and ministry vehicles.

Quinuenos today own sixteen small passenger trucks, or *colectivos*, and they have formed a transport committee in Ayacucho to protect their interests. Each of the trucks can carry up to 30 passengers, but they usually leave on a trip when they have 10. Since trucks pick up and discharge additional passengers along the route, they average 20 passengers each per trip—a conservative estimate. They generally make two trips per day, thereby carrying 80 passengers each, or since eight trucks are running on most days, a total of 360 passengers each day. In 1987, it cost $0.47 to travel in the back of the truck and $0.62 to ride in the cab. Consequently, Quinua peasants (and others) are paying an approximate total of $169.00 each day for this transportation, another measure of the importance of the cash economy.

Some of the passengers are teachers or others who live in Ayacucho or along the route, but the majority are peasants traveling to sell produce, make purchases, receive medical care, and solve legal and governmental problems. Motor transportation has increased in part as a result of the guerrilla violence in the community. Few people walk in the countryside today because of the danger.

Changes in transportation have altered other social phenomena. Because Quinuenos are using motor transportation instead of foot travel, the number of burros has declined. Footpaths have become less important and are no longer repaired as often or as well as they once were. Increased traffic has facilitated trade and cash-cropping. Peasants can take their produce to market easily, and outsiders can come to Quinua to make purchases. The paved highway has facilitated tourism; tourists have easy access to the battlefield monument, the archeological site of Huari, and the town, where they often bought ceramics and other crafts. Since the terrorist movement began in earnest in 1983, however, tourists rarely travel to Ayacucho and even less frequently to Quinua.

CENSUS DATA AND REGIONAL ECONOMIC CHANGES

Various Peruvian censuses confirm some of the changes described through more conventional anthropological techniques. Between 1972 and 1981, employment registered by the Peruvian census increased by 15.3 percent in Quinua and by 54.7 percent in the Province of Huamanga (Peru 1974 and 1983). Construction, commerce, transport, social services, and nonspecified economic activities (probably petty sales and artisan production) have grown the most in Huamanga, while agriculture and manufacturing activities have declined since 1940. Informant interviews establish that Quinua has experienced a similar expansion in the service and informal economy. Individual cash-cropping has increased rather than declined in Quinua, but the total number of agricultural workers and production may have declined as in Ayacucho as a result of migration and fallowing of fields.

Several measures of wealth demonstrate that Quinua is more prosperous than many other communities in Ayacucho. In 1972, 41.4 percent of Quinua households reported that they owned a radio or sewing machine, as compared to 29.8 percent for the entire depart-

Table 32. *Access to Cash Wealth: Comparison of Quinua with Other Peasant Communities in Province of Huamanga, 1972*

		Respondents in Quinua	
		No.	As % of Province of Huamanga
Censused Population		4,297	13.6
Home Amenities			
Electricity		49	96.1
Piped water		21	41.2
Cement floor		24	27.9
Wooden roof		7	26.9
Brick wall		5	23.8
Tile roof		956	21.8
Kerosene cooking		39	21.2
Type of Employment			
Other		49	32.4
Manufactures		78	19.3
Services		35	17.6
Agriculture		710	11.7
Commerce		32	11.3
Monthly Income			
Soles	US $ Equivalent		
0–199	0.00–4.66	0	—
200–499	4.68–11.69	41	41.4
500–599	11.70–14.01	15	27.8
1,000–1,999	23.40–46.78	8	25.0
2,000–2,999	46.80–70.18	0	—
3,000–3,999	70.20–93.58	15	16.7
5,000–9,999	117.00–233.98	9	29.0
10,000+	234.00+	0	—
Not specified		65	15.5

Source: Peru 1977b.

ment (Peru 1974:1204).[12] The reported monthly income for Quinua and the consequent home amenities are also substantially greater than in other registered peasant communities in the Province of Huamanga (table 32).[13] Although Quinuenos represented only 13.6 percent of the population of all peasant communities in Huamanga in 1972, they had 96.1 percent of the electricity found in those communities, as well as higher percentages of such other household facilities as kerosene stoves, running water, nonearthen floors, and nonthatch roofs. The disposable income found in Quinua was also significantly higher. Quinua, for example, commanded 41.4 percent of all the incomes between $4.68 and $11.68 a month found in these registered Peasant Communities.

SOCIAL INEQUALITY AND RURAL POVERTY

The economic changes in Quinua have been profound: there is now more material wealth as well as more opportunity for economic mobility. Nonetheless, people have participated unequally in the growth. Economic inequality throughout Peru has increased as a result of the processes described in this book (Caballero 1981 : 209; Cotlear 1988 : 221, Table 1; Degregori 1986; de Janvry 1981 : 121).

Quinuenos all say that they are poor (huakcha), yet it is quite clear to both informant and investigator that some people are much poorer than others. Precise figures on that poverty, however, are difficult to obtain. Nonetheless, Ayacucho is one of the three poorest departments in Peru (Banco Central de Reserva 1981),[14] and several measures from Quinua and other areas in the sierra suggest that Quinuenos have differential access to land, food, health, life, education, monetary income, and amenities.

Figueroa's (1984 : 52) economic survey of communities in the southern sierra found that households in the highest quartile (as measured by monetary income) had between four to thirteen times as much monetary income as the lowest quartile. Cotlear's (1988 : 220–221) data reaffirm these figures and, when reanalyzed, show that inequality increases with increasing cash income. Cotlear studied three geographic areas in Peru. The wealthiest families in the poorest region (average family income of $722.00) had 7.2 times the income of the poorest families. In the area with much higher income ($3,600.00), however, the wealthiest families had almost doubled the income disparity to 13.3 times the poorest.[15]

Figueroa's study also showed that the richest families had more income from all sources—agricultural, pastoral, and commercial activities, local skilled wages, and migrant wages—than did the poorest families. The only category in which the poor obtained more income than the rich was in local unskilled labor, primarily agricultural wage labor (1984 : 54–56). The general trends expressed in this study reflect the reality in Quinua; rich Quinua peasants and townspeople do not work for agricultural wages, but they obtain considerably more income from all other sources than do poor farmers.

As we have seen in chapter 4, most Quinuenos do not have enough land to feed themselves or their families adequately. Although informants report that most people, other than those driven from their homes by the guerrilla war, have sufficient food, other evidence suggests otherwise. The National Food Consumption Survey done in 1971–1972 (a good agricultural year) shows that 37 percent of all families in the central and southern highlands suffer caloric deprivation and another 16 percent are at risk of such deprivation, a total of more than half the population (Ferroni 1980 : 86; see also Parillón et al. 1983 : 43). Protein consumption is not as serious a problem; nonetheless, between 27 and 29 percent of the families in the southern and central highlands are at risk of "protein-energy malnutrition" (Ferroni 1980 : 94; see also Parillón et al. 1983 : 43). Brooke Thomas (1973 : 69) demonstrates serious caloric deficits for the population in Nuñoa. Here children under 13 consume only 63.4 percent of the recommended calories, children 13–19 eat 64.5 percent and adults 75.4 percent. Thomas's data, moreover, chillingly demonstrate that the Andean's small body size is an adaptation to low energy capture (1973 : 166). In another study in 1984 more than 70 percent of the homes of subsistence farmers and day agricultural laborers in Peru had children under 6 years of age with signs of chronic malnutrition (Franklin et al. 1985 : 37).[16]

Quinuenos share in this low caloric and protein intake. Only some townspeople and rich peasants eat meat, eggs, or cheese regularly. I do not have precise figures for Quinua, but per capita caloric consumption of the Department of Ayacucho overall is very low. Ayacuchanos on the average eat only 1271 calories per day (Peru 1986 : 13), 53 percent of the Food and Agriculture Organization (FAO) and World Health Organization recommendation of 2,400 calories for Peru (Franklin et al. 1983 : 29; Parillón et al. 1987 : 4–7). Daily per capita protein consumption in Ayacucho is 27 grams. The suggested minimum is 37 grams for a moderately active man, 29 grams for a similar woman, 38 for a pregnant woman, and 46 for a lactating woman (Passmore 1974).

Infant mortality provides another measure of poverty. Peru has one of the highest infant mortality rates in South America (Bobadilla 1987 : 5). In Quinua during the years 1965–1985, 26.6 percent of all deaths were those of infants under one year and 23.3 percent were those of children between one and four years of age (see table 2). These deaths result largely from respiratory distress and from dehydration caused by diarrhea. It is likely that poor nutrition aggravates these conditions. The incidence of diarrhea is at least partly determined by the quality of the water supply. The central town constructed a potable water system in 1967, but water outside the town is stored in contaminated cisterns next to the houses (see chapter 2). Even before the potable water system, central town water was purer than that lower down, since the densely populated town was (and is) the major contaminator of irrigation water. It is likely that rural Quinua children consequently die more frequently from diarrhea than do urban children, although data are not available to support this proposition.

Some Quinuenos are unable to supply the alcohol and ritual paraphernalia necessary for life-passage events. The lack of resources to give a proper fiesta deters many people from marrying either civilly or religiously. Parents sometimes do not have the resources to buy alcohol to bury a child (drinking is indispensable at a child's funeral), and they rely on better-off neighbors, kin, and ritual kin to provide it. Some people give the alcohol as a gift, and others place money in a plate set out for that purpose. It is likely, of course, that such families also suffer from nutritional stress. In one case in 1967 a woman had a spontaneous abortion in the seventh month of pregnancy. Informants attributed the miscarriage to the mother's inability to buy the meat and eggs that the fetus wanted. I do not know if malnutrition was the cause of the miscarriage, but I do know that the mother did not have enough money to pay for the alcohol needed at the funeral. At another funeral in 1967, the mother of a dead 4-year-old girl was too poor to own more than two spoons—and too distraught to obtain more from family and friends. She was criticized for having served a soup that had to be drunk from the bowl and a main course that had to be eaten with the hands.

The poor are less able to afford medical care. Although the medical post does not charge for a consultation, powerful townspeople receive the best attention. Moreover, poor Quinuenos must do without medicine, which is costly even for urban Peruvians. Children, those at greatest risk of dying, receive the least medical care.

Although many Quinuenos have intensified cash-producing economic activities in a major way, significant numbers have done so less successfully and remain poor. Cash incomes are lower for the rural areas of Quinua than for the urban center. The dominant merchants and the major ceramicists live in the central town, often having moved there from rural Quinua after having achieved success in the cash economy. Urban Quinuenos are also better educated, since education takes wealth. Although most Quinuenos now attend school, 16 percent of rural youth ages 15–19 and 13 percent ages 10–14 were still illiterate in 1981 (see table 31). This is a significant impediment to successful migration or participation in the cash economy. The corresponding figures for town youth are 2 percent and 10 percent. Townspeople also have better access to irrigation water, the police, and national and international programs. They received, for example, most of the food distributed by the Food for Peace program in the 1960s.

CONCLUSION

Quinua's economy has changed dramatically over the last half century. Nonfarm work is much more important than in 1940 and even than in 1966, when I first visited the community. The growing population has pushed against environmental resources: there is too little land suitable for cultivation to feed a growing population. These ecological constraints have been exacerbated by economic ones. The system of private tenure restricts access to idle land. The low value of agricultural goods in national markets makes nonfarm employment more attractive than farm employment. Prices of manufactured goods have inflated at a faster rate than prices of farm produce. The decline of the cotton plantations in the 1960s restricted an important source of employment, and Quinuenos began to seek alternate sources of income.

It is true that nearly everyone in Quinua still is a farmer, but nonfarm employment has become much more important to the household economy than forty years previously. Quinua's proximity to Ayacucho, the growth in transportation, and the extraordinary success of ceramic manufacture have laid the basis for much of this growth. Similar responses to inflationary forces have been common throughout the highlands. In reaction to the inflation of the 1970s, for example, 41 percent of the peasants studied by Gonzales in rural Cuzco worked more in wage labor than previously, 19 percent sold more cattle, 14 percent sold more artisan products, and 12 percent received more remittances from migrant relatives (1987:137).

The economic changes in Quinua have led to social ones. Almost everyone now goes to school. People complain that children no longer show the respect for adults that they once did. Women must work even harder in the fields to compensate for absent husbands. And people have dramatically changed their religious and sociopolitical organization. In the course of less than twenty years, they have abandoned much of the *cargo* system, and many have adopted Protestantism. It is to these changes in sociopolitical and religious organization that we now turn. They are of great theoretical interest because they have happened so quickly and because they contradict

Weber's hypothesis explaining the development of capitalism. The changes in sociopolitical organization also lend credence to the proposition that the economic changes in Quinua are fundamental in nature and not simply a continuation of the economic system that had existed prior to the 1940s.

7.

FEASTS AND *CARGOS,*
1966–1974

THE ECOLOGICAL and economic changes in Quinua are themselves of considerable interest, but they have also transformed social organization. No longer the society it once was, Quinua has undergone a revolutionary change that is well illustrated by the changes in religious practices. When I first went to Quinua twenty years ago, their religion was a syncretism of aboriginal and Catholic beliefs. People worshiped Catholic saints in public ceremonies that structured much of the political and economic life of the community. In their homes and fields Quinuenos dealt with aboriginal spirits and demons that had an everyday impact on health and luck (cf. Allen 1988). Although they continue these home ceremonies, they have altered public ritual dramatically today, and many have become Protestant. The increased economic dynamism described in the last chapter has set processes in motion that have undermined traditional religion.

RELIGION IN 1966

The central supernatural figure in household religion is the mountain god (*tayta urqu*), often associated with a type of hawk (*killinchu* or *cernicalo*) known as the *huamani*. The mountain god intervenes in everyday affairs, appears in dreams, and protects animals. There are many mountain gods, each one associated with a particular mountain. The larger the mountain, the more powerful the god. People propitiate them to seek help or to avoid their wrath. Many stories warn of powerful mountains that can even bring down airplanes. Before sowing their crops, farmers place coca leaves, cigarettes, cane alcohol, and maize in the ground as an offering (*pagapu*) to the god to which the field belongs. They dedicate animals to the god during the branding in order to protect the animals when grazing on the puna. Diviners call on the mountain god to discover animal thieves and witches.

Quinuenos also populate their supernatural world with other beings. *Qarqachas* are the spirits of people who have committed incest. *Manchachikos*, who wander the Earth to frighten the living, are men who have been condemned at their death for having left unpaid debts or for having money hidden in such a way that their heirs cannot find it. *Amaru* are golden animals, such as pigs and chickens, who live under the earth guarding their gold and causing landslides when they move. *Aya*, the ancient people found around archeological sites, cause illness. *Ukumari* are beast-men possessed of extraordinary strength. Devils (*diablos*) are generally malevolent spirits who inhabit known locales and are best avoided by prudent individuals.

Quinuenos attribute disease to the hot-cold system, well known in Latin America, and to soul loss and object intrusion. They classify food and climatic phenomena (temperature, altitude, wind) as hot or cold. Improper combinations cause sickness. Earthly forces, if not treated with respect, can also enter the body, causing illness. Air, cold, wind, the earth, and mountain vapors are important natural forces that must be dealt with circumspectly.

Quinuenos call on curers, witches, and diviners to help with problems or to harm enemies. Curers (*hampih* or *curanderos*) diagnose illness by rubbing a guinea pig over the patient. They heal the illness by removing the offending object found in the animal's body and by making offerings to the mountain god and other spirits. Witches (*layqa* or *brujos*) are consulted in order to harm someone. Like the Navaho (Kluckhohn 1944), Quinuenos accuse others of witchcraft more often than they admit to such practices themselves. The same person is often a curer as well as a witch. Some Quinuenos are diviners (*pongos*) who speak with the mountain god in order to read the future or to ascertain the name of a thief. Other diviners, known as *hatipah*, are not curers but read the future in coca leaves, cards, cigarette smoke, and maize.

Catholicism centers on public ritual, the agricultural calendar, and the sociopolitical organization of the village. In 1966 nearly all Quinuenos were Catholics. Crosses dotted hillsides and footpaths. Nearly all homes had one or more crosses as household shrines. Ceramic churches dominated the rooftops of the village. People often prayed to and petitioned God the father (*diós yay* or *papa diós*), Jesus, various saints, and—especially—different manifestations of the Virgin. Quinua Catholicism is clearly polytheistic when behavior rather than official beliefs is examined. Educated Quinuenos profess monotheism, but most peasants treat the saints, Virgin, Trinity, crosses, and statues as separate deities with separate identities.[1] The Catholic church, San Pedro de Quinua, is the largest structure in town. Tradition dates the construction of the church to 1563. The bell tower is dated 1888. The Sunday market is held in front of the church, and people sometimes use the church, privately and without the assistance of the priest, in household curing rites. The church also houses the most important saints' images. Quinuenos keep other images in hamlet chapels. A very few saints' images are privately owned and kept in homes.

In 1966 a resident priest attended to Quinua's needs as well as to those of the nearby district of Acos Vinchos. Most priests were removed after a few years, often because of complaints from the community to the archbishop that the priest was a drunkard, a womanizer, or irresponsible. The last resident priest lasted only a few years; he left the community and the priesthood voluntarily in 1980. There has been no resident priest since that time. Priests are scarce in Peru, and Quinua is served today by priests from Ayacucho and elsewhere who visit the town on important feast days. In 1987 one of them was shot to death, presumably by Shining Path, while he was saying mass in Ayacucho.

In addition to the priest, a community of ten Oblate nuns lived in Quinua for a few years in the mid-1960s. They ran a girls' school where they taught reading, writing, embroidery, and cooking. When the nuns left Quinua in 1966, the resident priest expanded the school into a regular primary school with state recognition, although it has since ceased to exist. Catholic missionaries occasionally arrived during fiestas, to take advantage of the greater church attendance, but preached even so to small congregations, except on days of major processions.

The priest and nuns had little control over much local religious practice. The nuns were in Quinua for too short a period to have had any lasting influence. Those few priests who remained in Quinua for longer periods did become part of the local power structure and influenced decisions of the town elite. Nonetheless, they exercised little control over household religion and the politico-religious system. They were, however, involved in the decisions to sell important church lands (the *cofradía* lands described below).[2] They rarely attended fiestas, although they were often invited. Quinua priests correctly feared an irate community should they try to alter even minor aspects of popular religion.

Most peasants paid little attention to the formal requirements or admonitions of the church. Few went to confession or communion. Most continued to believe in the mountain god, spirits, and demons in spite of exhortations to put those beliefs aside. It was *compadrazgo* and the fiesta system that formed the core of Quinua Catholicism. Self-identity as a Catholic was also important. People frequently told me "we are Catholics" ("*somos católicos*"), which in a sense meant "we are human beings."

The priest's primary functions were and are largely to say mass at specified times; to fulfill important public roles during the fiestas; to baptize, confirm, marry, and bury the population; to maintain and dispense the records of these ceremonies; and to provide other help when requested. Baptism, marriage, and confirmation are important in *compadrazgo*. People need marriage and baptismal records often: to obtain identity documents, to contract marriage, to enter school. In 1988 a twelve-year-old shoeshine boy in the city of Iquitos told me he did not attend school because he had lost his birth certificate, a common problem for poor Peruvians. The church was the only source of birth records in Quinua until 1935, when the civil register was established. The church continued as an important source of such documentation until 1960, when Quinuenos began to register births systematically in the municipality rather than the church.

In addition to the priest, two sisterhoods, or *hermandades*, tended to church affairs.[3] Women from both the town and the countryside joined these sisterhoods and were affiliated with the worship of the Sacred Heart or the Virgin of Perpetual Sorrow. Although the two organizations were ostensibly separate, the membership overlapped. The sisterhoods generally acted informally in consultation with important members of the town to advise the priest. They were the primary guardians of public religion and oversaw the patronal fiesta to the Virgin of Cocharcas. Only two old women remain of these formerly powerful organizations.

THE FIESTA SYSTEM

The most spectacular aspect of public religion was the system of fiestas. The central town alone celebrated eighteen public fiestas a year (table 33).[4] The hamlets celebrated additional ones. Although each hamlet has its own patron and other saints, those of the central town are the most important and tend to dominate the ritual calendar of all but the most remote hamlets.

Quinuenos believe that the proper celebration of the saints maintains the spiritual health of the community. They also use feast days

Table 33. *Calendrical Cycle of Central Town of Quinua, 1966*

Early August	Animal branding (Señal, or Senal)
August 14	Virgin of Carmen
August 15	The Assumption (Virgin de la Asumpción)[a]
Mid to late August	The Irrigation Festival (*Yarqa Aspiy*)
September 8	Mama Cocharcas (coincides with the Feast of the Nativity of the Virgin Mary in the official church calendar)
October 4	Saint Francis (San Francisco)
November 1	All Saints Day (Todos Santos)
December 8	Immaculate Conception (Virgin Purísima[b])
December 9	Battle of Ayacucho[c]
December 25	Christmas (Niño Nacimiento)
January 1	New Year, Change of Varayoc (*Vara Muray*), and the Infant of Prague
February 2	Candlemas (Candelaria)
February[d]	Compadres and Comadres
February	Carnival (Carnavales)
April	Holy Week (Semana Santa)
May 3	Holy Cross (Santa Cruz)
June 17	Trinity (Trinidad)
June 21	Corpus Christi
June 22	Saint Isidore (San Isidro)
June 29	Saints Peter and Paul (San Pedro y Paulo)

Source: Informant data and personal observation.
[a] Also called Mama Asunta.
[b] Also called Mama Limpia, Concepción, and Imaculada.
[c] A secular celebration of townspeople and outsiders.
[d] Compadres takes place two weeks and Comadres one week before Carnival.

to mark such important agropastoral events as the time for irrigating fields or the transfer of cattle from the puna pastures to the savannah. When discussing the agricultural calendar and the intricate irrigation schedule, informants usually referred not to calendar dates but to saints' days. Feasts associated with important events in the agricultural cycle are more important than those that are not.[5]

The ritual cycle of the central town begins in August with the branding of animals (*señal,* or *senal*), followed by the celebration of the irrigation system (*yarqa aspiy*), and then the patronal celebration of Mama Cocharcas in September.[6] The fiestas follow one after the other, so that August and early September are the months of greatest public ritual activity. Mama Cocharcas is especially miraculous. Quinuenos tell few stories about the origin of Quinua, but they sometimes relate one that concerns the appearance of Mama

Cocharcas at a spring where she commanded that a church be built. She is celebrated on September 8, the date of this appearance.[7] This feast begins the agricultural year. Although some planting takes place earlier, people initiate most of the sowing and the formal distribution of irrigation water (the *patacha*) around this time.

The agroceremonial year continues with the feast of Saint Francis on October 4, which initiates the beginning of the formal irrigation turns and rainy-season sowing in the barrio of Hanan Sayoc. All Saints Day, on November 1, is not only an important festival commemorating the dead but also signals the time to irrigate and cultivate fields lower in the savannah. Candlemas and Carnival in February celebrate the early harvest of the dry-season cycle. Holy Cross on May 3 marks the main harvest of maize and the return of animals from the high-altitude pastures. Corpus Christi, a movable feast in May or June, has strong harvest associations.

THE *CARGO* SYSTEM

The *cargo* system is both a system of worship and a key part of social organization.[8] It consists of posts known as *cargos* that people occupy in both the fiesta system and peasant political organization (the *varayoc*). The Peruvian *cargo* system is less structured than the well-known system of closely linked civil and religious posts in Mesoamerica.[9] In Peru there is no clearly designated ladder (a term used frequently to describe the Mesoamerican system), only a series of more and more costly *cargo* positions.

Festival officials (religious *cargo* holders) organize the fiestas of the saints, creating public processions, spectacles, and feasts. Fiestas differ in the number and types of festival posts. In Quinua the fiesta to Mama Cocharcas is the most elaborate festival and the only one that still continues with something of its former strength. The fiesta of the irrigation system—*yarqa aspiy*, "cleaning the canals," or *yarqa ruhuay*, "working on the canals"—is unique because of its complete separation from the formal church and its relationship to corvée labor. I will describe both fiestas and the peasant political organization to illustrate the operation of Quinua's *cargo* system.

THE FIESTA OF COCHARCAS

The fiesta for Mama Cocharcas actually commemorates four saints on consecutive days: Mama Cocharcas, the Infant Jesus (Niño Manuelito), Immaculate Conception (Mama Ascepción), and the Blessed Sacrament (Santísimo Sacramento). The celebrations begin with the

Table 34. *Fiesta of Mama Cocharcas: Calendar of Events*

August 30– September 6	The Novena
September 7	The Eve (*Vispera*) and last day of Novena (*Hatun Novena*)
September 8	Mama Cocharcas
September 9	The Infant Jesus (Niño Manuelito; also called Niño, Niño Manuel, and Niño Emanuel)
September 10	Immaculate Conception (Mama Ascepción; also called Mama Asumpción, a local confusion with the Assumption of the Virgin)
September 11	Blessed Sacrament (Santísimo Sacramento; also called Espiritu)
September 12	Benediction (*Bendición*); Combined processions of all three saints
September 13	The departure (*Avio* or *Qaru Chuqay*)
September 14	The head curing (*Uma Hampi*)

Source: Informant data and personal observation.

Novena on August 30 and continue day by day, increasing in intensity until the final half day on September 13 (see table 34 and photographs 5 and 6).

The feast is a public extravaganza that lasts for two weeks. The entire town enjoys the public processions and vast quantities of food and drink. One of the festival officials (the *trono*) dresses Mama Cocharcas in her beautiful burgundy gown, white veil, and (until they were stolen in 1973) gold earrings and a silver crown. Men carry Mama Cocharcas and the other saints around the plaza on wooden palanquins covered with white papier-mâché and candles. The people follow and surround the float, many with rapturous faces and some holding candles. The processions are very exciting. The church bell tolls and bands play. Costumed participants, dressed as tropical forest Indians and colonial military, add color, while the groaning of oxhorns punctuates the processional music of the band. In the past, the peasant political leaders walked among the crowd, whips in hand, ready to chastise anyone showing disrespect.

Before and after the processions, the festival officials proffer maize beer, wine, cane alcohol, and commercial beer to the celebrants. They make frequent forays through the town, accompanied by bands and dancing in the streets. In their houses they serve special foods: hominy stew, noodles, rice, guinea pig, chicken, mutton, and beef. By the time night falls, many people are drunk. The number of inebriates is one measure of the *cargo* holder's generosity. I have partici-

Procession during the fiesta to the Virgin of Cocharcas, 1967; note the standard-bearer with the staff of the Virgin.

Food sales during the fiesta to the Virgin of Cocharcas, 1967.

pated in two fiestas to Mama Cocharcas but have never been able to remain in the community for the entire two weeks. My body gives out after a week of intense feasting, drinking, and dancing and I am forced to escape.

Ideally, each of the saints during Cocharcas has a complete set of festival officials. The reality, however, is often different. Not all *cargo* posts of all saints are filled every year. Festival officials also differ in their willingness and ability to put on the fiesta. Quinuenos expect that the arrangements for Cocharcas should be the most elaborate, but even these festivities sometimes fail to rise above a minimal level. Nonetheless, the principal officials of the four saints compete with one another to provide the best celebration, and their combined efforts are usually stupendous.

Quinuenos rank the festival posts in prestige according to expense. Informants disagree on the exact order, but most group them from greater to lesser expense as follows: (1) standard-bearer (*al-*

ferez); (2) throne (*trono*) and altar (*altar*); (3) melodist (*melodio*); (4) mayordomo; (5) novenist (*novenante*), militia (*milicia*) and castle (*castillo*); (6) deputy (*deputado*); and (7) candle-bearer (*centilla*).

Everyone agrees that the standard-bearer is the most expensive and therefore the most important *cargo* post. Each saint is supposed to have a standard-bearer. Each standard-bearer is expected to bring a band, but only the one to the Virgin of Cocharcas always does so. This standard-bearer is the principal actor. He receives the silver standard of Cocharcas during a special ceremony, after which he removes it to his home, keeping vigil over it throughout the fiesta. During the processions he precedes the float of Mama Cocharcas, carrying her standard, and is followed by his band. He also pays the priest to say the mass and carries the money to him in a public ceremony, accompanied by family, friends, important members of the community, and the band. He also provides two bulls for the bullfights in the plaza.

The throne shares with the altar the next most important rank of *cargo* posts. The throne decorates the float on which the image of the saint is carried and sets off firecrackers during the procession. He may also provide a band from outside the community for one or two days, although this has become increasingly rare. Each saint has its own throne, but that for Mama Cocharcas is the most expensive and important. The monstrance (Santísimo Sacramento) has no throne, but is instead carried by the priest around the plaza under an awning.

The altar for Cocharcas decorates the church altar with cloth, flowers, and candles. The altars for the other saints reimburse him for this work and provide new candles during their feast days. The altar sometimes brings a band for one or two days.

The melodist, the next most expensive *cargo*, provides church music during the nine days of the Novena and for the mass on September 8. He hires a cantor, saxophonist, violinist, and portable organ. A single melodist provides the music for all four saints. He also brings two bulls and horn players (playing the *huaqra puku*, a circular instrument made of oxhorns) for the bullfights in the plaza. This post is unique in that the melodist has to find his own replacement.

The mayordomo is in charge of the fiesta, but while his expenses are significant, they are not as great as those of the standard-bearer, throne, altar, or melodist. Unlike all other festival officials, the mayordomo often serves for several years. The sisterhoods recruit the mayordomo, who in turn recruits the other festival officials. Ideally, Mama Cocharcas has two mayordomos, one for Hanan Sayoc and another for Lurin Sayoc. They alternate in giving the fiesta and com-

pete to see which barrio gives the better fiesta. In 1966 the Virgin
had lands in Lurin and Hanan Sayoc for the mayordomo of each
barrio. Each of the other three saints has only one mayordomo.

The mayordomo and sisterhoods begin to recruit the important
cargo holders around July, more than one year before the fiesta in
which they will serve, but only two months before the official start
of the current year's celebrations. Quinuenos are thinking about the
coming fiesta at this time; many *cargo* holders have already begun
the celebrations with festive work parties (*yanta huaqtay*) to obtain
firewood. The mayordomo and sisterhoods review the festival histories, economic resources, and willingness to serve of various community members. They discuss their decisions with the priest and
other notable people. People rarely ask to serve, although a Lima migrant sometimes does so and will be given preference. Migrants have
more money than peasants and give better fiestas.

After deciding on a candidate, the mayordomo and members of the
sisterhood visit the prospect (a process known as *yaykupaku*), ply-
ing him and his wife with drink until one of them accepts. During
the last days of the current fiesta, the mayordomo gives a special
meal, known as the election (*eligión*), in which he recruits the
minor *cargo* holders and makes public the list of all the coming festival officials. Participants at this meal often fight over who has
served what and when in the *cargo* system, and what kind of costs
they have had to assume. People who wish to avoid *cargo* posts do
not attend this or any of the other meals during a fiesta, a difficult
but not impossible feat. At least one week before the fiesta is to
begin, the mayordomo visits all the festival officials. He brings a
bottle of cane alcohol to each one to remind them of their coming
obligations.

There are supposed to be nine novenists, one for each day of the
Novena, the nine-day period before the festival proper. There are
never enough novenists for each of the saints, and the posts are generally filled only for Mama Cocharcas. Each novenist pays the priest
for one day of the Novena, adorns the church altar with flowers and
candles, and brings rockets and other noisemakers to the celebration. The Novena ends elaborately on September 7, with the band of
the standard-bearer adding to the celebration.

The post of militia (sometimes called *estandarte*) combines civil
pageantry with religion. This festival official contracts for costumed
men, also known as militia, who represent soldiers in the Battle of
Ayacucho (the final battle in Peru's independence from Spain) fought
in Quinua in 1824. Wearing the clothing of either the Royalist or Pa-
triotic forces, the militia stand guard in the church door with lances

during the bullfight. The holder of this post also provides drum, flute, and violin music and carries a special standard (*estandarte*) throughout the fiesta.

The post of castle contracts for the building of firework structures and provides rockets and other explosives. The firework structures are large and very roughly resemble castles.

The deputy (commonly pronounced *reputado* in Quechua) is one of the least expensive posts and is often filled by poor peasants. A parent frequently accepts this post in the name of a child. The eight to twelve deputies in the fiesta rent bulls for the bullfights and hire horn players who also care for the bulls. Some deputies travel great distances to get good horn players.

The deputies organize bullfights on the afternoons of the five major days of the fiesta (September 8 through 12). They each bring a bull on their particular saint's day. The standard-bearer and melodist also bring bulls on September 8, the day of Mama Cocharcas. The final bullfight on September 12, which celebrates the benediction, sports the best bulls from all of the preceding days.

Bulls roam the plaza during the bullfights while men—often drunk—confront them. The men use their ponchos as capes and sometimes attract the bull with the poncho even while they are wearing it. Everyone scatters to safety when a bull charges. Women and children pull their drunken male relatives away from the bull-fight, intervening as they often do to save men from the consequences of their machismo. The authorities, important members of the central town, and important migrants sit on chairs in front of the stores drinking beer. Other notables look on from the second-floor veranda of the municipal hall. The rest of the people stand and watch from the sides of the plaza. The bulls are usually not killed, but if one strays too close to the church, one of the militia may kill it with his lance to fulfill his obligation of protecting the church.

Quinuenos judge the quality of the fiesta partly by the quality of the bulls. A human death during the bullfight is a sign that the deputies have fulfilled their obligation to bring fierce bulls. Traditionally the peasant political leaders were supposed to erect barricades for the bullfight, but often did so several days after the start of the bull-fights. As a result, bulls frequently broke loose into the streets of the town, causing panic and sometimes injury and death. The lieutenant governors now erect the barricades, although they do so no sooner.

The candle-bearer, the most minor post, carries a large candelabra (*centilla*) in front of the float during the procession.

In addition to their major responsibilities, festival officials may contract for special entertainment if they so desire. A few always provide people costumed as tropical forest Indians known as *chunchus*. Carrying panpipes and arrows, these costumed participants add color to the proceedings as they accompany the processions and visit the festival officials.

All of the festival officials must ensure that they are accompanied in the fiesta by family, ritual kin, friends, and neighbors. The deputy and his wife, for example, travel throughout their hamlet with their horn players, offering people alcohol. They remind them of the fiesta and their role in it and ask their neighbors to accompany them. This entourage journeys to the central town. The horn music is heard over great distances, announcing the approach of the participants and helping create a link between town and countryside. Similar activities by all the festival officials assure the attendance of large numbers of people at the fiesta. It is difficult to refuse these demands to accompany the officials.

THE IRRIGATION FESTIVAL—*YARQA ASPIY*

The term *"yarqa aspiy"* means "canal cleaning," but it contains an added meaning of "the celebration of the irrigation system"—a terminological distinction made in Spanish but not in Quechua.[10] In Hanan Sayoc in 1966 people cleaned the system at the same time they were celebrating it. In Lurin Sayoc the actual cleaning was held in July, about one month before the celebration of the system. Today, however, the celebration and the work are combined in both barrios. The switch from earthen to cement canals at the intakes has reduced the amount of labor needed, consequently diminishing the importance of the irrigation corvée.

The following describes the fiesta and work as it existed in Lurin Sayoc in 1966 and 1967. The residents of Lurin Sayoc cleaned their canals and reservoir during two to four days of corvée labor every July. Initiated and supervised by the peasant political organization, the labor followed a practical order. The first day the upper canals were cleaned, the second day the reservoirs, and subsequent days the lower parts of the system. The workers removed rocks and debris and cut trees and brush on the banks. To prevent seepage, participants reinforced the earthen canals and reservoirs with sod and stones and patched the cement ones.

Approximately one month later, in August, the residents of Lurin Sayoc organized the celebration of the system. At this time they inspected the canals and made additional repairs. They also inspected water flow to make initial assessments of the distribution of water

The cooking fires of the *cargo* holders of the irrigation festival, 1966.

among the major regional canals. Last, but not least, they celebrated the system with a fiesta.

The irrigation festival was one of Quinua's most beautiful fiestas. During the early morning the wives, daughters, and daughters-in-law of the festival officials set out from their homes for the main canal intakes located in the spectacular heights of the moist forest and prairie. They left early to prepare meals at assigned places along the system. The other celebrants set forth a little later, but still in the dark, under a dry-season sky alive with stars, August Perseids occasionally streaking across the horizon. They were greeted at the main intake at dawn by the smoke of the women's cooking fires blending with morning mists. Unlike other celebrations, where bands, radios, and record players produce a cacophony, Quinuenos had left their competing music behind and listened only to the drums and flutes provided by the festival organizers. The high-pitched sounds and drumbeats further welcomed them on their arrival.

After the celebrations at the intake, the participants, sporting special flowers in their hats, followed the canals downward. They walked in the direction of the water flow, until they had inspected, cleaned, and feted the entire canal system. On the second day, they commemorated the reservoirs, and on the third day, the peasant leaders held celebrations in their homes, serving alcohol and a special meal called *combidu*. On the fourth day, people celebrated the departure (*despedida*) of the cooks, chicha preparers, musicians, and dancers who had been living with their respective captains and peasant political leaders.

The fiesta ended on the fifth day with the curing of the head (*uma hampi*). All fiestas end with the head curing. People assemble at the home of the giver of the fiesta, where they are served a hearty breakfast (often eggs and a chili sauce) and corn beer or other alcohol in order to cure their hangovers. Many people, however, continue to drink throughout the day, and the head-cure often turns into its own fiesta. *Uma hampi*, nonetheless, marks the end of the festivities and the return to normal routine—even if this only happens on the next day.

The irrigation festival was the only public fiesta in which the priest did not participate in any way, not even celebrating a mass. The participants venerated a cross known as father irrigation (*cequia taytacha*) or father canal (*tayta yarqa*). (There are three such crosses in Lurin Sayoc but only one in Hanan Sayoc.) These crosses remained in chapels for most of the year, but during this fiesta the mayordomos carried them, wrapped reverentially in white cloths, in their arms along the canals and reservoirs. At two customary rest stops, where peasant political leaders had constructed brush shelters, the crosses were set in places of prominence. The fiesta organizers and other important people rested in the shelters. Other participants stood outside, and a prayer leader recited prayers (*loctrina* or *doctrina*) to celebrate the crosses and the irrigation system. The participants ate, drank, and watched the antics of costumed dance groups.

The two major *cargo* posts were mayordomo and captain (*capitán*). The three irrigation mayordomos (*cequia mayordomos*) represented the three major regions of the Lurin Sayoc irrigation system: Moya, Sicsa Ura, and Lurin Sayoc. They were considered the "owners" of their respective irrigation system. They were responsible for deciding on the general allocation of water for the year among the three geographical areas, and their discussions during the fiesta sometimes led to fights among the different users of the system. The

Dancers during the Lurin Sayoc irrigation festival, 1967.

mayordomos inspected the irrigation system throughout the year and called corvée labor groups to repair it when needed. During the irrigation festival, the mayordomos provided food, alcohol, music, and costumed dance groups. The dance groups, known as *qamille* or *allqucha* ("little dogs"), dressed as soldiers and danced out sexual allusions and jokes, accompanied by drum, flute, and horn. Pairs of women sang *qarahui*, customary songs that announced work parties and fiestas. The mayordomos were also responsible for obtaining the other festival officials.

One or two captains organized the actual work on the irrigation canals and reservoirs. Each one supervised a work party and provided singers, dancers, drum, flute, food, and drink. The barriowide rural political organization (*llahta varayoc*) helped organize the fiesta and aided the festival officials. During this festival the *varayoc* were referred to as irrigation *varayoc;* they were known as irrigation mayor (*cequia alcalde*), irrigation constable (*cequia albaser*) and irrigation alderman (*cequia regidor*).

Participants in the irrigation festival drank and ate well. The wives and female kin of the festival officials prepared large pots of soup, mutton or beef stew, potatoes, hominy, parched maize, guinea pig, and other festive food. The officials served one another in formal exchanges (*contrapunte*). They paired off, and the wife of the highest-ranking member of the pair served them food, after which the second wife did the same. Celebrants drank special maize beer (*hurka chicha*) from novel parrot-shaped ceramic cups. At the end of each day the celebrants retired from the irrigation system to the central plaza, where they continued their revelry with more dancing and drinking. On arriving at the entrance to the town the wives of the festival officials were waiting with more food and alcohol.

To receive water during the formal water distribution, each conjugal family had to send a worker to the cleaning and celebration. The family, however, was responsible only for those sections of the system that it utilized. Any family that did not send a worker was expected to collaborate with the fiesta and corvée work group by sending *hurka chicha*, cane alcohol, cigarettes, and coca leaves for the participants. Large landowners and haciendas sent maize beer and coca in addition to workers.

Those who neglected to collaborate with the irrigation work and celebration were fined the daily wage of an agricultural laborer before they could receive water in the formal system of turns. A list of workers and collaborators with the fiesta was kept for use during the water division. Nonetheless, peasants often argued over whether a family's participation had been sufficient to merit water. The rules exempting persons from the work and fiesta were ambiguous and open to varying interpretations. Major *cargo* officials were exempted from corvée labor, but Quinuenos did not always agree on what constituted a major office. They also lacked a precise definition of how much maize beer and other goods to send in lieu of work.

In 1966 the fiesta in Lurin Sayoc was extremely conservative and maintained old customs through a formal system of punishment known as the *sipu.* A person who was deficient in his duties was forced to kneel in front of the mayordomo, a string connecting his finger to the irrigation cross. The mayordomo chastised and fined the culprit (perhaps a half bottle of cane alcohol) and exhorted the celebrants to follow the old customs appropriately. Neither his efforts nor the *sipu,* however, were able to stem the ecological and economic forces that undermined the entire fiesta system. Although Quinuenos still participate in the communal repair of the system that continues to define rights to water, the irrigation festival is today celebrated only in a minor way in both barrios.

THE PEASANT POLITICAL ORGANIZATION—*VARAYOC*

Until about 1970 peasants also assumed *varayoc* posts, quasipolitical positions that differed from fiesta posts but shared many characteristics with them.[11] In its traditional form this organization was quite large, numbering from thirty to forty men (see figure 4). Each barrio had its own town organization, known as the town *varayoc* (*llahta varayoc* or *hatun varayoc*). The town organization of Hanan Sayoc was headed by a town mayor (*llahta alcalde*), as was that of Lurin Sayoc. The two organizations were equal in rank and power but functioned only within their own barrio. Each hamlet had additional peasant political officials known as the rural mayor (*campo alcalde*) and rural constable (*campo albaser* or *alguacil*). They served under the supervision of their respective town organization.[12]

There was no particular order to an individual's movement from the rural to the town peasant organization. The only definite rule was that someone who served in the rural system did not serve in the town's lowest rank of alderman (*regidor*). Only peasants with lands near the central town had to participate in the town system. Those who had served in the armed forces did not have to assume any peasant political post. Nor did townsmen ever serve. The *varayoc* were definitely associated with the status of peasant.

Organized in a strict hierarchy, the peasant political officials carried staffs of authority (the *vara*). Whenever they were together, they walked in a single file organized from higher to lower rank. The high-

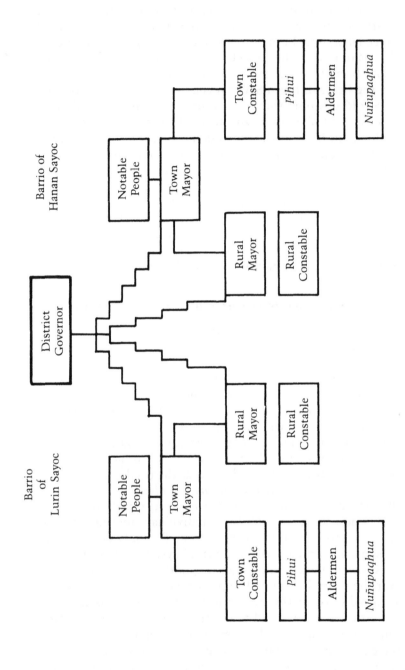

Figure 4. District peasant political organization (*varayoc*) of Quinua

The town mayor (*llahta alcalde*) of the Lurin Sayoc *varayoc*, 1966;
note his store-bought sneakers.

ranking officials were like fathers to the lower ones. They provided them with food during ceremonies, in return for which, the low-ranking aldermen worked in the fields and performed other tasks for the high-ranking mayor and constable. The first and last aldermen were called by kin terms which mean "oldest child" (*pihui*) and "youngest child" (*nuñopaqhua*), respectively.

These respected peasant officials organized corvée labor, ensuring that the roads, bridges, and other public facilities were kept in good repair. Quinuenos considered the town peasant officials (along with the irrigation mayordomos) to be the owners of their barrio's irrigation system and expected them to oversee it and to help organize its annual cleaning and festival. In Lurin Sayoc, they organized the distribution of irrigation water, an act which in effect determined the time of planting.

The *varayoc* were Quinua's police force. They carried whips, and at the apogee of their power, people feared them, although some of that fear had begun to diminish as the system declined in the 1960s. They punished petty crimes and sometimes sent a criminal to the authorities in Quinua. They might whip people who carelessly let their animals damage crops. They brought unmarried couples to the church to confess and to be married during mass weddings held on Palm Sunday and during missions. At the same time, they took children to be baptized. People called on the peasant officials to solve marital disputes, which they sometimes did by punishing the offending husband or wife. During processions or in church, the peasant leaders whipped anyone not showing the proper respect for the proceedings.

Responsible for the spiritual health of Quinua, the *varayoc* maintained roadside crosses, oversaw the system of festival posts (*cargos*), and played a major role in the fiestas. They accompanied the fiesta officials and helped them fulfill their obligations. They traveled to the tropical forest *montaña* with mules several weeks before Holy Week to obtain palms for Palm Sunday, spending at least a week on the journey. One consequence of their extensive participation in the fiestas was that they were frequently drunk. They visited the sick and helped bury the dead. They always participated in such mourning rites as the vigil held on the fifth day after a death (the *pichqa*) and that for the end of mourning (*huata unras*) one year later.

Immediately after assuming office on January 1,[13] the *varayoc* traveled to the houses of the town authorities and then inspected the houses in the town and hamlets (*huasi visitay*). They saw that the houses were clean and maintained properly with the required cross

The town mayor (*llahta alcalde*) of the Lurin Sayoc *varayoc* after accompanying a family during the end of the mourning ceremonial (*huata unras*), 1966.

of flowers on the wall. The trip throughout the community took the Lurin Sayoc officials a week, after which they traveled to Ayacucho to greet (*saludar*) the prefect. On this and other trips throughout the community, often undertaken during fiestas, the *varayoc* oversaw the behavior of children. Women, especially widows, would ask them to punish errant children. They complied by whipping the youngsters three times: for the Father, Son, and Holy Spirit. In an attempt to escape these punishments, children hid in trees and sometimes insulted the peasant leaders from their safe perches. The *varayoc* also helped widows to cultivate their fields.

The *varayoc* were not independent political officials, however, and they served the interests of townspeople in controlling peasant behavior and labor.[14] As direct subordinates of the governor, the peasant leaders gathered in the plaza every Sunday to greet him. Those not present were jailed briefly the following week. In the plaza they lined up in order, the Lurin Sayoc officials on one side of the plaza, and the Hanan Sayoc ones on the other. The governor gave them his orders for the week. They were usually assigned quotas of corvée laborers. In this role the *varayoc* recruited people to work not only on the projects that interested them, such as repair of the irrigation canals, but also on projects that primarily benefited the town elite, such as repair of the town plaza or water system (cf. Rasnake 1988:86). Peasants often resented such work. Even in those projects that profited peasants directly, it was the peasant who worked, while townspeople, who also benefited from the work, sent peons, coca leaves, cigarettes, and cane alcohol—or later paid fines.

Before the police post was established in 1953, the governor employed the *varayoc* as a small army to control the population (cf. Rasnake 1988:76–77). He and other town authorities had them forcefully round up young peasant men for the army (the *leva*) and arrest those accused of some wrong to bring them to jail. Town authorities used the *varayoc* as messengers (*chasquis*) (ibid.:70–72), sending the peasant officials on foot to Ayacucho and other towns. Certain of the peasant officials worked for important townspeople as servants. Each Sunday the aldermen swept the central plaza and communal hall. Two aldermen were assigned weekly to clean the governor's house, work in his fields, and graze his animals. The Hanan Sayoc organization provided the workers one week and Lurin Sayoc did so on the following. The peasant leaders also collected the fees charged by the town for grazing on communal lands (the *yerbaje*), a sheep from every non-Quinueno using the land. The control of this free peasant labor gave certain town officials a significant advantage in the local community (ibid.:78).

The subordination of the *varayoc* to town authorities was expressed symbolically. Peasant leaders addressed town authorities submissively, often slightly bowed, and during certain fiestas, they gave gifts of food to the governor and priest, using tones, words, and behaviors expressing their subordination. The peasant leaders did maintain some independence from town officials (ibid.: 83), but they were nonetheless subordinate to them on the whole.

I have no information on the origin of the *varayoc* organization in Quinua, but Rasnake (1988) suggests that similar authorities among the Yura of Bolivia have roots in both pre-Hispanic officials (the Ethnic Lords) and Hispanic ones (the *curacas*). The Quinua *varayoc* organization (or something like it) was probably responsible for recruiting Indian labor early in the colonial period. Indians provided labor service in Quinua as early as 1537, the time of the first Spanish contact, building houses and constructing a church (Rivera Serna 1966:21–22, 30). A document dealing with the late sixteenth and seventeenth centuries, labeled "Titulos de Quinua," reports that Quinuenos served as messengers and repaired roads and bridges among other tribute and labor obligations. I do not believe it is accidental that these very functions—the only ones specifically mentioned in these documents—were also important functions of the *varayoc* organization.

INDIVIDUAL PARTICIPATION IN THE *CARGO* SYSTEM

A person enters the *cargo* system after marriage, although older adults sometimes serve even when unmarried. Quinuenos accord male officials prominence, but it would be a mistake to think of the fiesta as something dominated by men. The head of the conjugal family, usually but not always male, assumes the post, but the entire conjugal family works together to fulfill it (cf. Allen 1988:79). The wife is an important participant. In rare cases widowed or older single women have accepted important festival posts.

Townspeople and peasants participate in the festival and political system differently. Peasants served in both the fiesta and *varayoc* system; townspeople served in local government posts and less frequently in the fiesta system, but never in the *varayoc* organization. Townspeople have always been unwilling to take on fiesta posts. They see festival posts as diverting money from business and other more productive ventures (cf. Smith 1977), an attitude also assumed by many rural peasants more recently.

Since most Quinuenos are reluctant to accept *cargo* posts, their neighbors employ various social pressures to get them to do so.

People often insult those who have not met their obligations. During the fiesta to the Virgin of Cocharcas, the *varayoc* officials used to establish themselves at the four corners of the plaza to harass the young men who had not yet served as aldermen. They sometimes imprisoned a person for a day if he refused to serve. Quinuenos also emphasize *cargo* contributions when wrangling over irrigation water, arguing that so-and-so has greater rights to water because of his greater participation in the system. Indeed, much of the fighting among peasants in Quinua was and is focused on participation in the *cargo* system.

Supernatural sanctions reinforce social ones. In some cases people accept *cargo* posts only after the saint has appeared in a dream, telling them to do so. Many tales warn of the evil consequences of failing to celebrate the Virgin of Cocharcas as one should: bad crops, accidents, deaths, and business failures are only some of the punishments she sends. In spite of these social and supernatural pressures, the mayordomo and sisterhoods usually must ply a couple with drink to get the pair to accept a festival post. Some people refuse the first offer of alcohol, as they are aware of the intentions of the mayordomo. The *varayoc* also sought out their replacements with alcohol, getting the person drunk in the process.

A person accepts *cargo* posts in no particular order other than the gradual assumption of more expensive ones. A peasant begins in the lower ranks of either the political or fiesta system and rises gradually in the hierarchy, moving between festival and political positions. Even the single fiesta of Cocharcas has no special order in which people pass the different ranks and most people serve only in one or two posts of the fiesta.

Many people from the countryside alternate between local and town festival and *varayoc* posts. Others, especially in the most remote hamlets, serve in only the hamlet system and know little about the town organization. The irrigation system is a significant variable in this participation. Inhabitants of hamlets that share the same irrigation water participate together in their barrio's fiesta and *varayoc* system. Those outside the irrigation network are likely to be outside the fiesta and political network as well.

After significant service in the *cargo* system, a peasant becomes one of an informal group of communal elders. Not a corporate body, this group has no formal name, and Quinuenos refer to its members simply as old people (*gente mayor, antiguos machus, viejos, ñawpa viejokuna,* or *ñawpa machukuna*). I have called them "notable people" in figure 4. Quinuenos regard all old people fondly; the death of the young is deemed happy, but the death of the old tragic. The old

who have passed many *cargo* posts are accorded especial respect because of their ritual associations and wealth. Notable people exercise
considerable influence in discussions about festivals, religion, and
the allocation of communal resources, but they do not necessarily
wield much influence in town political matters. Often illiterate, they
frequently lack rhetorical skills, so that they usually are not leaders
at community assemblies.

ECONOMIC COSTS OF *CARGO* PARTICIPATION

Participation in the peasant political and fiesta system was very expensive, the costs depending on the post and the will and financial
ability of the official.[15] People usually rested for several years between
major posts, to accumulate money for the next one. They sometimes
migrated to the coast to earn the money during this rest period or sent
their children to work on the coast. Many mortgaged their fields to
raise the necessary cash. The poor finished their service in the lower,
less expensive ranks.

The four standard-bearers during Cocharcas are expected to provide a band. A band consists of fifteen to twenty musicians, who are
generally from outside Quinua. They must be paid and fed, so that
the band is the single greatest expense. Some officials try to reduce
this expense by hiring a band for fewer days or by substituting a
cheaper orchestra that contains fewer musicians.[16] People criticize
such economy, especially for the standard-bearer of Mama Cocharcas and insist that this official at least provide a complete band for a
minimum of six days (September 7 to 12). Not all standard-bearers
are able or willing to comply.

Food and drink are the next major expenses, and the posts of standard-bearer, throne, altar, melodist, and mayordomo are expected to
provide prodigious quantities. The major festival officials employ
such specialists as women to wash and cut vegetables, cook, serve,
and clean up, other women to serve the maize beer, and men to su-
pervise and guard the plates, spoons, bottles, and other utensils lest
these be stolen by the guests.

A few social mechanisms alleviate some of the burden of fiesta expenses. Kinfolk, neighbors, friends, and ritual kin frequently contribute spontaneous gifts of beer during the fiesta when they are
drinking. Before the fiesta they pin money to the clothing adorning
the saint's statue. On the last day they pin it to the clothing of the
festival official. They may give food and drink in balanced reciprocity (*ayni*) before the fiesta, gifts which must be returned doubled by
the recipient when the donor has a fiesta. Such gifts in *ayni*, how-

ever, are infrequent; one standard-bearer, for example, only received two cases of beer and one bottle of cane alcohol in such a manner (case #1 below). Men help festival officials cut firewood in a cooperative work party, known as the *yanta huaqtay*. Kin and friends often work as cooks and servers in generalized reciprocity and out of respect for the Virgin, who is known to punish refusals of aid. All of this seemingly free labor, however, has indirect costs for the official; he must serve these helpers food and alcohol, as well as give the servers and musicians gifts of ceramic figures.

Special lands, known as *cofradía* lands (*mama allpa* or *tayta allpa*), were devoted to saints; the mayordomo cultivated or distributed these lands to the major festival officials to provide food for the fiesta. Most of these lands were of poor quality, and Quinuenos regarded their use as a symbolic rather than real contribution to the fiesta. The festival official cultivated them privately rather than communally. He alone provided the money for fertilizer, seed, and labor. As the fiestas have declined in importance, these saints' lands have been sold to raise money for church improvements. Many years ago the festival officials of Mama Cocharcas were also given access to a herd of sheep and cattle in addition to the lands. A few of these animals remained in the 1930s.

The priest who served in Quinua during most of the 1960s estimates that the standard-bearer of Mama Cocharcas was spending about $400.00 during that time, an amount that he estimates rose to $468.00 by 1973. However, these estimates are too low, as the following cases illustrate.

Case #1: In the early 1970s[17] the standard-bearer to Mama Cocharcas reported spending $842.00 on the fiesta. The major costs were: $515.00 for a band for six days; $42.00 for ten gallons of cane alcohol; $84.00 for such basic ingredients as rice, noodles, and salt; and $94.00 for a cow. These enumerated costs total $735.00. The remainder of the money was spent on unspecified cases of beer, rental of a bull for the bullfight, the preparation of maize beer, and gifts for the cooks and musicians. To the cash costs one must add such noncash expenditures as human energy and the value of the crops grown in the official's own fields and used in the fiesta (e.g., the maize used to make the beer). It is clear that while this festival official and others may exaggerate costs to maximize prestige, the costs are still substantial. The reported monetary cost for this official was 1,800 times the daily agricultural wage of $0.47.

To help defray some of the costs of the fiesta, the family borrowed $281.00 from a relative in Lima. They also postponed purchasing a plow and oxen they had planned to buy. Since they were agricultural innovators who cash-cropped a significant portion of their produce, the loss of the plow was felt deeply.

The family assumed the festival post with great reluctance only a few weeks before the start of the fiesta. Three Quinuenos had already refused the post, and the mayordomo and members of the sisterhood were desperate. They visited the male head of household several times, always bringing alcohol, trying to convince him and his wife to accept. They did so, but only after the male head of household reported that Mama Cocharcas had appeared in a dream telling him to take on the festival position.

Case #2: Expenditures vary according to the personality and social position of the festival officials. In the early 1970s the standard-bearer reported spending $2,000.00 on the fiesta. The extraordinary sum involved can be gauged by the fact that two highly inflationary years later he was earning $117.00 a month (or $1,404.00 a year) in his well-paid salaried profession. Although this income made him one of the richest men in the community, he nonetheless had to earn most of the money for the fiesta through sale of ceramics. The fiesta had cost him more than his annual salary two years later!

This individual's case illustrates how contemporary fiesta service is being used by some to facilitate their upward social mobility. He was a ceramicist born in the countryside, but he had obtained an important government position that brought him to the central town when he was twenty-three years of age. When he moved to the town in the mid-1960s, he was an uneducated Quechua-speaking peasant often insulted as an Indian. Up until that time he had worn rubber-tire sandals and chewed coca leaves, behavior incompatible with town social status. He initially deferred to other townspeople and took their insults quietly, but he often complained to me that people were envious. His wife wanted to open up a store but was reluctant to do so because people would say, "How rich she must be to be able to buy a store." To compensate he has carefully maintained all the dress and behavior codes appropriate to town status. Through ceramic manufacture and his profession, he has amassed great material wealth, which he has used to considerable advantage. He displays this wealth ostentatiously. He has constructed a two-story home in the town center and has more radios and record players than anyone else, making him a desired invitee to fiestas. He gives very elaborate birthday celebrations but avoided all participation in the *cargo* system (even though his father had served in the *varayoc*) until accepting the post of standard-bearer to Mama Cocharcas, the most important festival position of all. He accepted this post, even though he had told me previously that he would never accept any position, that it was a waste of money: "Of what use is a fiesta post?" He has not passed any other post, although he is today in his late forties. Careful use of this one fiesta post and of birthday celebrations have been sufficient to legitimize his social status.

Case #3: Even poorer people spend considerable sums. In the mid-1970s the melodist estimated an expenditure of at least $936.00. The couple spent $421.00 for fifteen days of music (organist-cantor, violin, and trumpet) and $140.00 for a cow. In addition, they slaughtered several guinea pigs and chickens and bought 50 kilos of rice, 50 kilos of noodles, 50 kilos of sugar, various quantities of condiments, four liters of cooking oil, half a truckload of potatoes (100 to 150 kilos), and half a truckload of firewood, although they sold the excess wood at the end of the fiesta. They ordered two large jugs (*maqma*) of maize beer from a professional brewer with ingredients bought in Ayacucho. *Molle* beer was made with one sack of *molle* berries given as a gift by the man's mother. They bought seventeen cases of beer (12 liters in a case), twelve bottles of pisco, and many bottles of cane alcohol, in addition to those they received as gifts. They had to pay the freight costs of the potatoes and firewood. They also rented a bull, two horn players, and two bullfighters for the bullfight in the plaza on the last day of the fiesta.

This couple is relatively poor. He is a carpenter and she ran a small store. At the time of the fiesta, they were living in Ayacucho and supporting six children, one of whom was attending school in Lima. They have never had much money and often rely on the largess of kinspeople to survive. This couple has not taken on any other festival post, even though the woman is deeply religious. Nor do they have elaborate birthday celebrations. They are never asked to be godparents; people know they are too poor for that. They reluctantly accepted the post of melodist only after the mayordomo and members of the sisterhoods exerted great pressure. They took the position in order to maintain their many emotional and material attachments to Quinua. They own a house and fields there but live there only when forced to leave Lima or Ayacucho by their many business reversals. They sometimes plant their fields in Quinua to supply their own food and cash-crops; they also use the town as a source of wood and laborers.

Case #4: Festival posts in other fiestas are generally less expensive than those in Cocharcas, but the costs are nonetheless high. One man spent a total of $36.00 to serve as mayordomo of Holy

Cross in the fiesta of *compadres* (one of the least elaborate and expensive posts) in the late 1960s: $32.00 for food, maize beer, cane alcohol, and fruit and $4.00 to the priest for the mass. He had accepted the festival post late in the year; he was unable to plant anything in the saint's land and only killed chickens for the food. Even though the total costs were low compared to other cases described above, this man had a hard time raising the money. He was a poor man and had to borrow $24.00 of the costs from a nephew.

Case #5: Even the festival post of deputy, one of the least expensive, has significant costs. In addition to providing food and drink, deputies rent a bull and horn players. In 1973 horn players alone cost around $11.70 each. One must add to these expenses those of travel and energy. A number of Quinuenos have traveled to Chuschi and Sarhua to obtain good horn players. This trip to southern Ayacucho would take them more than a week.

The man who initiated the custom of traveling to Chuschi for the horn players was a trader, who traveled around Peru to trade in coca and animals. He enjoyed *cargo* service and used his participation in the system to obtain high-altitude tuber fields.

Case #6: One of the most successful Quinua migrants in Lima accepted the post of standard-bearer to Mama Cocharcas in the late 1970s. I do not have data on his costs, but he ran such a spectacular festival that he brought someone to videotape it. He gave elaborate ceramic gifts to everyone who accompanied him. This man's situation illustrates the forces encouraging migrants to accept festival service in Quinua. He maintains elaborate ties with both Quinua and the migrant community. He uses these ties to obtain laborers for his two small manufacturing plants in Lima. At the same time he truly loves Quinua and its music and customs.

CONCLUSION

When I first studied Quinua's fiesta system in 1966, it was fully functioning, but I was unaware that it was on a trajectory that was to change it fundamentally. Quinuenos were in the process of modifying their system of festival posts, questioning the very religious system on which they were based. If someone in 1966 had predicted the changes I later witnessed, I would have thought the idea farfetched if not crazy. Although the *varayoc* organization was in the process of disappearing, the fiesta system seemed a stable and important part of Quinua life.

The changes in Quinua have been rapid and profound. Aside from intrinsic interest as data, they present challenges for standard anthropological theory. How do we explain them? I turn to the answer in the next chapter. As we shall see, Quinuenos modified their religious behaviors and ideas in response to the practical exigencies of their existence. Ideological changes followed closely on material ones. Unlike Weber's claim for Europe, economic changes preceded religious ones in Quinua.

8.

THE DYNAMICS OF RELIGIOUS CHANGE

I HAVE described the fiesta system as it existed—or how Quinuenos remembered it—in 1966. The *varayoc* organization was already diminished in 1966. It consisted of only the mayor, constable, and two aldermen of Lurin Sayoc; two rural officials (the constable and mayor) were also functioning in the hamlet of Llamahuillca. Much of my description of the *varayoc* is derived from informant memory. The system of festival posts still flourished, however, and all of the fiestas listed in table 33 were celebrated, although in some cases less elaborately than just a decade earlier. The ethnographic present represented by the data is approximately 1955, at which time both the *varayoc* and fiesta systems were thriving.

Quinuenos have changed their religion profoundly since that time. The fiesta system is much diminished in importance, and many Quinuenos are Protestant. Similar changes are occurring elsewhere in the highlands, where peasants are resisting participation in the *cargo* system and where Protestantism is growing concomitantly (Appleby 1976a; Carter 1965; Collins 1988:117; Lewellen 1978; Muratorio 1980, 1981).[1] We must not assume that there were no changes in Quinua before 1955.[2] It is tempting to suppose an eternal past that has changed only in the present, but such a view is false. Nonetheless, the recent, rapid and dramatic changes in Quinua religion cry for an explanation.

THE DECLINE OF *CARGO* POSTS AND FIESTAS

The *varayoc* organization has disappeared entirely, first in Hanan Sayoc in the late 1950s and then in Lurin Sayoc by 1972. The fiesta system declined at the same time, albeit more slowly. There is no longer a resident priest, and the sisterhoods have disappeared. Church lands have been sold. Festival officials are recruited with difficulty, as most people are unwilling to assume the cost. Only the patronal fiesta to Mama Cocharcas[3] has a mayordomo and is celebrated with any splendor. But even this fiesta has its problems. Festival officials often accept their post at the last minute, reducing the preparation time and quality of the fiesta, a strategy which reduces their costs. There are years when nobody accepts the *cargo* of standard-bearer for any of the saints during the festival. The mayor and other town authorities assume the post at such times, requesting financial help from migrants.

The lack of people willing to assume *cargo* posts has caused the number of fiestas to decrease from eighteen in 1975 to seven today. Carnival, Cocharcas, and the celebration of the Battle of Ayacucho are the only major public festivals celebrated in the district capital. San Francisco, Christmas, Holy Week, the irrigation festival, and Corpus Christi—all celebrated with some pomp in 1966, although not as grandly as people remembered them—have become so reduced in size as to be almost nonexistent as public ceremonies. Other fiestas are either not celebrated or celebrated in very minimal form.

THE RISE OF PROTESTANTISM

The first Protestant missionary arrived in Peru in 1822, but permanent mission work only began in the 1880s (Paredes-Alfaro 1980: 36–37, 110–137; see Marzal 1989:267–428 for a description of Protestant groups in Peru). Protestantism grew slowly at first, but in the mid–twentieth century began to expand more rapidly. Protestantism was established in Quinua in the 1950s, and began to thrive in the 1970s. In 1966 one small Pentecostal church stood in the hamlet of Murunkancha, a congregation founded in the early 1950s. In 1967, 10 to 15 people attended this native Peruvian church. In 1972, 54 Quinuenos (1 percent of the population) identified themselves as Protestants to the Peruvian national census. Only 12 men and 12 women of this total were over twenty years of age, suggesting the data represent 12 families. There were probably more Protestants, as informants in 1973 identified one hamlet (with a population of 167 people, 3 percent of the total population of the district) as entirely Protestant. In 1977 a report completed in Quinua mentions Seventh-Day Adventists and other Protestant groups (Peru 1977a).

Table 35. *Religious Change in Province of Huamanga, 1972–1981*

	% of Total		% Change
	1972	1981	1972–1981
Catholics	97.9	88.4	−0.7
Protestants	1.3	3.8	238.5
Other sects	0.8	7.8	941.6
Total number	457,441	503,392	10.0

Source: Peru 1974, 1983.

In the 1980s many Quinuenos began to openly identify themselves as Protestants and maintain churches and chapels. I do not have precise census data for Quinua, but in the province of Huamanga, of which Quinua is a part, the absolute number of Roman Catholics declined in the nine years between 1972 and 1981 in spite of phenomenal overall population growth (table 35). The people of Huamanga did not become irreligious but converted to other religions. Protestantism grew by 238.5 percent, and other sects[4] by a startling 941.6 percent. In 1981 non-Catholics represented 11.6 percent of this once all-Catholic province. Quinua has participated in this growth. Informants tell me that half the population is today Protestant. This figure, of course, may be exaggerated, but it is quite clear that non-Catholics have become a significant force in the village.

It was no easy matter for Quinuenos to become Protestants. Although I have no accounts of the bloodshed found in other areas of the Andes[5] (Collins 1988:53; Flora 1976:39–67; Lewellen 1978: 126–131; Muratorio 1981; Painter 1984; Paredes-Alfaro 1980), early Protestants encountered a hostile community. Members of the sisterhoods would ring the church bell at the appearance of any missionaries, summoning the peasants to throw them out. In 1967 Protestants occasionally came to the Quinua plaza on Sunday to preach and distribute tracts, but they were greeted with disdain in public. In consequence, many early Protestants hid their religion. One informant who had requested my sponsorship of his daughter's Catholic baptism in 1973 insisted that the service be held in the city of Ayacucho rather than Quinua. After the ceremony he served cherry syrup rather than wine. (I was very puzzled by this but never asked him or his wife about the cherry syrup for fear of offending them.) We repeated the ceremony for a second daughter in 1974. Many years later in 1983 I learned he was Protestant. He had protected his reputation with his fellow Protestants by hiding the baptisms from them, while at the same time observing the Protestant prohibition on alcohol.

Protestants are now visible and sometimes come to the central plaza (in front of the Catholic church) on Sunday to play music and recruit converts. Pentecostals maintain temples in the district capital and in six hamlets. Presbyterians, the next largest group, do not have formal churches but worship in special rooms set aside in houses, in the district capital and in various hamlets. The Israelites of the New Covenant (*Israelitas del Nuevo Pacto*), who also lack formal churches, are easily identifiable, as the men in this autochthonous Peruvian sect do not shave and wear caps over long hair. The women wear special habits and veils.

Although the fiesta system has declined and Protestantism has gained strength, traditional household religion remains very much intact. The important household ceremonies of the branding of the animals and All Saints Day continue with much the same force, as does *compadrazgo* (note my Protestant compadre), and birthday celebrations have become increasingly important.

CAUSALITY

Quinuenos explain the decline of the religious fiestas and the *varayoc* organization in personal terms. They say that people have become "civilized" and "knowledgeable" and therefore reluctant to assume the expenses of the *cargo* posts. Some stress the role of schoolteachers who taught the children that the peasant leaders were "brutish Indians." Everyone emphasizes the attitudes of important Quinua political officials who became opposed to the peasant political organization in the late 1950s. These officials had migrant experience on the coast; they turned from active support of the *varayoc* to active opposition saying that these *cargo* posts cost too much and were useless. At about the same time, in 1954, the prefect outlawed the *varayoc* in Ayacucho.

One informant expressed the sentiments of many when she decried the loss of the *varayoc* organization. She blamed the decline on the loss of traditional "values" and on people's unwillingness to assume traditional obligations. Like most people, she wanted *varayoc* leaders but did not wish to take on the expenses herself. She consequently reverted to the third person in her complaint made in 1974: "You don't find the *varayoc* now. I'm angry. Why have they lost it? I don't understand. Previously there were *varayoc*. If there were sick

people, if there were dead people, if there were unmarried couples—
they went to the houses and supervised as authorities. People no
longer want to take on the obligations. I'm sorry about that."

These interpretations of Quinuenos, however, do not adequately
explain why the politicoreligious system declined. They do not tell
us why people began to refuse service at the particular time they did.
The chewing of coca leaves is associated with Indian status, but
older peasants have not given up chewing coca although they have
given up the *varayoc* organization. The same authorities who now
oppose the *varayoc* had made use of this organization in earlier
times. One of them did so during most of his twenty-four years of
service as leader (*personero*) of the registered Indigenous Community.[6] In the early 1970s, shortly after the disappearance of the
varayoc, Quinuenos voted at a Sunday assembly to reinstate them,
but nothing came of this action.

Since *cargo* posts have always been expensive, we must explain
why certain expenses became a significant issue in the late 1950s.
Although by no means as great as fiesta expenses, birthday celebrations, godparenthood, and household ceremonies also entail costs,
yet people continue these celebrations. We must also explain why
the *varayoc* system continued in Lurin Sayoc, although in diminished form, long after it disappeared in Hanan Sayoc and long after it
had been outlawed by the prefect. Quinuenos say it continued because the people of Lurin Sayoc are more traditional and devote
more energy to the fiesta system. That may be so, but this explanation is inadequate, since the *varayoc* organization did disappear regardless of tradition.

RELIGION AND SOCIOPOLITICAL ORGANIZATION

The decline of the *cargo* system is best understood by analyzing its
changing personal and social functions. *Cargo* service provides few
immediate material advantages to participants (see Mangin 1961).
Major festival officials and the elders of the community are given
preference in receiving irrigation water, but this is not of great importance. In the rainy-season crop cycle, irrigation turns are determined by altitude, and water taken out of turn is nearly useless
(Mitchell 1980). It is helpful to have special access to water during
the dry-season sowing, but most festival officials, like most Quinuenos, do not plant this crop cycle. Major festival officials are exempted from corvée labor service, a significant personal advantage,
but these savings do not approximate the labor, food, and monetary

costs of the fiesta post. *Cargo* service also confers special rights to cultivate communal lands. This is a significant advantage to someone who has the household labor to cultivate them, but many people do not and are unable to take advantage of this benefit.

Cargo service does provide personal prestige. This prestige enhances a person's ability to influence the decisions of others, a reason why the politicoreligious system is frequently referred to as a prestige hierarchy. This function undoubtedly provides the individual with feelings of self-worth, an important consideration in any social system. However, I have encountered informants who remember their festival service with a great deal of pain. They feel that they were forced to do something against their will.

Fiestas do provide personal satisfaction to most participants. They are a form of worship that propitiates the supernatural world in the way that many Quinuenos believe that world wants. People adore the Virgin, who is miraculous and helps them get through difficult times. They incorporate the saints into their explanations of success and misfortune. Their adoration of the saints helps satisfy their desire for a meaningful world.

As spectacular events, fiestas also provide the major public entertainment (Mangin 1961; Smith 1975:13–14 and passim). People dance in the streets, masses are said, candles lit, and processions held. Bands play; firework displays and bullfights fill the plaza. People dress in their best clothing and feast on guinea pig and hominy stew. Young men and women use the opportunity to initiate courtship, while older people renew ties with family and friends who have returned to the community for the fiesta. In 1966 one migrant attended the fiesta to Cocharcas after an absence from the community of forty-six years, pleasing not only himself but old friends and relatives as well. His experience was duplicated by many others. An overwhelming sense of festivity and relief from everyday drudgery pervades the community.

Fiestas are also important economic events (Dow 1977; Poole 1982). They serve as an agricultural calendar that informs farmers of their tasks. Just as Memorial Day marks the beginning of the summer for many people in the United States, the animal branding, irrigation festival, and the fiesta to Mama Cocharcas begin the agricultural year in Quinua. During Cocharcas local and nonlocal vendors set up stands to sell cooked foods, specialty breads, beer, fruit, fruit juices, cotton candy, ices, and ice cream. Town stores do a roaring business in alcohol. Women sell *ponche,* the fiesta drink made with peanuts. At least one vendor always provides a bingo game. Festival officials spend a great deal of money not only on food but also on adornments and other goods. Even the poorest participant may purchase new clothing or have old clothing adorned by a seamstress.

The most important functions of the *cargo* system, however, are those associated with class structure and access to important resources. Used by the peasantry to define citizenship, politico-religious participation has determined who has rights to agricultural fields, irrigation water, labor, communal pastures, and woods (cf. Sallnow 1987:107). This is a major reason why there are so many fights during fiestas: people argue over who has served in what capacity and thereby who had rights to what. This is why hacendados always participated in the irrigation festival and cleaning: they maintained their rights to irrigation water that way. The help provided to the sponsor of a fiesta by kin, affines, ritual kin, and friends also validated the cooperation used in agriculture and other tasks. Nonparticipation often led to resentment and reluctance to help the offender at some future date (see also Collins 1988:116). The saints' lands (*cofradía* lands) also provide a symbol and focus of communal land rights, a focus that at least elsewhere in Peru has helped protect the integrity of all village lands (Celestino and Meyers 1981). In Guatemala, this focus on saints' lands often created peasant resistance to Protestant missionaries (Burnett 1989).

Fiestas, however, are also an important part of a system of domination and control established after the Spanish conquest that has continued in varied form into the present (cf. Allen 1988:52; Caballero 1981:250; Celestino and Meyers 1981:110 and passim; Muratorio 1980, 1981; Sallnow 1987:98).[7] This relationship is quite clear with respect to the *varayoc* leaders, who served as the police force and organized peasant labor at the behest of town authorities. The festival posts were an integral part of this system. They provided the *varayoc* with ritual and supernatural support for this indirect rule. In the case of the irrigation festival, moreover, there is a direct relationship between religious activity and the mobilization of peasant labor. Poor peasants repair the irrigation system while townspeople and rich peasants (who pay fines rather than work) nonetheless profit from the labor. These fines are levied on households rather than on size of landholdings, so that the poor carry a greater tax burden than the rich. In other areas of Peru, moreover, town merchants benefited by renting out saints' lands or selling the produce from them (Celestino and Meyers 1981). This type of commerce is probably true of Quinua as well, but I do not have the data to demonstrate it. Town merchants certainly benefited from the sale of the *primicia*, the first-fruits tribute given to the priest.

The *cargo* system has been the mechanism by which public religion, imposed through conquest and associated with government and the existing social order, is organized. Peasants bear the major costs of this religion (Muratorio 1981 : 508). Although the salary of the priest did not come entirely from the fiesta system, he was rewarded generously from the fiestas (through formal payments, or *derechos*) for saying mass. In the 1960s festival officials paid the priest approximately $12.50 to $27.50 for masses during the fiesta of Cocharcas alone. This was twenty-five to fifty-five times the value of the daily agricultural wage of under $0.77. The priest received additional income for registering births, for administering the sacraments of baptism and marriage, and for celebrating masses for health and the dead (Acosta 1982 : 132–133). He also profited from dispensing the documents relating to these life-passage events. The priest received labor and gifts of produce from the *varayoc* leaders and had at his disposition the labor of *fiscales*. The tradition whereby the priest obtained the first fruits of every field was clearly a form of tribute that benefited him and town merchants (Acosta 1982 : 133). Such fees paid to the priest often made him the richest person in his district during the colonial and early Republican periods (Acosta 1982; Lavallé 1982; Morner 1985 : 133).[8]

While religion is certainly not always the opiate of the people (e.g., liberation theology), it does help to preserve the status quo when people are occupied with an internal prestige system like the *cargo* system. Just as Marianism and the cult of the Virgin of Guadalupe were instruments of colonial rule in Mexico (Taylor 1987), the modern *cargo* system in Peru has been part of a system of domination (Morner 1985 : 185–186). The following statement of an unnamed parish priest to Indians who had established some schools in Puno does not prove this assertion, but is illustrative: "God has ordained that you should dedicate yourselves to pasturing your flocks and not to learning to read, which only grieves your fathers and mothers. This is why you suffer such misfortunes and why, year after year, your harvests are so poor" (quoted in Morner 1985 : 185). One objective of the 1920 uprisings in Puno was the "end of the *cargo* system, which was seen as draining valuable labor out of peasant communities" (Jane Collins, personal communication, 1989). The central Andes and Mesoamerica are the two areas of Hispanic America where a small elite class captured the labor of large native populations through semifeudal mechanisms of control. It is not a coincidence that they are also the two areas with the most highly developed *cargo* systems.

RELIGION AND ECONOMIC CHANGE

With the increase in population and changes in the economy after World War II, Quinuenos no longer participate in the *cargo* system the way they formerly did. The population growth eased some of the pressures to capture labor through semifeudal mechanisms of control, helping subvert such institutions generally (Caballero 1981; Thorp and Bertram 1978 : 297). At the same time, economic intensification has undermined many of the economic functions of politico-religious service, allowing people to act on their reluctance to assume its financial and temporal burden. Farming has declined in relative importance, a process that Caballero (1981 : 85) has noted for the highlands generally. A trader who travels throughout Peru selling clothing has little time to devote to a fiesta system tied to agriculture. Increased emphasis on cash relationships has undercut the traditional benefits of *cargo* posts (access to land, water, and labor). Peasants as well as townspeople use cash to purchase services and to legitimize relationships (cf. Caballero 1981 : 345). These cash relations help create business attitudes that override traditional values.

The response of one Quinua entrepreneur (he was a store owner, government employee, trucker, cash-cropper, and ceramicist, but his parents were monolingual Quechua speakers) to a complaint that he was taking advantage of his brother in a business deal was simply "well, that's business" (*"es negocio pues"*). Although known to be miserly (people make fun of him because he even charges his own mother for his services), this man is not unique. Many Quinuenos emphasize material self-interest at the expense of sentiment and notions of proper respect for religion. Weismantel (1988 : 189) describes similar processes in Ecuador where cash relations have replaced reciprocal ties.

I do not wish to overemphasize the point, for Quinuenos still hold many traditional beliefs dear. One truck owner accepted the post of standard-bearer to the Virgin of Cocharcas in the early 1970s but later reneged on his obligation and refused the post. Later, on a business trip to Huancayo, he hit and killed two people in separate accidents. Informants claimed that this was clearly a double punishment from the Virgin. They used this example to demonstrate the value of compliance with festival obligations. Nonetheless, the truck driver and my informants do what they must to get by, changing their practices and ultimately their beliefs accordingly.

Two groups continue to accept fiesta service with some regularity, but only in the patronal fiesta to the Virgin of Cocharcas. The first is a small local group of people who have recently risen in the stratification system. This process is illustrated in case #2 described in the preceding chapter. This group uses their fiesta service to validate their change from peasant to townsperson. Service in fiestas other than that of Cocharcas is not prestigious enough to have the same function. But even this group assumes the fiesta service reluctantly.

Migrants, however, still accept fiesta service with some of the old gusto because access to Quinua resources is still important to a significant number of them. When a migrant assumes a major post, usually during the fiesta to Mama Cocharcas, he celebrates it spectacularly (see case #6 in chapter 7). Migrants are the only ones who need to validate their claims to resources in the old manner, the only ones who gain a clear advantage by doing so. Many migrants maintain extensive economic contacts with Quinua: owning lands and houses, cultivating those lands, and using Quinua as a source of cheap labor. Others wish to return to Quinua when they retire. Migrants are able to exercise their rights in Quinua easily only when they continue to fulfill their social obligations and do not become strangers (see also Buechler 1970).

The data from Quinua differ from those in an Aymara community on the altiplano, where migrants do not contribute to the fiesta system (Collins 1988 : 145). Migration in this community is more seasonal than that in Quinua, creating different needs. Seasonal migrants often leave family behind in the community, so that the fiesta system complements rather than replaces other mechanisms to validate claims to resources. The permanent migrant from Quinua, however, not only has more cash but is forced to rely primarily on the fiesta system if he is to maintain his ties to Quinua.

The *varayoc* organization disappeared in Quinua as part of the general decline in the *cargo* system, aided by additional national changes. After the police post was established in Quinua in 1950, townspeople and peasants brought disputes to the more powerful police instead of to the peasant leaders. The police have also replaced the peasant organization in capturing young men for the army. Hamlet lieutenant governors have assumed the task of recruiting corvée laborers. The role of the *varayoc* as messengers for the town elite was undermined by the establishment of the post office and telegraph in 1940 and by increased motor traffic. The utility of employing the peasant leaders as sources of labor for the authorities dwindled as the numbers of peasants willing to serve in the organization declined. Once local authorities had no need for the *varayoc*, they stopped urging peasants to assume the posts and came gradually to oppose the organization itself.

The *varayoc* organization continued for a longer period in Lurin

Sayoc than Hanan Sayoc because it had stronger ties to peasant production. In Lurin Sayoc the peasant leaders distributed irrigation water and maintained the canal system. The town mayor and in recent times a water judge had always exercised these functions in Hanan Sayoc, so that there was less internal support for the peasant political organization in that barrio.

The visible florescence of Protestantism occurred after I was no longer able to travel to Quinua because of the guerrilla war. Before the 1980s, Protestants generally kept quiet about their religion, but my data from Quinua and subsequently from migrants in Lima indicate that the decline of the fiesta system and the rise of Protestantism must be understood together. Protestantism has provided some Quinuenos with an ideological justification for their actions (see Annis 1987; Carter 1965; Mallon 1983:331–332). Quinuenos often become Protestants because they perceive Protestants to be better people: rich, sober, healthy, honest, and helpful (see Annis 1987; Lalive D'Epinay 1969; Muratorio 1980). Many first go to a Protestant church to be cured of an illness, and after recovering they not only decide to remain but also recruit relatives and friends (see Annis 1987; Flora 1976:47–48, 61, 140–141; Lalive D'Epinay 1969:47, 204–207, and passim; Muratorio 1981). Because Protestants do not drink, they are probably healthier; because they do not spend money on festival posts they are undoubtedly richer. Informants claim that even a poor person becomes richer and healthier when he enters Protestantism. They point to people who were once poor but became Protestants and then became rich. One Catholic woman from a well-known and once rich family from the central town lamented to me that one former peon who had worked on her father's fields became a Protestant and is now better off than she. Of course, not all Protestants become rich and most rich people are still Catholic, but informant perceptions nonetheless illuminate some of the dynamics of conversion.

Comparative data from other areas of the Andes illustrate that Protestantism offers adherents opportunities in education, health care, knowledge, and trade (Appleby 1976a; Carter 1965; Lewellen 1978: 125–135; Muratorio 1981; Paredes-Alfaro 1980:183). In Colombia, Pentecostal women rely more on their church for help—including financial help—than do Catholic women (Flora 1976:196–198). In Chile, Pentecostal pastors place greater emphasis on obtaining work for their parishioners than do mainstream Protestant and (by implication) Roman Catholic pastors (Lalive D'Epinay 1969:61). Protestantism acted as an important source of opposition to the exploitation of the peasant by mestizo elites on the altiplano (Lewellen

1978:128–129) and elsewhere (Muratorio 1980, 1981). Reduced
drinking also appears to result in reduced family violence (Lalive
D'Epinay 1969; Muratorio 1981:523; cf. Flora 1976: 198). Protestant
missionaries in the Andes aimed their message to the poor (Paredes-
Alfaro 1980:202; cf. Skar 1982:80), as they did in Guatemala, because as one missionary explained, "The lowest classes have nothing on earth to lose [by associating] with us" (as quoted in Burnett
1989:129; cf. Flora 1976:130–132). In Chile, Pentecostalism is seen
as offering lower classes "a humanity which society denies them"
(Lalive D'Epinay 1969:48–50, 224). It is probable that Protestantism has at least supported Quinuenos in their quest for literacy, even
though Quinua does not have the Protestant schools found elsewhere in the sierra. Bible literacy among their converts is an important goal of Protestant missionaries (Lewellen 1978; Muratorio
1980, 1981; Paredes-Alfaro 1980).

Underlying these overt reasons, however, is the covert one related
to the traditional fiesta system: Protestantism is one way to avoid
the onerous financial burdens of *cargo* posts and the associated
drinking (Mallon 1983:332). Many informants in the 1960s and
1970s complained to me spontaneously about excessive drinking
and the high costs of fiesta service. One young man whose parents
had recently passed the post of standard-bearer of Mama Cocharcas
(case #1 in chapter 7) said to me in 1974 that he was opposed to Catholicism because of excessive drinking. On reflection, he changed
his mind and said it was not Catholicism per se, but the customs of
Quinua that were wrong. Other Quinuenos continued to identify
Catholicism with drinking and excessive spending and rejected the
religion completely. Why have people turned to Protestantism when
the politicoreligious system itself is disappearing? The answer is
that, as with many social processes, the two events are coterminous
responses to the same set of ecological and economic forces.

Some Quinuenos use the freed personal wealth obtained from
nonparticipation in the *cargo* system for capital, a process Annis
(1987) has also found among Protestants in Guatemala. Politico-
religious participation prevented the accumulation of capital necessary to buy land, animals, a truck, the stock for a store, or to educate
one's children. Others use the money that would have been spent on
cargos to purchase consumer goods. These consumer goods—radios,
phonographs, bicycles—have themselves become symbols of the
new economy, as well as profitable sources of income through rentals
to others. Many, probably most, use the money to purchase food, a
need that has increased as population has grown and rural-urban
terms of trade have worsened (cf. Lalive D'Epinay 1969:151). Infor-

mants often mention that the fiestas are poorer now because prices have risen and they do not have the money to create a good fiesta. Many Quinuenos are poorer today than previously and must purchase food with what cash they do have.

The competition between the labor demands of fiesta service and those of farm and nonfarm work has further undermined the *cargo* system (cf. Brush 1977:120). Because of male migration, peasants find it difficult to mobilize labor for their agricultural and nonfarm work. This hardship increases their reluctance to devote time to politicoreligious service when that service—in comparison to other forms of work—gives little in return (cf. Collins 1988:142–146).

The forces undermining the *cargo* system have left household ceremonies undisturbed. Household ceremonies continue to provide people the emotional support to deal with natural and supernatural forces. The fiesta system once provided this comfort for all and still does so for some but these ceremonies divert too much energy and cash from production. Household ceremonies are much less expensive.

At the same time, the birthday celebration of the male household head has increased in importance. These celebrations, even when most elaborate, never consume the wealth spent on the politico-religious system. In 1967 one couple (case #2 in chapter 7) gave a very elaborate birthday fiesta for the male head that lasted three days: the serenade on the night before the birthday, the birthday itself, and the head curing on the subsequent day. They invited twenty-seven people to the party, primarily fellow workers and leading townspeople. Many more—especially uninvited kin from the countryside—appeared in the house during the course of the three days.

The costs of the party were considerable, but nowhere near as great as those associated with fiesta service. Five women working in generalized reciprocity (*yanapay*) helped prepare the food which cost around $80.00: four chickens, seven guinea pigs, four bottles of oil, seven cases of beer, and unrecorded quantities of maize beer, cane alcohol, wine, cognac, noodles, and potatoes. The host's great uncle (his mother's father's sister's husband) brought four bottles of cane alcohol and a work companion brought one case of beer (worth $3.60) in balanced reciprocity (*ayni*). A recently indebted neighbor brought one bottle of cane alcohol, and a very indebted anthropologist brought a case of beer in generalized reciprocity (*yanapay*).

This birthday celebration—like all others—was clearly class associated. The townspeople sat in the front room (a store) in places of honor. The country kin sat in the rear of the house near the kitchen. Friends and relatives dedicated eighteen songs to him over the radio (a total of about one and a half hours worth of music at a cost of $.20 a song). The radio blasted notice of each song: "Attention Quinua! Greetings to [name of host] on his birthday from his compadre [name of donor] with the song 'Serenata Huayno.'" The songs were lovingly recorded and replayed throughout the rest of the year. The celebrant used this and other fiestas to establish his new identity as a townsman. Rural peasants have also shifted to birthday celebrations, if less fancy ones.

Peasants continue to actively support godparenthood, which is part of the system of domination. *Compadrazgo* provides them with important economic, political, and social resources that are more valuable than the costs in human energy required to fulfill their obligations. They must work for and help their godparents and compadres, but in return they receive a network of dyadic ties that increases their ability to get by. The rich benefit as well. They gain access to labor, which is worth the cost of providing influence and help. Migration and the increase in nonfarm work has caused that labor to be even more scarce, and special mechanisms such as godparenthood are required to recruit it.

Lewellen (1978) has rejected an economic explanation of the development of Protestantism and the decline of the fiesta system in the altiplano, attributing it instead to the desire for education. As we have already seen, peasants in Quinua view education as an important mechanism to achieve economic goals. Furthermore, Lewellen's view that "the fiesta system simply does not cost that much" (Lewellen 1978:123) is belied by his own data. It is certain that fiesta expenses were not high by *our* or even Lima standards; Lewellen's informants reported that on the average they spent only $157, $40, and $23, respectively, for the three largest fiestas. What is important, however, is not absolute costs, but relative ones. These figures represent 56 percent, 14 percent and 8 percent, respectively, of available annual average family income in this community! These monetary expenses, moreover, do not include the opportunity costs (the lost time and effort) of the fiesta nor the value of the food raised in the fields of the festival sponsors and served at the fiestas.[9]

It is unwise to reject an explanation, as Lewellen does, because informants do not use it. It is unlikely that informants would proffer economic motivations to explain religious conversion or other idealistic behaviors. Many students in the United States became passionately involved with the peace movement in the 1960s, only to have that passion decline with the end of the draft. Few were consciously aware that some of their passion was fueled by the threat to their own safety, yet that ignorance does not make the motivation any the less real.

In the next chapter, I turn to family history to illuminate the processes that have taken place in Quinua. Ecological and economic processes do not take place in some rarified realm of social structure but are played out at an individual level. Explanations are only valid in so far as we can demonstrate their utility in understanding individual decisions and behavior.

9.

THE INDIVIDUAL AND SOCIAL CHANGE

VARIABLES OF social causation operate at the individual level; people make choices formed in a specific ecological and economic context. Individual parents must feed and protect themselves and their children. As families grow in size, they are forced to make decisions: to endure hunger, abandon their children, or intensify production through cash-cropping, migration, and commerce. They also choose whether to have more children. As the value of their crops declines vis-à-vis wage work, they must decide whether to continue farming, abandon it partially, or abandon it entirely. All Quinuenos face these choices but make differing decisions that are appropriate to their life circumstances. Many of their solutions entail additional judgments about residence, education, and religion. Where does one live? Should children be educated? How can one increase production *and* spend money on the fiesta system?

Biography is an important clue to social processes, illuminating the interaction of living individuals with ecological and economic realities. The following history of CC and his family[1] reveals many of the dynamic changes that have transformed Quinua's social system. Starting out as a Quechua-speaking hacienda peon, CC rose to the status of a large landowner whose children have held some of Quinua's highest governmental posts. CC was an informant, but much of this story is told by his children.

A FAMILY HISTORY

CC was born in the thorn steppe of Quinua sometime before 1900. The third of nine children and the oldest male, he lived with his family on a small piece of land surrounded by haciendas. CC's family was poor. Farming is unproductive in the thorn steppe, and his family had insufficient land for its own subsistence. They acquired most of their unirrigated land and grazing rights by providing labor service and animals to haciendas. They resented this labor service and did not want to remain dependent on haciendas. CC's father repaired shoes for extra income. When the children became young adults, they began to raise animals, a common route to social mobility. They started with only a few sheep but ultimately ended up with a large herd of three hundred, changing their economic position from poor to rich. For additional income CC learned hat making from a neighbor and taught the craft to his siblings. The hats were used to obtain cash, not as goods for barter.

Tired of serving the haciendas, CC's father left Quinua after the death of his wife in 1917. He bought land in a neighboring town, where he became involved with another woman. His children remained behind in Quinua, so he had effectively abandoned them to care for themselves. He returned occasionally to see them and to sell some of the animals, which were in his name despite the fact that he had little to do with raising them.

CC wanted to buy irrigated savannah land to work in agriculture independently of the haciendas. He migrated to the coast around 1919 to raise the purchase price by working on cotton plantations. He remained on the coast for a year, living in the house of his father's brother. He became ill with malaria and was unable to work very hard. He returned to Quinua to recover, but a year later again left for the coast. He worked on the cotton plantations for a year, after which he returned to Quinua with enough money to buy land.

The uncle with whom CC had lived on the coast had already returned to Quinua. He had used his earnings to buy a former hacienda in the savannah and told CC that good neighboring land was for sale. CC bought the land in 1923 with his brother, who had earned money from hat making. They bought six and a quarter hectares of agricultural land and many more in pastures.[2] They put the land in their father's name but divided it between themselves. CC retained a little more than three hectares of good irrigated land, enough to make him one of the largest landowners in the community. Although the pastures were also divided, they were and still are used in common by themselves and their neighbors.

CC considered himself a farmer. He had many animals, he sold hats, he had traveled to the coast—but he was a farmer, a *campesino* (a term which does not carry the negative connotations of the English word *peasant*). And he was a highly respected farmer in the district, considered hardworking and diligent. He was proud of his farm, and with good reason. Every year he organized a number of festive work parties, using them to obtain the labor needed to till his maize fields. He was able to get these workers because of the abundant and well-prepared food he provided the men and their wives, as well as the maize beer, coca leaves, and entertainment. Women singing *qarahui* were always present at his festive work parties. Although he exchanged reciprocal labor with kin, he rarely participated in reciprocal labor exchanges with others. He believed he was rich enough to avoid such labor in most circumstances.

CC married in 1924. His wife was born to a moderately influential family. Her mother was a townswoman with an Argentine ancestor who had been one of the soldiers in the Battle of Ayacucho. Her father spoke Spanish, but he was the only uneducated son of educated parents. Her father sent all of his sons to school, but not his daughters, a neglect deeply felt by CC's wife, who is not only uneducated but, like her husband, a monolingual Quechua speaker.

Their first child was born in 1925. This child died, and their oldest living child was born in 1927. CC and his wife had thirteen children, but only ten of them lived to adulthood.[3]

The family began to obtain professional medical services in 1941. In that year the oldest child became ill while attending school in Ayacucho and was placed in the hospital for two weeks. Members of the family sometimes (although infrequently) sought medical care in Ayacucho; occasionally doctors even came to Quinua. CC traveled for medical care to Lima in 1954, when the doctors in Ayacucho were unable to cure him. In spite of the occasional use of modern medicine, however, both CC and his wife preferred to use two tradi-tional curers who lived in their hamlet.

In 1940, when CC had seven children, he bought an additional two hectares of farm land. He bought it with money earned by his children's hat making. Even though they were all young when CC bought the land (the oldest child was only thirteen years of age), the children's hat making was the major source of cash income for the household. They made hats in large quantities and sold them throughout Peru, traveling to Cuzco and elsewhere. They also raised and sold maize, potatoes, wheat, pigs, goats, sheep, and cattle. The children collected firewood in communal moist forest lands; their mother took it to Ayacucho on burros to sell. In the 1940s the children convinced their father to plant eucalyptus trees on poor land to provide building materials, fuel, and an additional cash crop. Today this plantation is a major source of income.

Sometime after 1940, CC's brother, three sisters, and their spouses left their natal hamlet in the thorn steppe to buy land near CC and their other brother and uncle. They also used money raised through hat making. These siblings bought the land together and had a single bill of sale, but they divided the land into separate farms for each conjugal family.

CC sent his sons to school to learn to read and write. He did not want them to be illiterate as he was. He regretted he could not speak Spanish and was angry that his parents had never sent him to school. Nonetheless, he was interested in educating his children only to the point where they could "defend themselves," a phrase people use frequently in Ayacucho.[4] He did not believe in educating them beyond a minimal level, nor did he want to send his daughters to school. He thought girls should attend to the house and animals. CC's wife, however, pushed for more schooling. She supported her sons in their desire to educate themselves further, as well as in their wish to educate their sisters.

CC's oldest son began school in Quinua in 1936 at the age of nine, but he left the school after a year because he was afraid of the teacher. He then went to a hamlet school where the single teacher for the school was the wife of an hacienda owner. She was more loving and the boy and his next older brother did well. When they returned home, they helped their younger siblings to learn Spanish and to read and write.

In 1942 when he was fifteen, the oldest son was forced to leave school to care for the family, which by then numbered nine children. CC's finger was infected, preventing him from working for several months and ultimately leaving him moderately crippled in that hand. His oldest son had to replace CC in the fields; he started his day before dawn to make hats before going to the fields. The boy was out of school for four years, well beyond the need occasioned by CC's injured finger. CC did not want his son to return to school: there were other things to do, other responsibilities to the whole family. Did that child think he was the only child?

The son fought, however. He fought his father to return to school, to reject fiesta posts, to beautify the house, to have mattresses, sheets, and pillows, to educate the girls, to buy shoes and pants. CC and his wife wore rubber-tire sandals; their children also wore them but stopped doing so when they started to leave Quinua when they were about nineteen years of age. The oldest son was supported in his aspirations by his mother and siblings. He accepted a scholarship to a technical school in Huanta, a nearby provincial capital, in 1946 when he was nineteen. He went there not to finish secondary school but to learn a trade; he learned carpentry, the trade that was to sustain him for the rest of his life.

This son gives no reason why he wanted shoes for his siblings or a beautiful house, other than to say he was born that way. He wanted his family to be different and for the house to be neat and orderly. He wanted the animals to be kept separate from the living quarters, not wandering freely as in other houses. He and his family transformed the house and created a beautiful home. They added outbuildings to the original structure, paved the patio with small stones, and planted a garden of roses and other flowers in its center.

Other sons were also educated beyond the levels offered in Quinua, primarily in Ayacucho. They lived together in the city in the house of a Quinua migrant located near the exit leading to Quinua, an area of the city inhabited by many Quinuenos. CC's children, like most Quinua students in Ayacucho, cooked their own food. They did not have a pension "like the rich" but carried the produce they consumed on their backs from Quinua, where they spent the weekends. They walked rather than rode, "because [they] were very poor and could not afford a truck and because there were very few cars then." The walk was grueling: they arose Monday morning around 3:00 A.M. and arrived in Ayacucho about 8:00 A.M.

A few of the children followed their older brother to Huanta to obtain a technical education, all on scholarships, but only one of them went as far as Lima. The scholarships paid for everything but clothing. They could afford the clothing of the provincial schools, which was similar to that worn at home, but they could not afford the special uniforms and clothing required in Lima. They did, however, pool their resources to educate one son in Lima, who later became an upper-white-collar worker, or professional (*profesional*). He became a financial mainstay of CC and his wife in their old age and has also helped many of his siblings financially. Although not the oldest son, this man has become de facto head of the family. He, however, never returns to Quinua and is ashamed of his past, claiming not to speak Quechua. (Such explicit shame is unusual among migrants from Quinua.)

CC liked assuming festival offices. He and his wife passed the office of altar (*esquina altar*) of Corpus Christi in the early 1930s, altar and throne of the Virgin of Cocharcas in 1936, and mayordomo of Saint Francis in 1943 and 1944. CC never entered the *varayoc* organization because he thought peasant political posts were beneath his social position. Even though he was illiterate, his large landholdings gave him the freedom to refuse such service without being harassed.

His children, again supported by his wife, were opposed to *cargo* service. They viewed it as competing with their desire to be educated and to beautify their house. *Cargo* service meant that there would be drunks messing up the house, nothing more. One of the reasons that CC's eldest son had left school was not only to replace his injured father but also to help raise money to pass the office of mayordomo of Saint Francis. He and his siblings fought further service, asking their father, Are you the only one who works, the only one who suffers to pass the *cargo*? The father acceded to their demands and assumed no further festive office after that for Saint Francis.

CC did not like to drink, so he avoided many of the fiestas where people fought over *cargo* service. But when he and his wife went to the central town, the mayordomos and members of the sisterhoods would frequently ask him to take on additional festival posts. He would reply by saying that he and his wife would think about it, a presence of mind made possible by his sobriety. They stopped bothering him eventually because he was rich and respected and because his service as the mayordomo of Saint Francis had been a major *cargo*.

CC died in Lima in 1982. None of his ten children live on the land he labored so hard to buy, although one of them owns a store in the central town, where he is a prominent man of the community. CC's children are all educated, some with college degrees. They are professional people, carpenters, and petty merchants. Two of them participated early on in the commercial development of Quinua. They opened stores and transportation services. One professional studied in other South American countries for many years. Two children have been school directors. Not all the children have done well, however. One daughter, a single mother, lives as a dependent in the Lima home of a richer brother, and one son, a carpenter, is unable to afford his own housing and lives in Lima with a younger and more successful brother.

Several of the children have served in various political posts in Quinua, forming part of the small group of townspeople and migrants who dominate the formal political positions of mayor, governor, and councilperson. They have assumed these posts out of genuine desires to help the community: to provide more irrigation water, to beautify the plaza, to build schools, to pave the roads. At the same time, some Quinuenos have accused them of using their positions to benefit themselves with jobs and other preferences. One son had to leave town as a result of such accusations. This son says the charges are false, the result of jealousy from an opposing political faction. Such accusations of official theft are frequent in Quinua and elsewhere in the highlands. The brothers are not unusual. I know of no official in Quinua who has not had such an accusation made against him by someone. It is always difficult to assess the validity of these charges.

CC's grandchildren have shared fates similar to those of their parents, some doing well and others not. Several grandchildren live abroad. They have undertaken journeys filled with great risk in an attempt to improve their opportunity. Peru is currently in a serious economic crisis, and there is no work for them in Lima. The eldest brother of one set of siblings migrated first and sent money to his younger siblings for the journey. He wanted his siblings near him for emotional reasons. He also wished to marry and have children but had been unable to do so because of the money he was sending to his parents in Peru. He planned for his siblings to replace him as the major remitter of money to Peru, thereby allowing him the financial resources to raise a family. A cousin subsequently joined the brothers abroad, sharing housing costs and sending remittances back home.

CC's widow still lives on the farm in Quinua, where she is happiest, but her children have urged her to move to Lima or Ayacucho to live with one of them. She visits Lima a few times a year but is unhappy there and feels out of place. She chews sugar instead of the coca leaves forbidden by the son she is visiting. In Quinua she lives with a daughter's illegitimate son, a teenage boy who grew up thinking that she was his mother. Several poor neighbors help her in return for money, food, and cultivation rights. She uses money sent to her by her children to hire additional agricultural workers, but she is not always able to plant all her lands. In some years she must leave many of them in fallow for lack of labor. Two of her sons also cultivate the lands that are still undivided and still registered in the name of CC's father. She sends each of her children food from the harvest. They in turn send her remittances, although only the unmarried son does so with any consistency. He earns an excellent salary and is particularly generous. In 1987 he sent his mother $16 to $31 in cash every month or so and around $94 in goods: rice, noodles, sugar, medicine, vitamins, and various treats.

LIFE HISTORY AND SOCIAL PROCESS

CC's family history clearly demonstrates the dynamic nature of Quinua society. People act to improve their material circumstances and in so doing are constantly modifying the social institutions around them. A family that started inauspiciously became very powerful: two sons serving as mayor and others having important posts elsewhere. First one and then another branch of the family moved from the hacienda and its ecologically poor land and bought good irrigated savannah land. In the process, CC, his uncle, his siblings, and their families became an important presence in the hamlet, although today most of the children of this family live elsewhere and many of the farms are inhabited only by widows.

CC's history, moreover, illustrates the changes in production and productive relations characteristic of many other families. Constrained by the hacienda economy and the low agricultural production of the thorn steppe, CC and his natal family intensified production in novel ways. They provided for growing numbers of children with animal husbandry, hat making, temporary migration, and finally cash-cropping on irrigated land. As CC's conjugal family grew in size, he, his wife, and their children increased their own production. They made hats, bought additional agricultural land, cash-cropped, raised animals, and developed a eucalyptus plantation. CC and his wife obtained the labor for these activities through working hard themselves and through the labor of their many children. Their generosity during festive work groups allowed them to obtain additional laborers at times of heavy labor demand.

CC's involvement in cash-cropping and hat sales forced him into other choices. Commerce is facilitated by the ability to read and write. Many merchants were and are notorious for taking advantage of peasant illiteracy. CC, like many of his contemporaries, wanted to educate his male children (but only up to a point) to improve his position and theirs in and outside of the community.

His children and wife pushed to extend that education. His wife compensated for her own deeply felt personal loss of education. His children wanted a new and glamorous world. Yet they were all aware of the economic and social importance of education. The mother and children were not planning migration careers for the children at first but were interested instead in securing access to the political and economic wealth of Quinua. Education and knowledge of Spanish were the key to commercial success and local upward mobility. Migration came later, in part as a response to the knowledge acquired—but that knowledge operating in the context of economic scarcity. Many Quinuenos were educating their children at the same time. This limited the chance of mobility within the central town, fostering the search for wider opportunities. At the same time, the ten children in this family could not all live on the farm with their families. The need for child labor ultimately produces a surplus as the child cohort grows up and begins to claim adult resources.

CC's family pooled their resources to make one of the sons a professional. This has become a common strategy in Quinua. Many parents speak of educating children in order for them to become professionals. Very few make it, but those who do often have greater wealth than their contemporaries.

Cash-cropping and the large expanse of good irrigated land gave CC's children an advantage vis-à-vis other children. Education and migration are investments that require a capital base to make them successful. CC was able to sustain his children with food and some cash as they left the village to go to school. Poor families are unable to provide such stakes, and their children are often forced to work as poorly paid day laborers in Quinua or to migrate to obtain other unskilled and low-paying jobs. This has created a cycle of poverty in which the lack of parental resources impedes the education and success of the children. The poor, moreover, are less able to maintain reciprocal ties with Quinua. They cannot send and therefore do not receive remittances. They are thereby cut off from an important strategy of their more prosperous brethren who use ties with Quinua to minimize the risks and costs of migration.

CC's household changed through time, always adjusting and adapting to new mouths to feed, new sources of labor and income, and the ecological and economic realities they confronted. The process is the intensification of production as a result of increased family size and ecological and economic squeeze—that is, population pressure. CC did not have to make the choices he did. Some of his contemporaries chose other alternatives: peonage, ceramic making, craft production, sharecropping, highway work, trade, commerce, and permanent migration. But he had to do something. His particular choices were shaped by his personal history evolving within ecological and economic constraints. He was a dedicated farmer who loved the land and agricultural work. He was also a proud, driven man. He always wanted to be better than his neighbors—the best farmer with the largest fields. He was aided in his choices by the large number of animals his natal family had possessed. It takes money to travel to the coast for work, and he was fortunate in being able to plan to go there and to return.

The competition between *cargo* posts, on one hand, and capital accumulation and education, on the other, is clearly delineated in this case history. CC was willing to assume further fiesta posts, but his wife and children were opposed as they saw that the service competed with the investment in education that they believed was necessary for future success. CC acquiesced and ended his career in the fiesta system. He received prestige through agricultural production and wealth instead. It is not coincidental that he ceased his service in 1944 when he had ten children (ages seventeen through infancy) to support. He had to make choices within his limited resources, even though they were abundant when compared to those of most of his contemporaries.

CC remained a Catholic, as have all his children. He was able to avoid undue participation in the fiesta system because of his wealth. The wealthy are not pressured too hard into taking festival posts. They are valuable assets to their neighbors in employment and other ways. The two male children who remain most closely tied to Quinua have substituted participation in formal government for fiesta service. Neighbors do pressure them from time to time to accept religious posts. They occasionally do so, but they limit such participation to minor positions.

COMPARATIVE CASE MATERIAL

CC's history is duplicated in the experiences of others. Poor in agricultural resources and curtailed in production by the surrounding haciendas, many in his hamlet of birth have developed alternate sources of income (especially hat making, trucking, and migration) to support their growing families. A number of these people are relatively wealthy today. In other areas of Quinua, people have worked on the highway or have sold food to travelers. Many have transformed ceramic production from a petty manufacture used to obtain agricultural goods in barter into a major industry to obtain cash.

DS is one of Quinua's great ceramicists. Born in 1909 in the lower savannah of Lurin Sayoc, a rural area about a 45-minute walk from the central town, DS moved from Quinua as a boy and was raised by his mother in her community. As an adult he returned to Quinua, where he worked on his father's farm. Although DS farmed irrigated land, he had only a small plot. He, therefore, produced ceramics to supplement his food production, using the ceramics to barter for needed food, but sometimes selling them for income.

After his father died in 1966, DS continued to cultivate his family land. Although DS had four siblings, they all lived in Lima. They had forfeited their rights to produce from the family land by not contributing to its production. In 1967, however, his younger sister came to Quinua to arrange to sell him her portion of the fields.

As his children grew in number—he ultimately had five boys and one girl (as well as four dead males)—DS had to confront the same problem faced by CC and most Quinuenos: how to provide for his children when his farm was too small to meet subsistence needs and when cash-cropping did not meet monetary ones? DS intensified his ceramic production in the 1950s. He was one of the first ceramicists to travel to Lima, where he produced ceramics while his wife and children remained in Quinua.

DS only participated partially in the politicoreligious system, since he was away in Lima for much of the time. He did serve in the lowest ranks of the *varayoc* organization, but he took on very few other posts.

DS is a monolingual speaker of Quechua. He was not educated and he never educated his children. He did not send them to school because he needed them to work on the fields and in ceramic production. He also never considered it necessary. DS never obtained any great social standing. He is still considered a rude peasant by townspeople and is sometimes insulted (but rarely to his face) as an upstart Indian (*chutu*) who "eats the land" (i.e., makes ceramics).

In spite of their lack of education, most of DS's children have done very well. To prevent being cheated in ceramic sales the eldest son taught himself to add by asking educated Quinuenos to teach him. He developed a cumbersome but accurate system to calculate the return on his family's ceramics. He told his father in advance what they should get and would produce the figure written on a sheet of paper when the traders arrived from Ayacucho.

Two of the children have become respected townspeople, but one of them (I have no data on the other) has suffered personally for his lack of education and his poor social origins. He is the young man who taught himself to add. He also taught himself Spanish. He only uses a single tense and has a limited vocabulary and rudimentary grammar. Nonetheless he is able to communicate in the language, which he has tried to teach to his children. He often admonishes them to speak Spanish rather than the Quechua with which they are more comfortable. He is also the man described in chapter 7 (case #2) who has used *cargo* service and birthday celebrations to validate his social mobility.

Other Quinuenos have rejected the ideological basis of the fiesta system. DO was a monolingual speaker of Quechua in his sixties or seventies when I interviewed him in 1973. He had been orphaned at an early age and grew up cared for by his grandmother. He was very poor. He had "nothing—no houses, fields—absolutely nothing." He migrated to work on coastal cotton plantations when he was a young man. He saved his wages, using them as capital to buy clothing, animals, and coca leaves. He sold these goods in itinerant trade throughout Peru. He also made ceramics and wove cloth for additional income. He bought land and a house in the rural area of Lurin Sayoc, about forty minutes from the central town, with proceeds from his wage work and trade. He used Quinua as a home base. He farmed the land and raised his children there, but he continued to travel throughout Peru to engage in petty trade. Of his nine children, only two were with him in Quinua when I interviewed him. The rest lived on the coast or in other areas of the highlands.

DO served in the politicoreligious system when he was a young man but gave it up when it conflicted with his needs to buy stock for his trade and to provision his children. He simply ignored the insults of those who complained about his lack of service. He was able to purchase land and food with the cash that he earned and had little use for the benefits that fiesta service brought. He resented the fiesta service he had fulfilled and proclaimed to me bitterly in 1974: "We spent [money on] *cargos* for no reason instead of making soup or buying clothing for our children. Useless expenses! The old people who have passed all the *cargos*, what do they have today? Nothing! The virgins and saints didn't ask us to give maize beer and food. They are calm. . . . Too many expenses, too many expenses! Even though we have to provide for our children, we have to pay for the *cargo*, sometimes leaving the children naked. . . . Newly married couples without food, land, or housing, still living off their parents, have to take on *cargos*. Very strange. . . . We have suffered because of this, we have suffered."

Many of the changes in Quinua are clearly seen in the aspirations of the young. BG is the educated son of monolingual Quechua-speakers. He shared with me in 1974 (when he was twenty-three) his dream of opening a bakery in Quinua. He had learned the trade by working in a bakery in Ayacucho while he attended school. He wanted a business that would allow him and his siblings to work together. Then, he exclaimed, "there would be money enough for everyone and money enough to go to school." He never opened his bakery but obtained a government post in the town. He became disillusioned with Catholicism and the expenses of the fiesta system. How could he open his bakery if he spent money on the fiestas? He also thought there was too much drinking associated with the fiesta system and that fiestas were not required by authentic Catholicism.

CONCLUSION

Quinuenos do not regard population pressure or the worsening rural-urban terms of trade as significant variables. They see themselves as simply trying to improve their lives and those of their children. Yet a significant portion of their economic decisions have been constrained by a growing population within a restricted ecological and economic context. Lack of water has prevented them from opening up new farmland. State policy has been unfavorable to farm products, reducing their value. The price of manufactured goods has inflated faster than farm prices. Because of migration there have been too few workers to produce many crops and certainly not enough for extensive potato cultivation, which provides the greatest monetary rewards. Quinuenos have earned less from cash-cropping than they have from other activities. Nonfarm work has produced an occasional radio; farm work has not.

Quinuenos have had to intensify their nonfarm economic activities to sustain themselves and their children. Many took part in the politicoreligious system, but often with less participation and enthusiasm than if they had remained just peasant farmers. The upwardly mobile did validate their new social position through ostentatious fiesta participation. But they did so through the celebration of the Virgin of Cocharcas. It was the major saint or nothing. Most of the other fiestas and the *varayoc* organization have consequently disappeared.

10.

QUINUA'S TRANSFORMATION

THE SOCIAL and economic transformation in Quinua has been profound. The decline of the *cargo* system and the rise of Protestantism have forever altered socioreligious organization. The signs of new material wealth are everywhere: new houses, stores, cars, televisions. Many Quinuenos have increased their monetary incomes severalfold. Others have not and some go hungry. Despite this hunger, some fields lie fallow. Although hunger in Peru is greatest in the cities, to which the poor have migrated, low food intake and high mortality persist in Quinua as in other rural areas. Quinua and the surrounding area are convulsed by the Shining Path guerrilla war.

These changes are not well described by explaining social change in terms of new ideas. Most of the ideas were present in 1966. What we must explain is the selective acceptance of these ideas. Peasants were always aware of the Indian status of the *varayoc*, but that status was not an important issue to them until recently. Nor are education and Protestant missionaries new. Calling on an alleged structure of Andean thought for an explanation is even less adequate; there is no evidence of mental change other than the phenomena we wish to explain.

ECOLOGY, ECONOMY, AND SOCIAL CHANGE

Focusing on ecology and economy helps us understand the changes in Quinua. Local ecology influences population size, settlement pattern, and the distribution and manner of farming and pastoralism along the mountain. People make choices in response to that ecology. They decide where and what to plant and where to live. The densest populations are found in the two most productive zones—

the irrigated savannah and valley bottom. These zones, however, represent only a fraction of the entire district. Most of the district is too unproductive to support more than scattered populations. These ecological relationships exist in a dynamic demographic and economic context. We must consequently turn to such phenomena as population growth, patterns of land tenure, competing labor demands, market relationships, migration, and international economic events to explain such changes as the abandonment of fields when hunger is rampant.

Prior to World War II most goods in Quinua were exchanged by means of barter, reciprocity, and redistribution. Peasants legitimized their access to productive resources—land, labor, and water—through participation in the *cargo* system. Like taxes, festival and peasant political posts were obligations of the citizenry. In a sense they were taxes. They rotated among families, and the wealthier peasants contributed more than the poor. Failure to participate in the system was punished by withdrawal of water rights and access to communal lands. Peasants were reluctant to participate in reciprocal and redistributive labor exchanges with those who did not complete their *cargo* obligations. Such people were not good citizens; that is, they had not proved their devotion to community ideals.

Townspeople, on the other hand, never participated conspicuously in the *cargo* system. Because townspeople controlled commerce and political administration, they could obtain agricultural resources through power—their control of the local and regional political system—and money. The politicoreligious system provided townspeople with a structure to control corvée labor. The *varayoc* organizations, closely allied to the fiesta system and the political expression of peasant leadership, acted as a police force to recruit peasant labor at the behest of town authorities.

Catholicism was intimately tied to this nexus of subordination and domination. The fiestas celebrated saints that were generally housed in the church. Proper worship of the saints ensured the spiritual health of the community and the success of crops and animals. Citizenship in the village—and all its attendant rights and obligations—was closely tied to participation in the *cargo* system. The celebrants consumed prodigious amounts of alcohol and food, at considerable expense to the donor, but vital to the quality of the celebration. People measured the donor's generosity partly by the number of drunken guests.

Prior to the 1940s, peasants migrated to work on coastal cotton plantations to supplement local production and to raise the funds for *cargo* service. This migration, however, was generally seasonal rather than permanent. Peasants also cash-cropped and produced crafts to supplement subsistence production. This migration and nonfarm work initially had a conservative function—helping maintain the existing social order—similar to that described by Salomon (1973) for the weaving industry of Otavalo, Ecuador.

Since World War II, the Peruvian economy has changed dramatically. Population has exploded and outstripped the ecological capacity of the prewar system. Economic constraints have acted in tandem with ecological ones. Subsidized food imports have depressed local farm prices. Urban wages have risen more rapidly than farm wages. Prices of manufactured goods have inflated more rapidly than agricultural prices. Peasants, like all of us, have weighed the relative advantages of their options, and many have chosen nonfarm employment.

Quinuenos have increasingly come to support their families through craft production and commerce. Ceramic manufacture, once confined to barter transactions by a few individuals, has become a household industry that supports many people. Cash-crop production has proliferated, and exchanges in the Sunday market have become increasingly oriented toward cash. Migration has increased, providing the capital for many of the new economic activities: cash for land, insecticides, fertilizer, trucks, schooling, and store stock. Schooling, the route to national economic participation, has become general among the young.

Both the land-poor and wealthy have turned to the nonfarm cash economy. The wealthy have done so in response to low agricultural prices in national markets that have depressed the return on agricultural products and made the purchase of consumer goods more difficult. The wealthy have also educated their sons to ensure that they would have the credentials to obtain monetary wealth. The poor have responded to their inability to feed their families and have switched to wage employment to do so (Gonzales 1987:145–146). Some have obtained enough money to change their social position. A few have become richer and bought more land than their brethren who had been less poor and consequently had not been pushed so strongly into the cash economy.

The labor diverted by migration and other nonfarm work has limited that available for agriculture, further reducing the relative importance of this sector. Many farmers are unable to mobilize sufficient labor to cash-crop potatoes, which are profitable but labor intensive. Migration and nonfarm work have thereby undermined farm production still further and accentuated the stress of population growth. Some Quinuenos have abandoned their lands in the midst of hunger and food scarcity, but concepts of private land tenure inhibit the use of these lands by the landless.

The mayor and other town authorities installed electricity and a potable water system in the town in 1967 by using peasant corvée labor. They and other Quinuenos have constructed new schools, providing children with some of the skills—especially Spanish literacy—necessary for the new commercial life. The town has also built symbols of the new (although selective) prosperity and economic order. In the twenty years I have worked in the community, I have seen three renewals of the central plaza and three successive monuments to the Battle of Ayacucho. Like the presidents of France who build Paris monuments, each mayor wishes to leave his mark by thus beautifying the town. These public works, however, are not just prestige symbols but also "social capital" that provides the elite access to labor and other community resources (Mallon 1983 : 201–202).

Nonetheless, many Quinuenos remain poor. Income disparity has increased generally in Peru and in Quinua as well. Certain families have become very rich, but most Quinuenos eke out an existence and continue to suffer poor nutrition and high infant mortality. A significant number are undereducated. Poorly schooled peasants are locked out of the most lucrative wage occupations except ceramic production and food sales to travelers. Although many poorly educated ceramicists have done well, they generally do not earn as much as the educated mid-level traders.

Social changes have followed demographic and economic ones. The natal family has grown more dispersed than in 1966, with most members living outside Quinua. There are more single mothers today than previously, suggesting that marriage bonds (consensual or otherwise) are more fragile. Most Quinuenos speak Spanish and have some schooling. They have also adopted the styles and symbols of the emerging national identity (Matos Mar 1984). Quinuenos consequently produce less Ayacucho music with their own instruments, but listen more and more to "prestige" music from other regional centers on radios and phonographs.

Ecological changes have occurred as well. The decline of communal systems of rotation and other control of land use has increased erosion throughout the sierra (Caballero 1981 : 81–82), a likely scenario for Quinua. The *varayoc* once exercised greater control over land use than is found today. There is less water available for cultivation in the thorn steppe than previously. Pastures are overgrazed (Flannery et al. 1989 : 18).

The *cargo* system began to change under these altered economic and social conditions. Reluctance to serve increased as fiesta participation no longer provided access to productive resources, as the time spent on them competed with wage work, and as the expenditures came to be viewed as incompatible with capital formation and survival. Today the *varayoc* organization, the group directly associated with labor recruitment for townspeople, has completely disappeared. The fiesta system has not disappeared but has become significantly modified. The only saint still venerated with any splendor is the patron—Mama Cocharcas—who is worshiped in September, at the beginning of the main agricultural cycle.

Protestant missionaries had been active in Quinua for some time, but in the 1960s few Quinuenos had converted. Missionaries became successful only after economic change began to undermine the *cargo* system. Protestantism has provided an intellectual rationale for the new economic forms. Protestants are prohibited by their religion from drinking and participating in the fiesta system. They have a ready ideology to explain their noncompliance with such service. Although many Roman Catholic priests had complained about the fiesta system, they bowed to the realities of traditional social structure and tended to leave it undisturbed.

The changes in Quinua are not isolated. They are part of an ecological and economic process that is taking place throughout the Andes (Adams 1959; Allen 1988: 30, 73, 106, 111, 181, 187, 229–236; Brown 1987; Brush 1977: 109, 114–115, 159–164; Caballero 1981; Celestino and Meyers 1981: 225–252; Collins 1988; Cotlear 1988;[1] Doughty 1968; Figueroa 1984; Gonzales 1987; Lewellen 1978; Long and Roberts 1978, 1984; Mallon 1983; Matos Mar 1984; Muratorio 1981; Painter 1981; Sallnow 1987: 108, 120–123, 162–163, 168; Samaniego 1978; Weismantel 1988). This process has led both to an increase in the size of cities and to new markets. The burgeoning urban poor and the need to supplement the low wages paid in the export sector have encouraged the government to subsidize food prices, which has diminished the value of agricultural production and led to still more migration to the cities. Migration has been further encouraged by the growth of income opportunities in the cities. There is usually some work there no matter how incidental. Poor cityfolk are often able to survive on such casual work (known as *cachuelos*). The growth of the cities has similarly increased pressures for transport facilities and trade. Peasant communities throughout the sierra have responded as Quinua has and have substituted a mercantile rationality for noncapitalist forms of production (Caballero 1981: 389).

Similar changes are also taking place elsewhere in the Third World. Scott (1976) has shown how population growth and the squeeze on peasant income by national elites fostered socioreligious and political changes in Southeast Asia, encouraging the many revolutionary movements of this century. Annis (1987:75–106) describes processes in Guatemala that are strikingly similar to those in Quinua. Population growth, ecological stress, and national political pressures have fostered nonfarm wage employment, which has in turn undermined traditional village organization and encouraged the growth of Protestantism. Indeed, his data show a clear relationship between Catholicism and traditional agriculture, on the one hand, and Protestantism and nontraditional wage and entrepreneurial work on the other.

The Shining Path guerrilla movement has developed out of the same social process. Despite high mortality and out-migration, the population of the Department of Ayacucho has nearly doubled since 1940, while that of the province of Huamanga has grown even more rapidly. This has created a young population many of whom are without regular work but who demand services. University-educated young people are particularly dissatisfied: their education has provided them with greater expectation than realization. Lima provided Ayacucho little economic help until recently, and resources have remained insufficient for the growth in population (see Degregori 1986; McClintock 1984, 1988). There have been periodic displays of military force and other abuses. The slaughter of marching students in 1969 and the buzzing of Ayacucho with Mirage jets when students demonstrated on the anniversary of the deaths caused increased resentment. In 1974 one middle-class man remarked to me ominously when jets buzzed low over the city, "What are they planning to do, kill us all?"

Shining Path at first flourished under these conditions. They promised to overturn an existing order that provided few benefits. As the war has dragged on, however, most Ayacuchanos that I know have come to view Shining Path as another repressive institution. Shining Path kills peasants just as the military does and at the same time tries to stop cash-cropping and other peasant survival strategies. This does not mean that Ayacuchanos are happy with the existing order. Many people—especially the young—are still without work. They struggle against difficult ecological and economic forces in an economy that is unable to absorb them.

Many people voice their misfortune by acknowledging their poverty and emphasizing it in their dealings with outsiders. "We are all poor here" is frequently expressed. Sometimes these same people—and others—articulate outrage at the rich. One informant in 1967, for example, was embittered by the economic and social discrimination against highland peasants and by his inability to get what he wanted in life because of limited educational and economic opportunities. He had finished the three school grades then available in Quinua but had been unable to continue because his father could not afford to send him to school in Ayacucho. He loved to learn and was always borrowing my books. He believed everyone in Quinua was equally poor—yet he was much better off than most Quinuenos. He had enlisted in the air force and now had an excellent job. Nonetheless, he felt limited in his ability to get what he wanted in life. He expressed his anger to me one day in a spontaneous and eloquent outpouring after listening to a radio broadcast in 1967: "Peru is exploited by imperialists and the rich," he told me. "Why must people from the sierra be treated as inferiors by the people of the coast? Why must we be treated as Indians (chutus) and brutes. I have encountered many abuses on the coast. . . . I don't like to say it but I hate the rich. Why should I be treated as inferior because my skin is brown and not white? Why are only the poor . . . taken into the army? The army serves the interests of the rich. . . . If Chileans [traditional Peruvian enemies] should come to my house in the countryside, what could they steal from me? Very little."

Since the 1940s the economy has become increasingly difficult for the Ayacuchano. Peru has entered a period of hyperinflation that exacerbates already difficult decisions for the young (and not so young). Peru shares with much of Latin America the problems of growing populations, high debt service, low prices for primary products, and the transfer of capital and income to the developed world (de Janvry 1981). Quinuenos experience these problems in the form of reduced employment, reduced real wages, and reduced remittances from migrants.

How many readers of this book would wait in line all night and all day to purchase food or to buy some subsidized but scarce good at a marginally cheaper price? The middle class of Lima do so all the time. The poor of Lima often lack the income to buy what is at the end of the line. The land-poor of Quinua nonetheless travel to Lima because it is still better for them there. Unless the economic situation is ameliorated—through redressing the problems mentioned above and by investment in rural agriculture—the situation in Peru and similar areas can only become more explosive.

CONCLUSION

The data from within and outside Quinua are consistent, each strand of information reinforcing the conclusion that population pressure in an ecologically restricted environment, operating within severe internal and external economic constraints, has encouraged Quinuenos to alter their sociopolitical organization in fundamental ways.

Reflecting on my twenty years of working with Quinuenos, I am particularly impressed by several things. First, and most important, I am impressed with the rapidity of the ideological change in Quinua. In 1966 I would have thought it impossible that so many villagers would abandon the fiesta system and adopt Protestantism so quickly. Rapid change is also found in other areas of culture.

Second, the role of population pressure in social change cannot be overstated. People have one, five, or ten children. These numbers create problems that must be solved. Should they ignore the children? Should they provision them? If so, how? Quinuenos see the problems not in terms of population pressure but as personal challenges that cause them to make immediate and personal decisions about their own lives and those of their own children.

Third, environmental and social circumscription as postulated by Carneiro (1970) is an important element in the equation. Ecological limits on agricultural expansion have encouraged people to intensify the nonfarm economy. Economic constraints—local, national, and international—have also stimulated peasants to abandon agriculture for nonfarm work.

Fourth, I am impressed with the dynamic and creative nature of the people we study. Rather than automatons blindly following custom and tradition, anthropological subjects are human beings like ourselves. They change their social institutions as they cope with the problems of everyday existence. They alter their beliefs to give emotional meaning to those changes. Quinuenos have reached to their past for guides to action, but have eliminated those rules antithetical to their new economic behaviors. Quinuenos, like the peasants described by Collins, have "rejected ideologies that [associate] ethnic identity with monolinguism, poverty, and ignorance," ideologies that "prevent them from functioning as full citizens of the republic" (1988:60).

Fifth, the data from Quinua strongly support Robertson's critique of Weber. It is not ideology that has caused the economic changes in Quinua, but the economic changes that have "created . . . [their] own spirit and set the churches to assimilating it" (Robertson 1959

[1933]:165). Quinuenos have adjusted to changed material circumstances with changed religious behavior and belief, not vice versa. In a sense Tawney (1962 [1926]) is correct in that the new religious behaviors and beliefs facilitate the transition to nonfarm work, but it is doubtful that Quinuenos would have changed their ideology had they not been forced to do so by changed material reality, a point Lalive D'Epinay (1969:146–158) has also made for the spread of Pentecostalism in Chile.

Sixth, the data have greater relevance than simply a critique of Weber's hypothesis. They demonstrate in a much broader way the theoretical utility of a materialist approach to social change. Analysis of the material constraints on behavior in Quinua illuminates processes that idealist analyses are unable to discern or explain. People certainly incorporate environment and economy into cultural constructs. As soon as those constructs lead to behaviors, however, they have real consequences that impinge upon and shape those behaviors and their ideational constructs. That is why cultural systems generally make sense. Once beyond mythology, they are not freefloating idea systems but are tied to empirical reality. That integration, however, is never complete. Environment and economy select for certain behaviors. Not all humans choose to comply, even though most generally do so.

Seventh, the processes that have taken place in Quinua are similar to those operating in much of the Third World. Population growth and other material forces are altering much of the world studied by anthropologists. Investigation of these contemporary transformations will expand anthropological theory and our understanding of social evolution. To take advantage of this opportunity, however, we must de-emphasize the traditional brief field study of one or two years and devote long-term research to the study of single communities.

Finally, development agencies must likewise direct their attention to these material forces if they are to have any impact in understanding and thereby ameliorating the frequently wretched conditions in which much of the world lives. Policy must be based on information about why people behave the way they do. Peasants are not conservative inhibitors of change, but rational people who adjust their behavior to the ecological, economic, and political reality around them. Some researchers have claimed that Andean peasants are unable to produce agricultural surpluses because they are impeded by an adherence to "blind tradition" (see Mitchell 1988 for a discussion of this issue, which was reported in the *Christian*

Science Monitor). Such an assumption is not true, a point that Caballero (1981:85) also emphasizes for Peru generally. Peasants do not produce large crop surpluses because of the ecological and economic crisis that has pushed them to the edge of subsistence. It does not pay them to do so. Tradition, blind or otherwise, has little to do with it!

APPENDIX 1

QUINUA CRUDE BIRTHS AND DEATHS, FIVE-YEAR INTERVALS: 1935–1965

	1935	1940	1945	1950	1955	1960	1965	1970	1975	1980	1985	Mean
Births												
Boys	11	35	23	6	85	83	107	118	117	129	126	76
Girls	14	36	19	5	60	80	111	113	110	120	134	73
Total	25	71	42	11	145	163	218	231	227	249	260	149
Sex ratio[a]	0.79	0.97	1.21	1.20	1.42	1.08	0.96	1.04	1.06	1.08	0.94	1.05
Deaths												
Men	—	—	—	—	41	50	35	66	33	45	33	43
Women	—	—	—	—	42	47	35	59	47	41	45	45
Sex ratio[a]	—	—	—	—	0.098	1.06	1.00	1.12	0.70	1.10	0.73	0.96

Source: Municipal birth and death records, District of Quinua. The Quinua birth register began in 1935, but people did not begin to register births there with any consistency until 1960.

[a] Males divided by females.

APPENDIX 2

MAJOR CHARACTERISTICS OF QUINUA ECOLOGICAL ZONES BEFORE 1983

Ecological Zone	Elevation (meters)	General Characteristics	Land Use
Rain tundra/ wet paramo	4,100+	Bunch grass	Herding
Prairie	4,000–4,100	Bunch grass; frost-resistant, small-sized vegetation	Herding; tuber cultivation
Moist forest	3,400–4,000	Dense under-brush of small trees and shrubs; eucalyptus plantation	Some herding; gathering of fuel and other wild products; cultivation of tubers and frost-resistant, quick-maturing crops
Savannah	2,850–3,400	Nearly all culti-vated; irrigated; terracing	Major cultivation zone; maize cultivation; trans-humant stock raising
Thorn steppe	2,500–2,850	Xerophytic vegetation	Some herding; non-irrigated cultivation of plants with low water needs
Valley bottom	ca. 2,500	Xerophytic vege-tation; irrigated; nearly all cultivated	Plentiful water from Rio Chacco; irrigated double-cropping; truck farming for city of Ayacucho

Crop Cycle	Fallow Period (years)	Population Density	Settlement Pattern	Land Tenure
None	Uncultivated	Uninhabited	Uninhabited	Communal
Rainy-season cycle	1–2: cultivation; 5–7: fallow	Low	Dispersed	Communal
Rainy-season cycle	3: cultivation; 1–5: fallow	Low	Dispersed	Communal/ private
Rainy- and dry-season cycles	Continuous cultivation	High; major population zone	Large nucleated town of Quinua; nucleated hamlets and dispersed dwellings	Private
Rainy-season cycle	2: cultivation; 0–3: fallow	Low	Small nucleated hamlets	Communal (former haciendas) and private
Rainy- and dry-season cycles	Continuous cropping	Low	Small nucleated hamlets	Communal (former haciendas) and private

APPENDIX 3

AGRICULTURAL CALENDAR: MAJOR AGRICULTURAL WORK OF RAINY-SEASON CYCLE (*HATUN TARPUY*)

	Average Rainfall	Moist Forest	Upper Savannah
August	Dry	Field preparation	Irrigation system repair; irrigating fields
September	Very light	Sowing of wheat, tubers, and broad beans	Irrigating fields; sowing
October	Light	Sowing	Irrigating fields; sowing; maize and potato cultivation
November	Light	Potato and barley sowing	Maize and potato cultivation
December	Heavy	Potato and barley sowing; potato cultivation	Maize and potato cultivation
January	Heavy	Potato cultivation	Maize and potato cultivation
February	Heavy	—	Maize and potato cultivation; fallow field plowing; weeding
March	Light	—	Fallow field plowing; weeding
April	Light	—	Early harvest
May	Very light	Harvest; crop drying and storage	Full harvest; crop drying and storage
June	Dry	Late harvest; crop drying and storage	Harvest; crop drying and storage
July	Dry	Crop drying and storage	Crop drying and storage

Lower Savannah	Thorn Steppe	Valley Bottom
Irrigation system repair	—	—
—	—	—
—	—	—
Irrigating fields; sowing	—	—
Maize and potato cultivation; sowing	Plowing; sowing	Plowing; maize sowing
Maize and potato cultivation	Maize cultivation	—
Maize and potato cultivation; fallow field plowing; weeding	Fallow field plowing; weeding	—
Fallow field plowing; weeding	Fallow field plowing; weeding	—
Early harvest	—	—
Full harvest; crop drying and storage	Harvest; crop drying and storage	Harvest; crop drying and storage
Late harvest; crop drying and storage	Harvest; crop drying and storage	Harvest; crop drying and storage
Crop drying and storage	Crop drying and storage	Crop drying and storage

APPENDIX 4

AGRICULTURAL CALENDAR: MAJOR AGRICULTURAL WORK OF DRY-SEASON CYCLE (*MICHKA*)

	Average Rainfall	Upper Savannah	Valley Bottom
August	Dry	Wheat and barley harvest; sowing of potatoes, peas, and maize	Potato sowing; green vegetable production
September	Very light	Potato cultivation	Potato cultivation; green vegetable production
October	Light	Potato cultivation	Potato cultivation; green vegetable production
November	Light	Potato cultivation	Green vegetable production
December	Heavy	Potato cultivation; pea harvest	Potato harvest; green vegetable production
January	Heavy	Full harvest	Green vegetable production
February	Heavy	Full harvest; wheat and barley sowing (*qipa michka*)	Green vegetable production
March	Light	—	Green vegetable production
April	Light	Field preparation	Green vegetable production
May	Very light	Field preparation	Green vegetable production
June	Dry	Field preparation	Potato sowing; green vegetable production
July	Dry	Wheat and barley harvest	Potato sowing; green vegetable production

APPENDIX 5

WORK REQUIREMENTS OF POTATOES AND MAIZE: UPPER SAVANNAH (ONE *YUGADA*)

THE FOLLOWING discussion analyzes each of the tasks depicted in appendixes 6 and 7 and summarized in table 18. The reader may refer to these charts for the substantiating data; the text summarizes the salient points. The numbers in parentheses after a task refer to the labor needed for the most common form of planting potatoes and maize in the savannah: the irrigated rainy-season planting; the maize field plowed once prior to the sowing and the potato field twice; potatoes sown with the hoe; and maize sown with the plow. Unless otherwise indicated, the data refer to the labor needed to plant a *yugada* of land. Since the information was obtained from a large landowner—who is able to obtain needed laborers—the data are optimal work requirements. When necessary, people reduce their labor inputs. See Skar (1982 : 136–164) for comparative data on agricultural work in the region of Andahuaylas. See also Collins (1988) and Painter (1981 : 142–160; 1984) for discussions of agricultural labor in Puno.

IRRIGATION (6 PERSON-DAYS FOR BOTH POTATOES AND MAIZE)

Irrigation is often a farmer's first agricultural task. During the dry season, soil becomes very hard and requires moisture before it can be plowed. In the savannah and valley bottom farmers soften the ground with irrigation to sow the rainy-season planting, although in other areas they wait for rain. Irrigation is labor intensive, requiring approximately 6 person-days for a *yugada* of any rainy-season crop in the upper savannah. People work even harder in the dry-season cycle, since they must obtain water about every two weeks, in contrast to the single turn in the rainy-season planting. The total for irrigation is broken down as follows:

Cleaning (1.25 Person-days)

Farmers toil constantly on irrigation maintenance, working both in corvée labor and in cleaning and shoring up canals as they use them. Conjugal families in the Hanan Sayoc–Lurin Sayoc irrigation network provide a laborer for 2 to 3 days in the corvée every year, creating a total of 2.5 person-days for all their fields. (When data are given as 2–3 days or 2–4 persons, I summarize them as 2.5 and 3, respectively.) Incidental cleaning throughout the year involves at least one man working for an additional 2 to 3 days. I have divided this labor between maize and potatoes, as most savannah farmers try to plant at least one field to potatoes and another to maize. Since the calculations exclude such nonagricultural uses of irrigation as providing household water, which would offset some of the maintenance labor for agriculture, I have estimated that half the labor involves agricultural uses of the system and have assigned 1.25 person-days to maize and another 1.25 to potatoes. Large landowners, of course, have less work per maize or potato field, while small landowners have more.

Distribution (1.25 Person-days)

In the rainy-season planting a farmer or his wife must travel to the central town or reservoir several Sundays in a row to petition the authorities for irrigation water. They usually receive it for a single field (usually a *yugada*) after two or three Sunday mornings spent in the effort.

Reservoir Storage (2 Person-days)

On the assigned night, two men (frequently the two farmers sharing the water) fill the storage reservoir. They may sleep during the night but must check the intakes lest someone steal the water, a frequent occurrence signaled by the lack of water rushing through the canal. A farmer given free-flowing stream water has about the same amount of work as one given water from the reservoir. He has the advantage of being able to work in the daytime, but he needs an extra guard for the intakes and may have to irrigate longer, as the stream water flows more slowly.

Guarding Water (1.25 Person-days)

After filling the reservoir, a farmer immediately begins to irrigate. Two or three people (men, women, or children) guard the water against theft. The number of people needed depends on the distance of the field from the headgate. The guards usually walk up and down the canals to check the intakes. If there are a sufficient number, they are able to wait by each of the intakes. Farmers sometimes contract with a neighbor of the intake to guard it.

Irrigating the Field (0.25 Person-days)

The actual irrigation takes the least work. One man works in a *yugada* for a few hours opening up canals to see that all the field is irrigated.

FERTILIZATION OF MAIZE (0.25 PERSON-DAYS)

Farmers usually fertilize a maize field just before or after irrigation. It takes one man a few hours to fertilize one *yugada*. The labor figures for fertilization do not include the time needed to obtain the fertilizer, nor the time spent throughout the year grazing animals in the field to fertilize it. Before the advent of commercial fertilizer, Quinuenos with large extensions of maize fields had to obtain animal fertilizer from pastoralists, an activity that might involve a day's work for one or two men, as well as enough pack animals to carry the load. Grazing one's own animals in a maize field needs little additional labor, as the animals have to be grazed anyway. Farmers usually fertilize potato fields during the crop cultivation (see below).

PLOWING (4 PERSON-DAYS FOR POTATOES AND 2 FOR MAIZE)

After irrigation or sufficient rainfall, farmers leave the field to dry for 2 to 3 days before plowing or hoeing it. Potatoes require considerably more work than maize from the plowing on. Maize fields are generally plowed only once (2 person-days for one *yugada*). This plowing (called *barbecho*) lasts one day. One man works the plow and another usually follows breaking up the clods of earth and preparing the field. Potato fields are generally plowed two times (*barbecho* and *cruze*—4 person-days for a *yugada*). A third plowing (*recruze*) is too costly in time and money to be used generally, and farmers employ it only for tubers, and then only when the soil requires it. If they have sufficient time and irrigation water, peasants may plow some fields in July to reduce the work during the normal sowing from September through December.

Farmers prefer to plow with oxen for efficiency, but they use the pickax, foot plow, and hoe when forced to do so by steep slopes, small fields, grasses, or lack of plows. At high altitudes they sometimes burn the grass cover before turning it, a practice that they have recently introduced into the savannah. The ashes fertilize the soil, while the fire destroys the habitat of crop pests. Fires out of control, however, sometimes burn parts of the eucalyptus plantation or other areas not meant to be burned.

SEED POTATO CURING (0.25 PERSON-DAYS)

Quinuenos soak seed potatoes in insecticide before planting. It takes one man a few hours to perform this process for one *yugada.* Maize seeds are not cured.

THE SOWING (6 PERSON-DAYS FOR POTATOES AND 2 FOR MAIZE)

Quinuenos plant potatoes in one of two forms. Cash-crop producers sow large seed potatoes in single rows approximately 90 cm apart (the *chulla ñahui* method), while small-scale producers plant two small seed potatoes together in rows about 1 m apart (the *iskay ñahui* method). The second method requires more labor, but people work more intensely and complete the task with the same number of person-days as in the first method.

Farmers sow potatoes using either the hoe, the animal plow, or the foot plow. They generally use the hoe because it gives better results than the plow and because potato terrain is not always suited to the animal plow. Hoeing requires 6 person-days for one *yugada:* four men hoe for an entire day, while one or two men or women assist them. In a hectare a farmer would use more laborers to complete the labor in as short a time as possible, but the total of person-days would still be 46. The animal plow requires much less time than the hoe, 2.25 person-days. The animals and plow, however, must be bought and maintained, costs (both of money and labor) that place plows out of the reach of most Quinuenos. One man opens up the rows in a *yugada* in half a day with the plow, while two men or women sow and one or two others prepare the seed potatoes and fertilize the field. In high-altitude areas, where grasses impede the hoe and animal plow, farmers turn the earth with a foot plow, a job requiring considerably more labor, approximately 12 person-days. (In high altitudes they do not measure fields by *yugadas,* as it is a measure tied to plow cultivation, but speak instead of *chacras.* To sow one *chacra* in a day, four men work the foot plow, each assisted by a man or woman turning the sod and another planting the seed potatoes. I have treated a high-altitude *chacra* as approximately a *yugada;* it is probably less.) Maize is planted more easily. Farmers always sow a *yugada* with the animal plow in 2 person-days. One man operates the plow while another man or woman follows behind planting the seed.

CROP CULTIVATION (8.25 PERSON-DAYS FOR POTATOES AND 6 FOR MAIZE)

Crop cultivation requires short periods of heavy labor. Farmers hoe, hill, and weed maize and potatoes twice. They often cultivate potatoes one extra time for a total of three. The heavy rains of January and February often restrict the days suitable for such work, heightening the labor demand. Large landowners are consequently forced to employ festive work groups to recruit the scarce labor.

Potato cultivation requires more work than does maize. Quinuenos first cultivate potatoes (*hallmay*) when they are about 10 cm high, approximately one and a half months after the sowing. This takes place in October through December in the upper savannah. Four men weed and hoe a *yugada* in 0.5 day. Up to three men or women add fertilizer, if this has not been done during the sowing and if the farmer has the money to purchase it. They cultivate potatoes a second time (*papa qutuy*) one month after the first cultivation, when the plants are in flower. This generally takes place in January and February. Five men hoe a *yugada* for an entire day. Two to three children nip the flowers to increase tuber production. They take two to three hours to do so. Many farmers hoe potatoes a third time (*misan quqary* or *nisachay*), but most invest the great labor (seven men hoeing for an entire day) in only a few special varieties. I have left this third potato weeding out of my summary calculations, thereby underestimating the labor requirements of some potato farmers.

Farmers in the prairie and moist forest cultivate potatoes differently. They turn the grass sod to cover the potato roots five to ten days after sowing and proceed with a second cultivation when the potatoes are in flower as in other zones.

Maize cultivation is less onerous, but even so large landowners must often use the festive work group to get enough laborers for all of their fields. Quinuenos first cultivate maize (*hallmay* or *almeo*) when the plants are 20 cm high, one month to one and a half months after the sowing. This occurs between the end of September and mid-January in the savannah. Two men weed and till the earth around the plants in one day in a *yugada*, while another man or woman may fertilize the field.

Maize is cultivated a second time (*kutipa*) when the plants flower. This takes place about one month after the first cultivation, from November to mid-February. Three to four men work the soil in a *yugada*, the number depending on the condition of the ground. Since labor is scarce at this time of year, farmers in lower altitudes often make do with a single cultivation. In higher altitudes they are unable to do this, as the plants grow more slowly and need the extra cultivation.

INSECTICIDE APPLICATION TO POTATOES (PERSON-DAYS DEPEND ON YEAR)

Farmers must guard potatoes against disease and insect damage continuously throughout the growing season. Previously they killed insects by hand, but since the 1960s most of them also use insecticides. A single man applies the insecticide, but the amount of work depends on the amount of damage. Some farmers feel trapped by pesticide use. They claim that pesticides improved things at first, but after a while they have had to use more of them to just keep pace with insect infestations.

THE HARVEST (8 PERSON-DAYS FOR POTATOES AND 7.75 FOR MAIZE)

Harvest time in the rainy-season crop cycle is surprisingly uniform regardless of the time of planting. Since plants mature more slowly in high altitudes, an early sowing ensures that they are harvested at the same time as crops planted lower down. Farmers commence the rainy-season harvest with green peas and potatoes in April. They continue with maize in May and finish with wheat in June and July. The dry-season crop is harvested in January and February.

The harvest of the rainy-season crop is a particularly beautiful time. The rains have ended and the skies are an intense blue. Many-hued maize ears, left in the sun to dry, color brown fields. Harvested green and yellow squashes, placed out of animals' reach on the roofs of most houses, speckle the red tile. Animals, brought down from the puna to help with the work, dot the fields, grazing on the stubble. Food is fresh and often abundant. Farmers cook squashes and tubers in earth ovens constructed at the harvest site. They eat special foods, such as *qumenta:* ground fresh maize mixed with cheese and spices and cooked in the husk. Women make fresh squash into puddings (*api*). In the not too distant past Quinuenos celebrated their success with public feasts honoring various saints, bands playing and people drinking. Many of the large landowners still give personal fiestas to secure laborers to thresh their wheat. Women sing in high-pitched voices, the sounds carrying for miles, to summon the young to the celebrations and work.

Women and children do more of the harvest work, and slightly fewer men are required than in the crop cultivation. The harvest is also more leisurely. There is no rain to interrupt work outdoors. Farmers leave most noncash crops to ripen and dry in the field as long as possible. There are risks in this strategy, however. Neighbors frequently steal one another's crops, perhaps requiring a guard placed in the field. A hailstorm, not unheard of in the dry season, may destroy the ripening food, or it may be eaten by birds and other predators.

Farmers devote 8 person-days to the harvest of one *yugada* of potatoes. Men are required for 5 of these person-days. Four to seven men uproot the potatoes (*papa allay*), a job that lasts from 0.25 to 1.0 day depending on the soil. Four women follow these men, gathering the potatoes (*papa pallay*) and piling them (*papa pilay*). At the end of the day, everyone packs the potatoes in sacks and loads the burros to transport the harvest home. If the harvest is a large one, they may need an additional one or two men to transport it.

They spend about the same amount of time on the harvest of maize (7.75 person-days for one *yugada*), but men are required for less of the work (only 3.25 person-days). Two men first cut and gather the plants in piles (*sara arcuy, sara juñuy,* and *sara barbay*). The maize is then left for two to three weeks to dry further. When the crop is dry, four to five women open the maize ears and cut them from the husk and stalks (*sara tipiy*). They harvest a few ears with the husk intact (*sara qehui*), saving the husk to make *tamales* and *humita.* Two to three men transport the maize ears to the drying enclosure (*tindal*)—level ground lined with maize stalks in which they place the cobs to dry.

CROP STORAGE (11.25 PERSON-DAYS FOR POTATOES AND 7.0 FOR MAIZE)

Women do most of the work of storage (9.75 of the person-days for potatoes and 5.75 for maize). They begin while the harvest is still taking place. They place maize and other grains to dry—and squash to ripen—in the sun. Women work alongside men in separating the fruit of wheat, quinoa, barley, oats, peas, broad beans and chick peas from the chaff. They prepare special forms of dried potatoes, maize, and squash—time-consuming work. After the initial preparations, they store the crop in the granary (*dispensa*).

Farmers work harder on potato than maize storage. The inspection, selection, and sorting of potatoes is especially labor intensive: 6 person-days for the harvest from a *yugada*. Three women inspect each potato for worms and other damage and separate the damaged ones to use in preparing a form of dried potatoes called *cocopa*. They sort the remaining potatoes according to size. The largest are kept for sale and future consumption, the middle size for seeds, and the smallest for immediate consumption. Farmers who specialize in cash sale sometimes separate potatoes by variety, but most people store and plant most varieties together. One man packs and carries the bags of sorted potatoes to the granary, an activity that takes 1 to 2 days depending on the harvest.

Farmers generally store potatoes and other tubers on the floor in a corner of the granary. Farmers sometimes keep seed tubers in bins of adobe or wood. They place loose tubers on top of mixed layers of eucalyptus branches, a plant called *chillka,* and an herb called *muña* (*Minthostaychys setosa* [Briq.] Epl.).

Women work hard to manufacture boiled and dried potatoes (*cocopa*) out of damaged ones, a process that often requires 5.25 person-days for the produce from a *yugada*. They use the *cocopa* milled in soups or diced as a very delicious main course. *Cocopa* commands a high market price, so it is also a significant cash crop. Depending on the size of the damaged crop, between two to five women spend 1 to 2 days peeling and boiling the potatoes, after which they place them in the sun to dry. One woman, man, or child guards the drying potatoes for 5 to 7 days. This activity requires great care, and the person must bring the *cocopa* under cover at the first sign of rain. Rain turns *cocopa* black, which significantly reduces its marketability.

In the moist forest and above, where nighttime temperatures fall below freezing, farmers manufacture freeze-dried potatoes (called *chuño* or *chuno*) to improve storage (potatoes keep for several years in this form) and variety in cooking (cf. Flannery et al. 1989:78–82). *Chuño* takes little work and requires only 1 person-day. One man needs about one hour to place four sacks (200 kilos) of potatoes on the ground to freeze. The next day, two men stamp the potatoes with their feet for about an hour to remove the peel. The potatoes are then soaked in water for five days, after which they are put in the sun to dry for another seven. A man or woman gives the soaking and drying potatoes only cursory attention. Since few farmers make *chuño* in the savannah, I have not included the data in the summary of potato labor in table 18.

People spend much less time in maize preparation and storage. One man constructs the *tindal* in two hours. Two to four women need only 1 day to sort the ears from a *yugada* by size and sometimes variety. They then leave the ears to dry for ten to fifteen days. A man, woman, or child cares for the drying maize each day by turning the ears and protecting them from barnyard animals. This work is light (unless it rains), and the person is usually involved in other tasks. After the ears are dry, two men or women pack the ears for storage in 0.5 day, while another man hauls them to the granary. Two or three additional men store the maize stalks in tree limbs for fodder. Commercial maize producers store all maize varieties in the granary separately, but everyone else separates only those grown in abundance, usually the *morocho* and *compites* varieties.

Families store maize in several different ways to minimize the risk of food loss during the year. They keep most maize as dried and husked ears. They are usually placed on top of beans in a barrel-like container (*taqi*) made of wheat straw. The best ears are stored at the bottom to be used as next year's seeds. They also keep a small number of loose ears on a raised platform called the *marka* to allow further drying, but such storage is limited because the ears are susceptible to mice predation. Most people also try to store a sack (50 kilos) of loose kernels to use for seed, beer, hominy, and cash sale. A woman takes about one day to remove a sack of kernels from the cob (*sara iskuy*). These loose kernels are sometimes stored in large clay vessels (*maqma*) to protect them from mice.

Women boil and dry the small and damaged ears for *chochoca* (also pronounced *chochoqa*), which they sell or use at home in soups. One to two women boil the damaged ears from a *yugada* in about 0.5 day. The boiled ears are then left to dry in the sun for seven days. A man, woman, or child gives the drying *chochoca* only cursory attention to see that it is not rained upon nor eaten by the barnyard animals.

A few people process maize into *sora* (or *jora*), fermented and dried kernels used to make beer. Very few people do so as this requires a great deal of work (about 7 person-days to make 200 kilos) and because they have too little maize for food to spare for beer. Most people contract to have maize beer prepared by a specialist when they need it.

APPENDIX 6

LABOR REQUIREMENTS OF POTATOES (*RUYAQ SISA* VARIETY): NUMBER OF LABORERS PER *YUGADA*—RAINY-SEASON CROP CYCLE, UPPER SAVANNAH

Labor	Days	Men	Women	Men or Women	Total Laborers	Person-days[a]
Irrigation						
Canal cleaning[b]	2.00–3.00	1	0	0	1	1.25
Distribution	1.00–1.50	0	0	1	1	1.25
Reservoir storage	1.00	2	0	0	2	2.00
Guarding water	0.50	0	0	2–3	2–3	1.25
Irrigation	0.25	1	0	0	1	0.25
Plowing						
First	1.00	2	0	0	2	2.00
Second	1.00	2	0	0	2	2.00
Seed Potato Curing	0.25	1	0	0	1	0.25

Sowing						
With hoe *or*	1.00	4	0	0	5–7	6.00
With animal plow *or*	0.50	1	0	3–4	4–5	2.25
With foot plow	1.00	4	0	8	12	12.00
Crop Cultivation						
First	0.50	4	0	0–3	4–7	2.75
Second[c]	1.00	5	0	0	5	5.00
Nipping flowers[c]	0.25	0	0	2–3	2–3	0.50
Third[c]	1.00	7	0	0	7	7.00
Insecticide Application: depends on the year—a male task						
Harvest						
Uprooting	0.25–1.00	4–7	0	0	4–7	3.50
Gathering	0.50–1.00	0	4	0	4	3.00
Transport	1.00	1–2	0	0	1–2	1.50
Storage						
Selection/storage	1.00–2.00	1	3	0	4	6.00
Preparing cocopa						
Peeling and boiling	1.00–2.00	0	2–5	0	2–5	5.25
Drying[d]	5.00–7.00	0	1	0	1	—
Preparing *chuño*	14.00	1	0	0	1	1.00

[a] Midpoint of "Days" multiplied by midpoint of "Total Laborers" rounded to nearest quarter day (intervals of .25).

[b] The work is distributed among the various uses of irrigation to give 1.25 person-days (see text).

[c] Fields are often replowed a second time but rarely a third.

[d] Guarding against animal and rain damage; turning occasionally; data not included in summary because of light labor demands.

APPENDIX 7

LABOR REQUIREMENTS OF MAIZE (*ALMIDON* VARIETY): NUMBER OF LABORERS PER *YUGADA*— RAINY-SEASON CROP CYCLE, UPPER SAVANNAH

Labor	Days	Men	Women	Men or Women	Total Laborers	Person-days[a]
Irrigation						
Canal cleaning[b]	2.00–3.00	1	0	0	1	1.25
Distribution	1.00–1.50	0	0	1	1	1.25
Reservoir storage	1.00	2	0	0	2	2.00
Guarding water	0.50	0	0	2–3	2–3	1.25
Irrigation	0.25	1	0	0	1	0.25
Fertilizing Field	0.25	1	0	0	1	0.25
Plowing						
First	1.00	2	0	0	2	2.00
Second[c]	1.00	2	0	0	2	2.00
Sowing						
With animal plow	1.00	1	0	1	2	2.00

Crop Cultivation						
First						
Hoeing and weeding	1.00	2	0	0	2	2.00
Fertilizing	1.00	0	0	0–1	0–1	0.50
Second	1.00	3–4	0	0	3–4	3.50
Harvest						
Cutting and gathering	1.00	2	0	0	2	2.00
Husking	1.00	0	4–5	0	4–5	4.50
Transport	0.00–1.00	2–3	0	0	2–3	1.25
Storage						
Constructing *tindal*	0.25	1	0	0	1	0.25
Sorting	1.00	0	2–4	0	2–4	3.00
Drying[d]	10.00–15.00	0	0	1	1	—
Storage	0.50	1	0	2	3	1.50
Storing the stalks	0.25	2–3	0	0	2–3	0.50
Degraining (1 sack)	1.00	0	0	0	1	1.00
Preparing *chochoca*	0.50	0	1–2	0	1–2	0.75
Drying *chochoca*[d]	7.00	0	0	1	1	—

[a] Midpoint of "Days" multiplied by midpoint of "Total Laborers" rounded to nearest quarter day (intervals of .25).

[b] The work is distributed among the various uses of irrigation to give 1.25 person-days (see text).

[c] Fields are rarely replowed, as it is too costly in time and money.

[d] Guarding against entry of animals; turning periodically; data not included in summary because of light labor demands.

APPENDIX 8

PRODUCTION OF WHEAT, MASHUA, AND ONIONS

	(a) Census Yield	(b) Census Yield	(c) Calculated Yield	(d) Calculated Yield	(e) Food and Land Requirements per capita	(f) Food and Land Requirements per capita
	tons/ha	kg/traditional yugada	Gross kg/ yugada	Consumable kg/ yugada	Food eaten (kg)	Yugadas needed
Wheat	.438	110	330	281	64.24	.229
Mashua	.588	147	441	375	56.21	.150
Onions	.706	176	528	449	46.35	.103

Column a: figure reported in 1972 agricultural census.
Column b: column a divided by 4 *yugadas* per hectare (the traditional equivalent) times 1,000 kg/metric ton.
Column c: column b times estimated error factor of 3. The census reports Quinua's combined maize and potato yields as 520 kg/traditional *yugada*; informants report a combined median gross yield of 1,600 kg/traditional *yugada*. 1,600 ÷ 520 ≈ 3.
Column d: column c less 15% estimated postharvest loss.
Column e: daily consumption figures reported in table 22 times 365 days per year.
Column f: column e divided by column d.

NOTES

1. The Transformation of a Peasant Society

1. Pronounced with an initial velar voiceless spirant designated /h/ in the Parker (1969:17–20) orthography. Quechua words using this sound (e.g., *hampi, hatun, hampih, hatipah, hawinka, llahta*) are spelled with the symbol *h*. Elsewhere I use standard Spanish orthography whenever possible in my transcriptions.

2. *Varayoc* is a Quechua word with Spanish (*vara*) and Quechua (*-yoc*) roots. It literally means "with the staff," but refers to the "peasant political organization." When people use the term "*varayoc*," they might mean either the organization itself or the persons in it, the meaning being clarified by the context. I follow this practice as well throughout the text. Except for this first parenthetical introduction of the term "*varayoc*," I use the English glosses ("peasant political organization" or "peasant political leaders") until chapter 7, where the *varayoc* are discussed in more detail; I thereafter use the Quechua word.

3. *Gringo*, a term that means "light-skinned person," or a "foreigner," especially a white North American. The term *gringo* usually does not carry negative connotations and is often used as a term of affection. In this context, however, it is quite clear that gringos are to be feared.

4. The scholarship on the Weber hypothesis is voluminous. I chose to review those three works (those by Weber, Tawney, and Robertson) that are most famous and that reflect divergent theoretical positions. A review of the entire corpus would take a book itself, but the reader might wish to consult Eisenstadt 1968; Fanfani 1935; Green 1973; Kitch 1967; Samuelson 1961; and Sombart 1915.

5. Idealism is used in the social sciences to refer to theories of historical change that emphasize the role of ideas and knowledge as opposed to materialist theories that emphasize ecology and economy, a usage that differs from the philosophical idealism of Plato and Berkeley.

6. Weber's position is more complex than *The Protestant Ethic* would

lead us to believe (Kitch 1967:xiv–xv; Muratorio 1980; Guy Oakes, personal communication, 1987). Weber wrote this book with the polemical purpose of refuting certain notions of vulgar Marxism. His position is that historical causation is unique to the particular event being described. He would not deny that capitalism could develop without Protestantism; it is European capitalism—not capitalism per se—that developed out of Protestantism. In other works he accords economic forces a role in social causation, and in his work on religion he refers to ideas as *switchmen* determining which way underlying economic forces will go (Weber [1922–23] 1958b:280). See also Adams's (1975) concept of "trigger" for the use of a similar concept in anthropology.

7. Weismantel does speak to causation, which she clearly places in the material realm.

8. Prof. Allen certainly recognizes the importance of economic factors in Peru's violence (1988:221), but she emphasizes the breakdown of culture and ritual in her discussion (1988:215–227). I argue that it is not culture change per se that leads to violence, but only those changes that prevent people from controlling their own destinies. Poverty, hunger, and relative deprivation are preeminent among such causes of violence.

9. Long and Roberts (1984), for example, successfully employ population dynamics in their excellent discussion of changes in the Mantaro Valley in Peru but curiously accord population little theoretical importance.

10. Lewellen (1978) anticipates some of my conclusions concerning the role of population pressure in economic change in the Andes, but he oddly denies it a role in the development of Protestantism.

11. See Shaw 1976:13 for the use of absorptive capacity in demography and Weiss 1985 and Mitchell 1987b for a discussion of the role of increased parental longevity on migration. See Easterlin 1980 for a discussion of generation size and economic success in the United States.

12. I am especially grateful to Pamela Rosi for her critique of my position. Her defense of the role of values and ideas in social causation has helped me sharpen my own views.

2. Population Growth and Ecological Limits

1. The administration of antibiotics, of course, is itself a risk and may cause death.

2. The data from the death (as well as birth) registry were obtained for five-year intervals: 1955, 1960, 1965, 1970, 1975, 1980, and 1985. The total of 247 deaths, therefore, represents only the deaths in those specific seven years, not the total for the entire thirty years between 1955 and 1985.

3. Quinuenos are very concerned about the cleanliness of their surrounding environment and their bodies. Without water, however, it is difficult for them to achieve that cleanliness.

4. Comparative data on population, birth, mortality, and migration for the Andean area are sorely lacking. In some areas infant mortality rates ap-

pear to be higher than Quinua, and out-migration is consequently less. See Rasnake 1988: 31–32 for a brief yet somewhat contradictory (pp. 36, 178, 180, 181, 262, 263) description of this phenomenon among the Yura of Bolivia.

5. *Tiumpu* is sometimes used instead of *uku*.

6. Although the data in table 7 are for the city of Ayacucho, the conditions in Quinua are similar, except that Quinua is at a higher altitude and therefore somewhat colder.

7. Ecozonation is a relatively well-described feature of Andean adaptations. See Brush 1976, 1977; Fonseca 1972; Fonseca and Mayer 1978; Gade 1975; Golte 1980; Guillet 1983; Masuda 1986; Masuda, Shimada, and Morris 1985; Mayer 1985; Murra 1972; Orlove 1977c; Orlove and Guillet 1985; Pulgar Vidal n.d.; Rhoades and Thompson 1975; Thomas 1973; Valée 1971; Webster 1972; and Winterhalder and Thomas 1978 for comparative treatments.

8. My discussion of these zones is based on Arnold's (1975) analysis of Tosi's (1960) classification for Peru. The English terms for these zones are derived from Holdridge 1947, which was the basis of Tosi's work. My classification of Quinua's zones is etic rather than emic. The people of Quinua distinguish terminologically only between the high altitudes called *sallqa* or *urqu* (the moist forest and above) and the low altitudes called *quechua* (the savannah and lower zones), a classification that corresponds to Pulgar Vidal's (n.d.). Mayer (1977: 62–64, 1985) uses the phrase "production zone" rather than "ecological zone" to emphasize that these zones are not strictly environmental but a result of human productive activities in a particular environmental setting. I prefer to use the phrase ecological zone, for it properly includes human productive activities within its meaning. Mayer is correct, however, in asserting that such zones are not strictly environmental.

9. Brush writes (1977: 10–16) as if his "three types of zonation" (Compressed, Archipelago, and Extended) are mutually exclusive ecological zones. In fact, his useful typology refers to the size and nature of the geographic area being exploited. Any community can employ the three types of adaptations (cf. Skar 1982: 116). Quinuenos exploit their compressed ecological zone, but also employ a contemporary archipelago exploitation in which migrants send remittances from Lima and the eastern tropical forest.

10. Botanical identifications are derived largely from Gade 1975; Horkheimer 1973; Parker 1969; Sauer 1948; Soukup 1970; and Towle 1961. Deborah Pearsall checked the identifications and provided additional ones. A collection of botanical specimens from Quinua is available for analysis by interested scholars.

11. Table 8 is constructed from the national agropastoral census made in 1972. Farms include *chacras, maizales, solares,* and *huertas* (but not fruit orchards). It is probable that many upper-altitude fields were counted as "natural pasture" because of the long fallow system found in those zones. Peruvian census data are useful but present problems (Degregori 1986: 89–91). Peasants often dissimulate to census takers out of fear that the in-

formation will be used to collect taxes or harm them in some other way. The various population censuses, moreover, do not cover the same area, as the district boundaries before 1940 were not the same as they are today. Nonetheless, the censuses are a systematic source of comparative and group information that, when used with care, illuminate trends that would be otherwise impossible for a single researcher to discern. The census data were discussed with informants, and I only use the information that makes sense to them or to me. I have confidence in the trends expressed rather than in absolute values.

12. Unfortunately, I am unable to provide data on the number of individuals per hectare for each of the zones as I do not know their absolute size. In relative terms the zones range in size from larger to smaller: rain tundra/paramo, thorn steppe, savannah, prairie/moist forest, and the valley bottom.

3. Resource Ownership and Control

1. I do not have the patronym of three households, so the incidence of virilocal residence could be higher.

2. The *comunidad* was established in 1940; the major effort in doing so was taken by a migrant resident on the coast. Although grafted on local custom, the *comunidad* is not a complete reflection of local reality.

3. All monetary figures are given in United States dollars. Dollar conversions are based on the official rate at the time of the transaction. In 1966, the *sol* was worth $0.0375 US, a rate which continued until it fell to $0.0249–$0.0257 US in 1967–1968. In 1973 and 1974, the sol was worth $0.0234 US, and in 1980 it was $0.0037 US. The value of the sol declined rapidly throughout the 1980s, one sign of the inflationary pressures in Peru. A new monetary unit, the *inti* (100 soles), was introduced in 1986. All dollar values of the inti reflect the official exchange rate at the end of 1987 of 1 inti to $0.03125 US; the black market rate varied from $0.03 to $0.02 US.

4. These loans are probably no longer given, since current inflation would rapidly destroy the value of the original capital.

5. Sometimes called a *yunda* or *yundayoc*.

6. It is likely that many discussions of Andean field sizes translate the Andean category of *yugada* into hectares in the same rough way as do Quinuenos without facing the methodological issue (cf. Burchard 1974:245, note 18). This is certainly true of Peru's 1972 agricultural census, at least for the materials dealing with Quinua.

7. The actual measurements were 0.1544, 0.1320, 0.1440, 0.13866, 0.0891, and 0.1184 hectares per *yugada*. The average figure of 0.1294 hectares per *yugada* that I have calculated for Quinua is close to the figure of 0.1250 used by Skar (1982:241) to translate the native category of *tarea* into hectares in Andahuaylas.

8. Someone in Quinua (perhaps the president of the community) prepared this report for SINAMOS, a government agency providing rural mobi-

lization and aid. The data in the report must be used with great caution, since the questionnaire was self-administered and is often wildly inaccurate. The data, nonetheless, represent the perceptions of at least one authority (*autoridad*) in Quinua. I use the figures in the report only when they seem reasonable based on my own experience and that of my informants.

9. Units of contiguous and noncontiguous agricultural and pastoral land utilized by a single household or other corporate body. In Quinua I estimate that 1,566 of the agropastoral units are households, the remaining 5 units being the peasant community, two cooperatives, and two entities whose definition is unclear (see table 14).

10. I assume in this analysis that informants spoke and thought in terms of *yugadas* and that they and the census workers converted these *yugadas* to hectares, using the folk conversion of 4 *yugadas* to the hectare. To convert the census figures to actual hectares, I multiplied the census hectares by 4 to give the data in *yugadas* and then divided that figure by 7.7 to give the data in actual hectares. Unless otherwise noted in the text or tables, I have converted all hectare figures for Quinua (but only Quinua) derived from informants or the Peruvian census by using the same formula (census hectares multiplied by 4 divided by 7.7).

11. To obtain this figure I discounted the data on 34 agropastoral units described in this census as resulting from the agrarian reform because these units probably contain several families each, even if they were not labeled cooperatives. At the very least they represent a new form of tenure.

12. My data on animal husbandry largely comes from the savannah. The reader can refer to Flannery et al. (1989) for a description of herding in Quinua's prairie and Flores (1979) for comparative material on stock raising in the Department of Cuzco.

13. Cotlear (1988) has found that the poor tend to have more animals than the rich in the areas he studied. In these potato-producing regions, agricultural intensification depends on costly chemical fertilizers and insecticides, causing poor people to pasture animals.

14. Brush (1977: 104) finds that Uchucmarca is self-sufficient in labor, although individual households may experience shortages from time to time. Uchucmarca is unusual in that there are almost as many adult men as women: 22.1 percent of the adult population (age 15–64) was male in 1971 while 24 percent was female (ibid: 38). Nonetheless, the dependency ratio is still very high (51.4 percent of the population was under age 15), and I suspect that even in Uchucmarca labor may be more difficult to obtain than Brush indicates. Such scarcity would explain the high frequency of payment in kind in Uchucmarca in spite of the much higher cost to the landowner (ibid: 107–108). Ten percent of the households in Uchucmarca, moreover, are single females and 7 percent single males (ibid: 39). These households (17 percent of the total) would have great difficulty in farming without obtaining additional labor.

15. People also employ festive work groups during the cutting of firewood, the roofing of a house, the training of oxen to plow (*toro huatay*), and

the making of roof tiles. Most laborers at these events, however, are working in generalized reciprocity and are not paid a wage.

16. Some informants regard the cutting of firewood for the *cargo* holder of a fiesta as a corvée work group, since every household in the barrio in which the *cargo* holder resides is expected to contribute two days of labor to the cutting of the firewood. Others, however, regard this work as generalized reciprocity. I have not included this work in my calculations of time spent in corvée labor.

17. Burchard (1976, 1978) indicates that coca improves the efficiency of carbohydrate metabolism, increasing the efficiency of the gastrointestinal tract in food absorption and helping maintain a steady blood-sugar level.

4. Agricultural Production and Food Consumption

1. Since it is likely that nonirrigated land is underreported in the census, it is probable that irrigated fields constitute an even smaller proportion of the terrain.

2. Lower soil fertility and slower organic decomposition probably increase the need for fallowing in the cold prairie and moist forest.

3. Compiled from informant data and records, rather than observation, table 18 and appendixes 5 through 7 must be used with care. The data were obtained in Lima, using the memory and current production records of an informant heavily involved in cash-cropping. They were checked against other informant data obtained in Quinua on earlier field trips. The figures are gross calculations, submerging such variables as differences in soils, moisture, disease, and annual production. Memory data, moreover, are notoriously unreliable. In spite of these caveats, the data are important indications of the relative work requirements of these two important crops and the reasons for those differences. They confirm, moreover, the general statements of informants that potatoes require more labor than maize, illustrating where and when the differences occur.

4. I collected the data on labor for one *yugada*. Quinuenos think and work with *yugadas*, not hectares. Very few people are able to plant an entire hectare in potatoes or maize. To obtain the figures on person-days for a hectare, I have multiplied the data on a *yugada* by 7.7.

5. Kilo weights are estimates. People do not measure production directly in kilos, but in *sacos*. A *saco* is a large plastic sack that contains between 50 to 60 kilos of potatoes or maize. I have counted a *saco* as 50 kilos. Burchard (1974:246), on the other hand, uses a figure of 80 kilos for a *saco* of potatoes in the Huánuco area. Maize weight varies significantly with the type of product measured: green maize, dried cob and kernels, or dried kernels alone. Most maize is stored in the dried cob and kernel form.

6. Unfortunately, I do not have data on large quantities of maize weighed by myself. The ratio of .933 is obtained from data supplied by a research assistant in 1989 who weighed ten cobs of dried maize (a mixture of the *almidon* and *puka moro* varieties). He obtained a weight of 1.5 kilo-

grams for the combined cob and kernel and 1.4 kilograms for the cob alone. Informant estimates of the ratio are lower (from .5 to .8), but I have used .933 in my calculations.

7. In the 1986–87 agricultural year a large-scale producer heavily involved in cash-cropping on his family's 6 hectares, for example, used 8 kilos of *almidon* seeds in a *yugada* and harvested between 500 to 750 kilos of husked and dried cobs or between 475 to 700 kilos (with figures rounded to the nearest 25 kilos). His production figures are comparable to the first informant, although his lower seed weight is more typical of actual practices than the higher weight of the first informant. His experience with potatoes, however, is very different, since he uses introduced methods. He plants 500 to 600 kilos of seed potatoes on a *yugada*, a greater weight than the more traditional first case, as he uses larger seed potatoes in the *chulla ñahui* method. Although they cost more money from a seed vendor, larger seed potatoes produce a better crop. He also uses insecticides and fertilizers regularly. His usual yield is around 2,500 kilos per *yugada*; he sometimes harvests very large yields of 6,000 kilos, but in other years he has lost his entire crop because of lack of rain. Subtracting seed weights from his usual yield gives us a net yield of 1,900 kilos per *yugada* or 14,630 kilos per hectare.

8. Brush's data from Uchucmarca demonstrate much greater productivity for potatoes vis-à-vis maize. In Uchucmarca potatoes are 4.4 times more productive by weight than is maize (Brush 1977 : 174–175).

9. As is clear from table 20, production figures vary widely and probably represent methodological problems (especially the use of informant figures for yield and size of land planted), as well as true differences in yield caused by differing soils, technologies, and seeds. My data share in these methodological problems. While high, my data on Quinua potato production do fall within the range published for the Mantaro Valley (1,200–17,900 kilos per hectare), although they are much higher than the range published for Cuzco (2,630–5,000 kilos per hectare) (Franco et al. 1983 : 60). Painter (1984) calculates potato production in Puno at 5,229–6,000 kilos per hectare. My maize production figures, however, are higher than any published figures I have encountered.

10. Brush obtains different figures for the village of Uchucmarca in the Department of Cajamarca. He calculates that potatoes produce 673,273 calories per *yugada* (i.e., 2,693,093 calories per hectare) and maize 629,768 calories (i.e., 2,519,074 calories per hectare) (see Brush 1977, Table 17). Potatoes produce 13,465 grams of protein and maize 14,813 grams. His higher caloric figures for potatoes result from the considerably higher weight yields of potatoes compared to maize in Uchucmarca, a ratio which is higher than that in Peru generally (table 20). He also uses a much higher figure for converting weight to calories (1,000 calories per kilogram of potatoes compared to 790 in my analysis). My analysis is also based on net consumable yield, while Brush uses gross yield. The discrepancies between his figures and mine nonetheless remain. They are probably the result of real differences in yield as well as problems of methodology.

11. In spite of the many descriptions of food production in the Andes, scholars have devoted little attention to food consumption. See Weismantel (1988) for an excellent exception. See also Ferroni (1980) and Orlove (1987).

12. See Ferroni 1980:107–115 for somewhat contradictory findings. His analysis of the National Food Consumption Survey of 1971–1972 shows that caloric consumption is highest during the harvest and lowest in the period immediately after.

13. Fiesta foods and maize beer are excluded from these estimates.

14. His figure of 0.106 kg for maize consumption is considerably lower (cf. Orlove 1987:498–499). My maize data, however, are strikingly consistent with the annual per capita consumption figure of 182 kg calculated by Annis (1987:38) for rural Guatemala and only slightly higher than the 160 kilos of maize suggested as the annual amount of maize eaten per capita in aboriginal Mexico (Sanders and Nichols 1988:42). Flannery et al. (1989: 42–43) estimated plant intake in the high altitude and nonmaize-producing areas above Quinua as 40 percent potatoes, 20 percent maize, 20 percent broad beans, and 20 percent divided among *mashua, olluku,* quinoa, *cañihua,* squashes, and wheat. Of course, people in the savannah, the area we are considering, eat much more maize.

15. Ferroni 1980:153–154 estimates that a family of five requires 2.5 hectares (or one-half hectare per person) to meet food needs. Since he relies on the 1972 agricultural census for his data on production per hectare, it is not unreasonable to convert his data to actual hectares using the formula established for Quinua (censual hectares multiplied by 4 divided by 7.7). If we do so, Ferroni's family of five requires 1.3 hectares (or 0.26 hectares a person). This figure is about double my estimate that a Quinua adult requires 0.1294 hectares.

5. The Structure of Economic Change, 1966–1974

1. See Brush 1977:110–113 and Mayer 1971 for other discussions of disparities between barter and exchange rates.

2. Collins (1988:119) has found that families purchased 7 to 12 percent of the food they consumed in 1980 in one Aymara community in the altiplano. Ferroni (1980:60) has calculated that purchased foods represented 35 percent of the monetary value of all foods (both home produced and purchased) in rural Puno, 45 percent in the rural southern sierra, 69 percent in the rural central sierra and 69 percent in rural Junin.

3. The small amount spent on production in this study, as compared to the information from Quinua, results from aggregating alcohol, coca leaves, and cigarettes as consumption rather than production expenses.

4. See de Janvry 1981 and Meillassoux 1981 for a discussion of the impact of export economies on peasant production. I have relied heavily on Thorp and Bertram's (1978) excellent economic history of Peru for much of my economic analysis. See also Appleby 1982; Caballero 1981; De Soto 1986; Gonzales 1987; Mallon 1983; Matos Mar 1984; Morner 1985; Ortiz de Zevallos 1989; Painter 1981, 1984; Reid 1985.

6. The Dynamics of Economic Change

1. See Tschopik 1947 for an early description of Quinua and Montero 1974 for a brief analysis of some of the changes found in Quinua in 1973.

2. These percentages are probably higher, as I counted the men classified as *obreros* as farm laborers, and at least some of them work primarily in manual labor rather than in agriculture.

3. Even with the decline in the wheat market, this grain is more salable than *achita* and quinoa, which had hardly any cash market—a situation that may have changed somewhat for *achita* in recent years as a result of President Alan Garcia's campaign to plant and eat the grain. The *achita* of Quinuenos is called *kihuicha* elsewhere in Peru.

4. Although the general trend in the Andes has been to increased cash sale (Cotlear 1988), periodic crises have sometimes led to increased barter (Appleby 1982; Collins 1988:14; Orlove 1986:94–95). Such fluctuations occur in Quinua, but they are restricted to particular crops rather than to the overall pattern. In Quinua the deterioration in rural-urban terms of trade has tended to encourage greater cash-cropping to earn the cash needed for such important expenses as education. At the same time, the growth of the nearby city of Ayacucho and the increased food sales to travelers have created new markets for Quinua produce. In other areas (but not Quinua), increased cash-cropping of such tropical products as coffee has resulted in declines in the cash-cropping of subsistence crops (Painter 1984).

5. Similar bulking is found in markets in Puno (Appleby 1976a).

6. These figures must be used with caution. See note 8, chapter 3.

7. The data on coastal migrants is from a study that commenced in 1983 in which 107 migrants from Quinua were interviewed. These data are only partially analyzed, and the figures reported may change when the study is completed.

8. The hamlet of Moya and the small locality of Otguchullko.

9. This information is from the Pueblo to People (Houston, Texas) Spring 1990 catalog. That Quinua ceramics are advertised in this catalog is, of course, another indication of the importance of ceramic production in the local economy.

10. In the city of Ayacucho, 84.7 percent of white-collar workers in the 1980s were government employees (Degregori 1986:73). At the end of 1987 Shining Path guerrillas murdered three engineers working on the Rio Cachi irrigation project, causing some professionals to abandon Ayacucho. I do not know what the impact of this has been on professional and government workers in Quinua.

11. In 1987–1988 I was frequently panhandled by children in rural Peru asking for ballpoint pens, which they said (in response to questions) they wanted for school. I had never had so many children ask for pens (as opposed to photographs or money) on previous trips and believe the requests reflect many of the underlying economic strains in rural areas.

12. If the city of Ayacucho were removed from these figures the differences would be even more dramatic.

13. Constructed from data in a census comparing registered Peasant Communities, the sample universe in table 32 is a restricted population that excludes more prosperous nonregistered communities.

14. Only the departments of Apurimac and Huancavelica are poorer according to the Central Reserve Bank's criteria. The Province of Huamanga, however, stands out as being less poor according to the criteria, although still considerably poorer than most of Peru.

15. His region with intermediate average income (average family income is $1,234 US), however, is anomalous, as it is in many of his measures. The wealthiest quartile here has only 5.2 times the income of families in the poorest quartile.

16. There is some controversy as to whether studies using body size as a sign of malnutrition are adequate. Nonetheless, evidence suggests that Andean stature is related to nutrition (Gresksa 1986).

7. Feasts and Cargos, 1966–1974

1. Quinuenos call these objects of devotion (God the Father, Jesus, the Virgin, and the saints) *santos*. I translate this term as "saints."

2. I have contradictory information on the role of priests in the sale of the *cofradía* lands. Some people maintain that the priests and the archbishop sold the lands, but with the approval of the *hermandades*, while one popular priest, who served in Quinua for nearly ten years and was one of those said to have sold some lands, reported that he did not know where most of the saints' lands were located.

3. *Hermandades* are usually associated with men, but women in Otuzco (Department of La Libertad) also run an *hermandad* as in Quinua (Smith 1975:38).

4. The animal branding (which is a private fiesta) and the celebration of the Battle of Ayacucho (which is primarily governmental) are not included in this count.

5. See Brush 1977:66–67, 101–103; Poole 1982; Rasnake 1988:178–182; and Urton 1981:27–29, 77–78 for other discussions of the relationship between feast days and the agricultural calendar.

6. A patronal fiesta is one that celebrates the patron of a community. The term *"mama"* means "mother" but in this context is synonymous with "virgin" and is the preferred usage in speaking of female saints. In this case, Mama Cocharcas means "the Virgin of Cocharcas." A male saint is often called *"tayta"* ("father") as in Tayta San Francisco.

7. The celebration of the Nativity of the Virgin Mary occurs on the same date in the official Catholic calendar. See Sallnow 1987 and Vargas Ugarte 1956, 2:128–133 for additional data on the Virgin of Cocharcas in the Andes.

8. The term *"cargo"* means "burden" and refers to any public office undertaken for the communal good (cf. Allen 1988:115–119). In addition to the peasant religious and political posts described in this monograph, the

term is also applied to posts in the formal political system, such as town mayor and governor, which are occupied by townspeople.

9. Andeanists have devoted little research to the social organization of religious and political *cargos*. Rasnake (1988) is a notable exception, but he is concerned primarily with the political offices similar to Quinua's *varayoc*. Sallnow focuses on pilgrimage and the symbolic meaning of religious practices but also provides some excellent material on *cargo* organization (1987:119–121, 147–175, and passim). Smith (1975) concentrates on the affective aspects of fiestas, and Celestino and Meyers (1981) on the history of the *cofradías*. Marzal (1989) has studied religion in a broad sense, including *cargos* (see also 1971). Other descriptions of the Andean *cargo* system are found incorporated in general ethnographies. The literature on the Mesoamerican *cargo* system is voluminous. See especially Cámara 1952; Cancian 1965, 1967; Carrasco 1961; Chance and Taylor 1985; Dow 1977; Greenberg 1981; Harris 1964; Price 1974; Rus and Wasserstrom 1980; Smith 1977; and Wolf 1959.

10. In Spanish, people speak of the "cleaning of the canals" (*limpia de la cequia*) or the "celebration" of them (*celebración de la cequia*). In Quechua, they refer to either the cleaning of the canals (*yarqa aspiy* or *yarqa ruhuay*) or the cleaning of the reservoirs (*qucha aspiy*) and mean by those terms the celebration of the system as well. "*Cequia*" is a regional variant of the standard Spanish "*acequia*."

11. See Adams 1959:31–32; Arguedas 1964; Castillo 1970:32–33, 40–42, 169; Castillo et al. 1963; Escobar 1961; Escobar 1967:24–41, 68–69; Isbell 1978; La Barre 1948:153–157; Mishkin 1946:443–447; Ordoñez 1919–1920; Rasnake 1988; Snyder 1960:344–364; Stein 1961:184–197; Vazquez 1964; and Webster 1971 for other descriptions of the *varayoc* or native leaders similar to them.

12. Associated with but separate from the *varayoc* was the minor post of *capilla regidor*, who was assigned the care of hamlet chapels but was found in only a few hamlets. The *fiscal*, another post, was servant to the priest and was occupied by the poor.

13. The change in office of the *varayoc* was known as *vara muray* in Quechua.

14. See Rasnake 1988:70–91 for comparative data on the subordination of *varayoc* officials to townspeople.

15. There is little comparative information on the costs of politico-religious service, except for general statements indicating that such posts are also expensive in other communities. Sallnow (1987:147–148) provides some information on relative costs but does not provide data on their relative significance to the peasant economy. See also Lewellen 1978; Marzal 1989:141–143; and Rasnake 1988:69, 86.

16. Quinuenos distinguish between *orquestas* and *bandas*, the band being the larger and more elaborate group.

17. Descriptions of the *cargo* holders have been disguised to protect them from envy and gossip. For the same reason, dates are reported only for the general time period.

8. The Dynamics of Religious Change

1. Rasnake (1988:76, 83–85, 177, 193, 222, 250, 271–272, 279–280) and Brush (1977:66) suggest that similar changes may be commencing in other areas of the highlands as well.

2. See Chance and Taylor 1985 and Celestino and Meyers 1981 for a discussion of the ever-changing *cargo* system in Mesoamerica and Peru, respectively.

3. In addition to the celebration of Mama Cocharcas in the district capital, the following hamlets still celebrated their respective patronal fiestas with mayordomos in 1987: Suso (Exaltación, September 14); Chacco (Espíritu Santo, movable feast in June); Orqu Suyu (Mama Rosario, October 7); and Mitoqasa (Santa Rosa, August 30).

4. The term "other sects" is a censual one ("*otros sectas*") and probably refers to such groups as the Israelites of the New Covenant and Jehovah's Witnesses.

5. Sketchy information, however, suggests that Protestants are one of the groups being systematically attacked by Shining Path guerrillas.

6. The *Comunidad Indigena*, which is now known as the Peasant Community (*Comunidad Campesina*).

7. The shape and form of this domination have varied over time (Chance and Taylor 1985), of course, and ethnohistoric research is needed to establish the historical antecedents of the modern *cargo* system.

8. I do not know how they obtained their wealth, but the two resident priests I have known in Quinua were well-off, one of them having been the owner of an hacienda elsewhere in Ayacucho. The other owned his own car. My remarks are not meant to disparage these priests; they appeared to have been fine men, truly concerned about the people of Quinua. Nonetheless, they seem to have benefited financially from their relationship with the community.

9. Smith (1975:45) also believes that fiestas are not excessively expensive but provides us with no specific monetary data. It is hard to see, however, how bands were provided at the festivals he describes without someone incurring great costs.

9. The Individual and Social Change

1. Important particulars of his name and story are disguised to prevent personal identification.

2. In this and all informant accounts given in hectares, I have taken the hectare figure reported by the informant and multiplied it by 4 (the traditional equivalent in *yugadas*); I then divide that figure by 7.7 (the number of *yugadas* in a hectare as actually measured in the field). This calculation gives us a better approximation of the actual hectares than using informants' figures (see chapter 3).

3. The years of birth of the living children are as follows: 1927, male;

1929, male; 1931, male; 1932, male; 1935, male; 1936, female; 1938, female; 1940, male; 1942, female; 1944, female.

4. Note Billie Jean Isbell's (1978) use of it in her title *To Defend Ourselves*.

10. Quinua's Transformation

1. Cotlear's (1988) data, however, show that the major source of economic differentiation in the three regions he studied is agricultural, rather than nonfarm, commerce.

BIBLIOGRAPHY

Acosta, Antonio
  1982 Los clérigos doctrineros y la economía colonial (Lima, 1600–1630). *Allpanchis* 19:117–149.
Adams, Richard N.
  1959 *A Community in the Andes: Problems and Progress in Muqui-yauyo.* Seattle: University of Washington Press.
  1975 *Energy and Structure: A Theory of Social Power.* Austin: University of Texas Press.
Ahora
  1987 Pistacos o son mercenarios? Ayacucho: *Ahora: Revista ayacuchana de opinión e información,* Sept. 1.
Allen, Catherine J.
  1988 *The Hold Life Has: Coca and Cultural Identity in an Andean Community.* Washington, D.C.: Smithsonian Institution Press.
Altamirano, Teofilo
  1984a Regional Commitment Among Central Andean Migrants in Lima. In *Miners, Peasants, and Entrepreneurs: Regional Development in the Central Highlands of Peru,* ed. Norman Long and Bryan Roberts. Cambridge: Cambridge University Press.
  1984b *Presencia andina en Lima metropolitana.* Lima: Fondo Editorial, Pontificía Universidad Catolica del Perú.
  1985 *Migración de retorno en los Andes.* Lima: Instituto Andino de Estudios en Población y Desarrollo (INANDEP), Programa de Investigación Sobre Población en America Latina (PISPAL).
  1988 *Cultura andina y pobreza urbana: Aymaras en Lima metropolitana.* Lima: Fondo Editorial, Pontificía Universidad del Perú.
Americas Watch
  1986 *Human Rights in Peru after President Garcia's First Year.* New York: The Americas Watch Committee.
  1988 *Tolerating Abuses: Violations of Human Rights in Peru; An Americas Watch Report.* New York: Americas Watch.

Amnesty International
  1985   *Peru.* London: Amnesty International Publications.
Annis, Sheldon
  1987   *God and Production in a Guatemalan Town.* Austin: University of Texas Press.
Ansión, Juan
  1987   *Desde el rincón de los muertos: El pensamiento mítico en Ayacucho.* Lima: GREDES (Grupo de Estudios para el Desarrollo).
Appleby, Gordon
  1976a The Role of Urban Food Needs in Regional Development, Puno, Peru. In *Economic Systems,* ed. Carol A. Smith, pp. 147–181. Vol. 1 of *Regional Analysis.* New York: Academic Press.
  1976b Export Monoculture and Regional Social Structure in Puno, Peru. In *Social Systems,* ed. Carol A. Smith, pp. 291–307. Vol. 2 of *Regional Analysis.* New York: Academic Press.
  1982   Price Policy and Peasant Production in Peru: Regional Disintegration during Inflation. *Culture and Agriculture* 15 : 1–6.
Arguedas, José Maria
  1964   Puquio, una cultura en proceso de cambio. In *Estudios sobre la cultura actual del Perú,* José Maria Arguedas et al., pp. 221–272. Lima: Universidad Nacional Mayor de San Marcos.
  1968   *Las comunidades de España y del Perú.* Lima: Universidad Nacional Mayor de San Marcos.
Arnold, Dean E.
  1972   Native Pottery Making in Quinua, Peru. *Anthropos* 67 : 858–872.
  1975   Ceramic Ecology in the Ayacucho Basin, Peru: Implications for Prehistory. *Current Anthropology* 16 : 183–203.
  1983   Design Structure and Community Organization in Quinua, Peru. In *Structure and Cognition,* ed. Dorothy Washburn. Cambridge: Cambridge University Press.
Baird, Vanessa
  1985   Travels through the Emergency Zone; Andahuaylas Food Store of the Southern Sierra. *Lima Times,* no. 527, June 14, 1985, pp. 6–7.
Banco Central de Reserva
  1981   *Mapa de pobreza del Peru 1981.* Lima: Banco Central de Reserva.
Banfield, Edward G.
  1958   The Moral Basis of a Backward Society. Glencoe, Ill.: Free Press.
Barlett, Peggy, ed.
  1980   *Agricultural Decision Making: Anthropological Contributions to Rural Development.* New York: Academic Press.
Barth, Fredrik
  1956   Ecologic Relationships of Ethnic Groups in Swat, North Pakistan. *American Anthropologist* 58 : 1079–1089.
Bennett, Philip
  1984   Peru: Corner of the Dead. *Atlantic* (May), pp. 28–33.
Berry, Sara S.
  1980   Decision Making and Policymaking in Rural Development. In *Ag-*

ricultural *Decision Making: Anthropological Contributions to
Rural Development,* ed. Peggy Barlett, pp. 321–335. New York: Academic Press.
Blankenship, James C., and R. Brooke Thomas
 1981 Improved Health Services and Increasing Population Pressure in an
       Andean Community: Simulating a Dilemma. In *Health in the
       Andes,* ed. J. Bastien and J. Donahue, pp. 151–172. Washington,
       D.C.: American Anthropological Association.
Bobadilla, José L.
 1987 *Report on the International Workshop, 1985, on Child Survival:
       Problems and Priorities.* Mexico City: The Population Council,
       Regional Office on Latin America and the Caribbean.
Bolton, Ralph
 1973 Aggression and Hypoglycemia among the Qolla: A Study in Psy-
       chobiological Anthropology. *Ethnology* 12:227–257.
 1976 Andean Coca Chewing: A Metabolic Perspective. *American An-
       thropologist* 78:630–634.
 1979 Guinea Pigs, Protein and Ritual. *Ethnology* 18:229–252.
Bonner, Raymond
 1988 A Reporter at Large: Peru's War. *New Yorker,* January 4, pp. 31–51.
Boserup, Ester
 1965 *The Conditions of Agricultural Growth: The Economics of Agrar-
       ian Change under Population Pressure.* Chicago: Aldine Publish-
       ing Company.
 1981 *Population and Technological Change: A Study of Long-Term
       Trends.* Chicago: University of Chicago Press.
Bromley, Raymond J.
 1976 Contemporary Market Periodicity in Highland Ecuador. In *Eco-
       nomic Systems,* ed. Carol A. Smith, pp. 91–122. Vol. 1 of *Regional
       Analysis.* New York: Academic Press.
 1981 Market Center and Market Place in Highland Ecuador: A Study of
       Organization, Regulation and Ethnic Discrimination. In *Cultural
       Transformations and Ethnicity in Modern Ecuador,* ed. Norman E.
       Whitten, pp. 233–259. Urbana: University of Illinois Press.
Brown, Paul F.
 1987 Population Growth and the Disappearance of Reciprocal Labor in a
       Highland Peruvian Community. *Research in Economic Anthropol-
       ogy* 8:225–245.
Brush, Stephen B.
 1976 Man's Use of an Andean Ecosystem. *Human Ecology* 4:147–166.
 1977 *Mountain, Field and Family: The Economy and Human Ecology of
       an Andean Valley.* Philadelphia: University of Pennsylvania Press.
Buechler, Hans C.
 1970 The Ritual Dimension of Rural-Urban Networks: The Fiesta Sys-
       tem in the Northern Highlands of Bolivia. In *Peasants in Cities:
       Readings in the Anthropology of Urbanization,* ed. William Man-
       gin, pp. 62–71. Boston: Houghton Mifflin.

Burchard, Roderick
1974 Coca y trueque de alimentos. In *Reciprocidad e intercambio en los Andes peruanos*, ed. Giorgio Alberti and Enrique Mayer, pp. 209–251. Lima: Instituto de Estudios Peruanos.
1976 Myths of the Sacred Leaf: Ecological Perspectives on Coca and Peasant Biocultural Adaptation in Peru. Ph.D. diss., Department of Anthropology, Indiana University, Bloomington.
1978 Comment on "Coca Chewing and High Altitude Stress: Possible Effects of Coca Alkaloids on Erythropoiesis," by Andrew Fuchs. *Current Anthropology* 19:283–284.
Burnett, Virginia Garrard
1989 Protestantism in Rural Guatemala, 1872–1954. *Latin American Research Review* 24:127–142.
Caballero, José María
1981 *Economía agraria de la sierra peruana: Antes de la reforma agraria de 1969*. Lima: Instituto de Estudios Peruanos.
Cámara, Fernando
1952 Religious and Political Organization. In *Heritage of Conquest*, ed. Sol Tax, pp. 142–173. Glencoe, Ill.: Free Press.
Cancian, Frank
1965 *Economics and Prestige in a Maya Community: The Religious Cargo System in Zinacantan*. Stanford: Stanford University Press.
1967 Political and Religious Organization. In *Handbook of Middle American Indians*, ed. Robert Wauchope, vol. 6, ed. Manning Nash, pp. 283–298. Austin: University of Texas Press.
Carneiro, Robert
1970 A Theory of the Origin of the State. *Science* 169:733–738.
1988 The Circumscription Theory; Challenge and Response. *American Behavioral Scientist* 31:497–511.
Carrasco, Pedro
1961 The Civil-Religious Hierarchy in Mesoamerican Communities: Pre-Spanish Background and Colonial Development. *American Anthropologist* 63:483–497.
Carter, William
1965 Innovation and Marginality: Two South American Case Studies. *América Indígena* 25:383–392.
Castillo, Hernan
1970 *Pisac: Estructura y mecanismos de dominación en una región de refúgio*. Mexico City: Instituto Indigenista Interamericano.
Castillo, Hernan, et al.
1963 Carcas: The Forgotten Community. *Socio-Economic Development of Andean Communities, Report No. 1*. Ithaca: Department of Anthropology, Cornell University.
Cavero, Luis E.
1953 *Monografía de la provincia de Huanta*. Vol. 1. Lima: Empresa Editorial Rimac.

Celestino, Olinda, and Albert Meyers
1981   *Las cofradías en el Perú: Región central.* Frankfurt am Main: Verlag Klaus Dieter Vervuert.
Chance, John K., and William B. Taylor
1985   Cofradías and Cargos: An Historical Perspective on the Mesoamerican Civil-Religious Hierarchy. *American Ethnologist* 12: 1–26.
Chilcote, Ronald H., and Dale Johnson, eds.
1983   *Theories of Development: Mode of Production or Dependency?* Beverly Hills: Sage Publications.
CIDA (Comité Interamericano de Desarrollo Agrícola)
1966   *Tenencia de la tierra y desarrollo socio-económico del sector agrícola.* Washington, D.C.: Unión Panamericana.
Cohen, Mark Nathan
1977   *The Food Crisis in Prehistory: Overpopulation and the Origins of Agriculture.* New Haven: Yale University Press.
Collins, Jane
1983   Fertility Determinants in a High Andean Community. *Population and Development Review* 9:61–75.
1988   *Unseasonal Migrations: The Effects of Rural Labor Scarcity in Peru.* Princeton: Princeton University Press.
Cook, Noble David, ed.
1975   *Tasa de la visita general de Francisco de Toledo.* Lima: Universidad Nacional Mayor de San Marcos.
Cotlear, Daniel
1988   La economía campesina en las regiones modernas y tradicionales de la sierra. *Allpanchis* 31:217–244.
Custred, Glynn
1980   The Place of Ritual in Andean Rural Society. In *Land and Power in Latin America: Agrarian Economies and Social Processes in the Andes,* ed. B. S. Orlove and G. Custred, pp. 195–209. New York and London: Holmes and Meier Publishers.
Dalton, George
1967   *Tribal and Peasant Economies: Readings in Economic Anthropology.* Garden City, N.Y.: Natural History Press.
de Janvry, Alain
1981   *The Agrarian Question and Reformism in Latin America.* Baltimore: The Johns Hopkins University Press.
Degregori, Carlos Ivan
1986   *Ayacucho, raíces de una crisis.* Ayacucho: Instituto de Estudios Regionales José María Arguedas.
1987   *El regreso de los pistacos.* Lima: El Diario de la República, Sept. 27.
DeQuine, Jeanne
1984   Peru's Enigmatic Killers: The Challenge of Shining Path. *Native* 239:610–613, December 8.
De Soto, Hernando
1986   *El Otro Sendero.* Lima: Instituto Libertad y Democracia.

Dew, Edward
   1969   *Politics in the Altiplano: The Dynamics of Change in Rural Peru.*
          Austin: University of Texas Press.
DeWalt, Billie R., and Kathleen Musante DeWalt
   1980   Stratification and Decision Making in the Use of New Agricultural
          Technology. In *Agricultural Decision Making: Anthropological
          Contributions to Rural Development,* ed. Peggy Barlett, pp. 289–
          317. New York: Academic Press.
Dobyns, Henry E., and Paul Doughty
   1976   *Peru, A Cultural History.* New York: Oxford University Press.
Doughty, Paul L.
   1968   *Huaylas: An Andean District in Search of Progress.* Ithaca: Cor-
          nell University Press.
Dow, James
   1977   Religion in the Organization of a Mexican Peasant Economy. In
          *Peasant Livelihood: Studies in Economic Anthropology and Cul-
          tural Ecology,* ed. Rhoda Halperin and James Dow, pp. 215–226.
          New York: St. Martin's Press.
Durham, William H.
   1979   *Scarcity and Survival in Central America: Ecological Origins of
          the Soccer War.* Stanford: Stanford University Press.
Easterlin, Richard A.
   1980   *Birth and Fortune: The Impact of Numbers on Personal Welfare.*
          New York: Basic Books.
Eisenstadt, S. N., ed.
   1968   *The Protestant Ethic and Modernization, A Comparative View.*
          New York: Basic Books.
Erasmus, Charles
   1956   Culture Structure and Process: The Occurrence and Disappearance
          of Reciprocal Farm Labor. *Southwestern Journal of Anthropology*
          12:444–469.
Escobar, Gabriel
   1961   *Estructura política rural del departamento de Puno.* Cuzco: Edi-
          torial H. G. Rozas, S.A.
   1967   *Organización social y cultural del sur del Perú.* Mexico City: Ins-
          tituto Indigenista Interamericano.
Fanfani, Amintore
   1935   *Catholicism, Protestantism and Capitalism.* New York: Sheed and
          Ward, Inc.
Ferguson, Brian
   1988a A Response to Isbell's "An Anthropological Dialogue with Vio-
          lence." *COSP Newsletter* 6, 2:8.
   1988b Rejoinder to Isbell. *Human Peace.*
Ferroni, Marco A.
   1980   The Urban Bias of Peruvian Food Policy: Consequences and Alter-
          natives. Ph.D. Diss., Cornell University, Ithaca, N.Y.

Figueroa, Adolfo
1984 *Capitalist Development and the Peasant Economy in Peru.* Cambridge Latin American Studies, vol. 47. Cambridge: Cambridge University Press.
Fioravanti-Molinié, Antoinette
1982 Multi-Levelled Andean Society and Market Exchange: the Case of Yucay (Peru). In *Ecology and Exchange in the Andes,* ed. David Lehmann, pp. 211–230. Cambridge: Cambridge University Press.
Flannery, Kent V., ed.
1976 *The Early Mesoamerican Village.* New York: Academic Press.
Flannery, Kent V., et al.
1989 *The Flocks of the Wamani: A Study of Llama Herders on the Punas of Ayacucho, Peru.* New York: Academic Press.
Flora, Cornelia Butler
1976 *Pentecostalism in Colombia: Baptism by Fire and Spirit.* Rutherford, N.J.: Fairleigh Dickinson University Press.
Flores Ochoa, Jorge A.
1979 *Pastoralists of the Andes: The Alpaca Herders of Paratía,* trans. Ralph Bolton. Philadelphia: Institute for the Study of Human Issues.
Fonseca Martel, Cesar
1972 La economía "vertical" y la economía de mercado en las comunidades alteñas del Perú. In *Visita de la província de Léon de Huánuco en 1562,* ed. John Murra, vol. 2 : 315–337. Huánuco: Universidad Nacional Hermilio Valdizán.
Fonseca Martel, Cesar, and E. Mayer
1978 Sistemas agrarios y ecología en la cuenca del Rio Cañete. *Debates en Antropología* (Lima) 2 : 25–51.
Foster, George M.
1965 Peasant Society and the Image of Limited Good. *American Anthropologist* 67 : 293–315.
Franco, Efraín, et al.
1983 *Producción y utilización de la papa en la region del Cuzco: Resultados de una encuesta de visita unica.* Lima: Centro Internacional de la Papa.
Frank, André Gunder
1966 The Development of Underdevelopment. *Monthly Review* 28 : 17–31.
Franklin, David, et al.
1983 *An Assistance Strategy Towards the Improvement of Nutrition in Peru.* Report Prepared for USAID/PERU. Lima: Sigma One Corporation.
1985 Consumption Effects of Agricultural Policies: Peru; Trade Policy, Agricultural Prices and Food Consumption: An Economy Wide Perspective. Report Prepared for USAID/PERU. Raleigh, N.C.: Sigma One Corporation.
Frére, M., et al.
1975 *Estudio agroclimatológico de la zona andina (informe tecnico).*

Rome: Food and Agriculture Organization (Proyecto Interinstitucional FAO/UNESCO/OMM en Agroclimatologia).

Fujii, Tatsuhiko, and Hiroyasu Tomoeda
    1981   Chacra, laime, y auquénidos; Explotación ambiental de una comunidad andina. In *Estudios etnográficos del Perú meridional,* ed. Shozo Masuda, pp. 33–63. Tokyo: University of Tokyo Press.

Gade, Daniel
    1975   *Plants, Man and the Land in the Vilcanota Valley of Peru.* Biogeographica, vol. 6. The Hague: Dr. W. Junk B.V.

Gebhardt, Susan
    1988   Nutritive Value of Foods. Washington, D.C.: Department of Agriculture, Human Nutrition Information Service, Home and Garden Bulletin no. 72.

Gladwin, Christina H.
    1980   A Theory of Real Life Choice: Applications to Agricultural Decisions. In *Agricultural Decision Making: Anthropological Contributions to Rural Development,* ed. Peggy Barlett, pp. 45–85. New York: Academic Press.

Golte, Jurgen
    1980   *La racionalidad de la organización andina.* Lima: Instituto de Estudios Peruanos.

Gonzales de Olarte, Efraín
    1987   *Inflación y campesinado; Comunidades y microrregiones frente a la crisis.* Lima: Instituto de Estudios Peruanos.

Gonzales, Raúl
    1986   Gonzalo's Thought, Belaunde's Answer. *NACLA Report on the Americas* 20, no. 3 : 34–36.

Green, Robert W., ed.
    1973   *Protestantism, Capitalism, and Social Science.* Lexington, Mass.: D. C. Heath and Company.

Greenberg, James B.
    1981   *Santiago's Sword: Chatino Peasant Religion and Economics.* Berkeley and Los Angeles: University of California Press.

Gresksa, Lawrence P.
    1986   Growth Patterns of European and Amerindian High Altitude Natives. *Current Anthropology* 27 : 72–74.

Guillet, David
    1979   *Agrarian Reform and Peasant Economy in Southern Peru.* Columbia and London: University of Missouri Press.
    1980   Reciprocal Labor and Peripheral Capitalism in the Central Andes. *Ethnology* 19 : 151–167.
    1983   Toward a Cultural Ecology of Mountains; The Central Andes and the Himalayas Compared. *Current Anthropology* 24 : 561–574.

Halperin, Rhoda
    1989   Ecological versus Economic Anthropology: Changing "Place" versus Changing "Hands." In *Research in Economic Anthropology,* ed. Barry L. Isaac, vol. 11. Greenwich, Conn.: JAI Press.

Halperin, Rhoda, and James Dow, eds.
1977 *Peasant Livelihood: Studies in Economic Anthropology and Cultural Ecology.* New York: St. Martin's Press.
Harner, Michael J.
1977 The Ecological Basis for Aztec Sacrifice. *American Ethnologist* 4:117–135.
Harris, Marvin
1964 *Patterns of Race in the Americas.* New York: W. W. Norton and Co.
1974 *Cows, Pigs, Wars and Witches: The Riddles of Culture.* New York: Random House.
1977 *Cannibals and Kings: The Origins of Cultures.* New York: Random House.
1979 *Cultural Materialism: The Struggle for a Science of Culture.* New York: Random House.
Harris, Marvin, and Eric B. Ross
1987 *Death, Sex and Fertility: Population Regulation in Preindustrial and Developing Societies.* New York: Columbia University Press.
Harris, Olivia
1986 From Asymmetry to Triangle: Symbolic Transformation in Northern Potosí. In *Anthropological History of Andean Polities,* ed. J. Murra, et al., pp. 260–279. Cambridge: Cambridge University Press.
Harrison, Lawrence
1985 *Underdevelopment Is a State of Mind: The Latin American Case.* Lanham, Md.: University Press of America.
Hayden, Brian
1981 Research and Development in the Stone Age: Technological Transitions among Hunter-Gatherers. *Current Anthropology* 22:519–548.
Herskovits, Melville J.
1952 *Economic Anthropology: A Study in Comparative Economics.* New York: Alfred A. Knopf.
Holdridge, L. R.
1947 Determination of World Plant Formations from Simple Climatic Data. *Science* 105:367–368.
Horkheimer, Hans
1973 *Alimentación y obtención de alimentos en el Perú prehispánico.* Lima: Universidad Nacional Mayor de San Marcos.
Horton, Douglas
1983 Potato Farming in the Andes: Some Lessons from On-Farm Research in Peru's Mantaro Valley. *Agricultural Systems* 12:171–184.
INCAP-ICNND (Institute of Nutrition of Central America and Canada–Interdepartmental Committee on Nutrition for National Defense)
1961 *Food Composition Tables for Use in Latin America.* Bethesda, Md.: National Institutes of Health.

Isbell, Billie Jean
  1978 *To Defend Ourselves: Ecology and Ritual in an Andean Village.* Institute of Latin American Studies, Latin American Monographs no. 7. Austin: University of Texas Press.
  1987 An Anthropological Dialogue with Violence. *Human Peace* 5, no. 4:2–8.
  1988 Dialogue with Violence Continued: Isbell Responds to Ferguson. *Human Peace* 6, no. 3:7.
Isbell, William H., and Katharina J. Schreiber
  1978 Was Huari a State? *American Antiquity* 43:372–389.
Johnson, Allen
  1980 The Limits of Formalism in Agricultural Decision Research. In *Agricultural Decision Making: Anthropological Contributions to Rural Development,* ed. Peggy Barlett, pp. 19–43. New York: Academic Press.
Johnson, Allen, and Timothy Earle
  1987 *The Evolution of Human Societies: From Foraging Group to Agrarian State.* Stanford: Stanford University Press.
Jurado, Joel
  1983 Política económica y condiciones de vida en la región central. Mimeo. Lima: Servicios Populares (SERPO). (As cited in Degregori 1986.)
Kawell, Jo Ann
  1989 The Addict Economies. *NACLA Report on the Americas* 22, no. 6:33–41.
Keesing, Roger M.
  1987 Anthropology as Interpretive Quest. *Current Anthropology* 28: 161–176.
Kirkby, Anne
  1973 *The Use of Land and Water Resources in the Past and Present Valley of Oaxaca, Mexico.* Ann Arbor: University of Michigan, Memoirs of the Museum of Anthropology, no. 5.
Kitch, M. J., ed.
  1967 *Capitalism and the Reformation.* New York: Barnes and Noble, Inc.
Kluckhohn, Clyde
  1944 *Navaho Witchcraft.* Papers of the Peabody Museum of American Archaeology and Ethnology, XXII. Cambridge: Harvard University Press.
Knapp, Gregory W.
  1987 Comment on "Terracing and Irrigation in the Peruvian Highlands," by David Guillet. *Current Anthropology* 28:420–421.
  1988 *Ecología cultural prehispanico del Ecuador,* pp. 28–29. Quito: Bibliografía de Geografía Ecuatoriana 3, Banco Central del Ecuador.
LaBarre, Weston
  1948 The Aymara Indians of the Lake Titicaca Plateau, Bolivia. Memoir no. 68. Washington, D.C.: American Anthropological Association.
Laite, A. J.
  1978 Processes of Industrial and Social Change in Highland Peru. In

Peasant Cooperation and Capitalist Expansion in Central Peru,
ed. Norman Long and B. R. Roberts, pp. 72–98. Austin: Institute
for Latin American Studies, University of Texas.

Lalive D'Epinay, Christian
1969 *Haven of the Masses: A Study of the Pentecostal Movement in
Chile.* London: Lutterworth Press.

Lappé, Frances Moore, and Joseph Collins
1977 *Food First: Beyond the Myths of Scarcity.* Boston: Houghton Mifflin.

Lavallé, Bernard
1982 Las doctrinas de indígenas como núcleos de explotación colonial
(siglos XVI–XVII). *Allpanchis* 19:151–171.

LeClair, Edward, and Harold K. Schneider
1968 *Economic Anthropology: Readings in Theory and Analysis.* New
York: Holt, Rinehart and Winston.

Lehmann, David
1982 *Ecology and Exchange in the Andes.* Cambridge: Cambridge University Press.

Lewellen, Ted C.
1978 *Peasants in Transition; The Changing Economy of the Peruvian
Aymara: A General Systems Approach.* Boulder: Westview Press.

Long, Norman, and Bryan R. Roberts
1978 *Peasant Cooperation and Capitalist Expansion in Central Peru.*
Austin: Institute for Latin American Studies, University of Texas.
1984 *Miners, Peasants, and Entrepreneurs: Regional Development in
the Central Highlands of Peru.* Cambridge: Cambridge University
Press.

McClintock, Cynthia
1981 *Peasant Cooperatives and Political Change in Peru.* Princeton:
Princeton University Press.
1983 Sendero Luminoso: Peru's Maoist Guerrillas. *Problems of Communism* 32, no. 5:19–34.
1984 Why Peasants Rebel: The Case of Peru's Sendero Luminoso. *World
Politics* 37:48–84.
1988 Peru's Sendero Luminoso Rebellion: Origins and Trajectory. In
Power and Popular Protest: Latin American Social Movements,
ed. Susan Eckstein. Berkeley and Los Angeles: University of California Press.

McKenna, Thomas M.
1988 Persistence of an Overthrown Paradigm: Modernization in a Philippine Muslim Shantytown. *Journal of Anthropological Research*
44:287–309.

Maletta, Héctor et al.
n.d.   *Perú: Las provincias en cifras, 1876–1981,* vols. 1–3. Lima: Universidad del Pacifico, Ediciones AMIDEP.

Mallon, Florencia E.
1983 *The Defense of Community in Peru's Central Highlands: Peasant*

Struggle and Capitalist Transition, 1860–1940. Princeton: Princeton University Press.

Maltby, Laura
  1980 Colonos on Hacienda Picotani. In *Land and Power in Latin America: Agrarian Economies and Social Processes in the Andes,* ed. B. S. Orlove and G. Custred, pp. 99–112. New York and London: Holmes and Meier Publishers, Inc.

Mangin, William
  1961 Fiestas in an Indian Community in Peru. In *Patterns of Land Utilization and Other Papers,* ed. Viola Garfield. Seattle: American Ethnological Society.

Marzal, Manuel
  1971 *El mundo religioso de Urcos.* Cusco: Instituto de Pastoral Andino.
  1989 Los caminos religiosos de inmigrantes en la gran Lima; El caso de el Agustino. Lima: Pontificía Universidad Catolica del Perú, Fondo Editorial.

Masuda, Shozo, ed.
  1986 *Etnografía e historia del mundo andino: Continuidad y cambio.* Tokyo: University of Tokyo Press.

Masuda, Shozo, I. Shimada, and C. Morris
  1985 *Andean Ecology and Civilization: An Interdisciplinary Perspective on Andean Ecological Complementarity.* Tokyo: University of Tokyo Press.

Matos Mar, José
  1984 *Desborde popular y crisis del estado.* Perú problema 21. Lima: Instituto de Estudios Peruanos.

Matos Mar, José, and José Manuel Mejía
  1980 *La reforma agraria en el Perú.* Lima: Instituto de Estudios Peruanos.

Mayer, Enrique
  1971 Un carnero por un saco de papas: Aspectos del trueque en la zona de Chaupiwaranga, Pasco. *Revista del Museo Nacional* (Lima) 37:184–196. (Actas y Memorias del 39 Congreso Internacional de Americanistas, vol. 3.)
  1974 Reciprocity, Self-Sufficiency and Market Relations in a Contemporary Community in the Central Andes of Peru. Ph.D. diss., Department of Anthropology, Cornell University, Ithaca, N.Y.
  1977 Tenencia y control comunal de la tierra: Caso de Laraos (Yauyos). *Cuadernos,* no. 24–25:59–72.
  1985 Production Zones. In *Andean Ecology and Civilization,* ed. S. Masuda et al., pp. 45–84. Tokyo: University of Tokyo Press.

Meillassoux, Claude
  1981 *Maidens, Meal and Money: Capitalism and the Domestic Community.* New York: Cambridge University Press.

Merrick, Thomas W.
  1986 Population Pressure in Latin America. *Population Bulletin,* vol. 41, no. 3. Washington, D.C.: Population Reference Bureau.

Mintz, Sidney W., and E. Wolf
  1950   An Analysis of Ritual Co-Parenthood (Compadrazgo). *Southwest Journal of Anthropology* 6:341–368.
Mishkin, Bernard
  1946   The Contemporary Quechua. In *Handbook of South American Indians*, vol. 2, ed. Julian H. Steward, pp. 411–470. Washington, D.C.: Smithsonian Institution.
Mitchell, William P.
  1973   The Hydraulic Hypothesis: A Reappraisal. *Current Anthropology* 14:532–534.
  1976a Irrigation and Community in the Central Peruvian Highlands. *American Anthropologist* 78:25–44.
  1976b Social Adaptation to the Mountain Environment of an Andean Village. In *Hill Lands: Proceedings of an International Symposium*, ed. J. Luchop, J. D. Cawthon, and M. J. Breslin, pp. 187–198. Morgantown: West Virginia University Press.
  1977   A Systems Approach to the Evolution of Primary Civilizations. Paper presented at the 76th annual meeting of the American Anthropological Association.
  1979   Inconsistencia de status social y dimensiones de rango en los andes centrales del Perú. *Estudios Andinos* 15:21–31.
  1980   Local Ecology and the State: Implications of Contemporary Quechua Land Use for the Inca Sequence of Agricultural Work. In *Beyond the Myths of Culture: Essays in Cultural Materialism*, ed. Eric B. Ross, pp. 139–154. New York: Academic Press.
  1986   Guerrillas and Migrant Networks. Paper presented at symposium, Politics and Culture in Latin America, 85th annual meeting of the American Anthropological Association, Philadelphia.
  1987a The Myth of the Isolated Native Community. In *Global Interdependence in the Curriculum: Case Studies for the Social Sciences*, ed. Judy Himes. Princeton: Woodrow Wilson National Fellowship Foundation.
  1987b Methodological Problems in Determining the Cause of Migration. *American Ethnologist* 14:379–380.
  1987c Comment on "Terracing and Irrigation in the Peruvian Highlands," by David Guillet. *Current Anthropology* 28:422.
  1988   Peruvian Farm Production. *Christian Science Monitor*, October 7.
  n.d.   Dam the Water: The Political Economy of Irrigation in the Ayacucho Valley, Peru. In *Irrigation at High Altitudes: The Social Organization of Water Control Systems in the Andes*, ed. William P. Mitchell and David Guillet.
Montero, Edith
  1974   Quinua: Una experiencia de lucha campesina (1973). *Ideología* (Revista de Ciencias Sociales y Humanidades, Universidad Nacional de San Cristobal de Huamanga, Perú) 4:38–49.

Morner, Magnus
   1985 *The Andean Past: Land, Societies, and Conflicts.* New York: Columbia University Press.
Muratorio, Blanca
   1980 Protestantism and Capitalism Revisited, in the Rural Highlands of Ecuador. *Journal of Peasant Studies* 8 : 37–60.
   1981 Protestantism, Ethnicity and Class in Chimborazo. In *Cultural Transformations and Ethnicity in Modern Ecuador*, ed. Norman Whitten, pp. 506–534. Urbana: University of Illinois Press.
Murra, John V.
   1972 El "control vertical" de un máximo de pisos ecológicos en la economía de las sociedades andinas. In *Visita de la província de Léon de Huánuco en 1562, Iñigo Ortiz de Zuñiga, visitador*, ed. John Murra, vol. 2 : 427–476. Huánuco: Universidad Nacional Hermilio Valdizán.
NACLA
   1989 Coca: The Real Green Revolution. New York: *NACLA Report on the Americas* 22, no. 6.
National Research Council
   1978 *Postharvest Food Losses in Developing Countries.* Washington, D.C.: National Research Council (Board on Science and Technology for International Development, Commission on International Relations).
Ordoñez, Pastor
   1919–1920 Los varayoc. *Revista universitaria del Cuzco*, nos. 27, 28, 31.
Orlove, Benjamin
   1977a Inequality among Peasants: The Forms and Uses of Reciprocal Exchange in Andean Peru. In *Peasant Livelihood: Studies in Economic Anthropology and Cultural Ecology.* ed. Rhoda Halperin and James Dow, pp. 201–214. New York: St. Martin's Press.
   1977b Alpacas, Sheep, and Men: The Wool Export Economy and Regional Society in Southern Peru. New York: Academic Press.
   1977c Integration through Production: The Use of Zonation in Espinar. *American Ethnologist* 4 : 84–101.
   1980 Ecological Anthropology. *Annual Review of Anthropology* 9 : 235–273.
   1986 Barter and Cash Sale on Lake Titicaca: A Test of Competing Approaches. *Current Anthropology* 27 : 85–106.
   1987 Stability and Change in Highland Andean Dietary Patterns. In *Food and Evolution: Toward a Theory of Human Food Habits*, ed. Marvin Harris and Eric Ross, pp. 481–515. Philadelphia: Temple University Press.
Orlove, Benjamin, and Glynn Custred, eds.
   1980 *Land and Power in Latin America: Agrarian Economies and Social Processes in the Andes.* New York and London: Holmes and Meier Publishers, Inc.

Orlove, Benjamin, and D. Guillet, eds.
1985 Convergences and Differences in Mountain Economies and Societies; A Comparison of the Andes and Himalaya. *Mountain Research and Development*, vol. 5, no. 1.
Orlove, Benjamin S., and Ricardo Godoy
1986 Sectoral Fallowing Systems in the Central Andes. *Journal of Ethnobiology* 6:169–204.
Ortiz de Zevallos, Felipe
1989 *The Peruvian Puzzle, A Twentieth Century Fund Paper.* New York: Priority Press Publications.
Painter, Michael
1981 The Political Economy of Food Production: An Example from an Aymara-Speaking Region of Peru. Ph.D. diss., University of Florida, Gainesville.
1984 Changing Relations of Production and Rural Underdevelopment. Journal of Anthropological Research 40:271–292.
Palmer, David Scott
1986 Rebellion in Rural Peru: The Origins and Evolution of Sendero Luminoso. *Comparative Politics* 18:127–146.
Paredes-Alfaro, Ruben Eli
1980 A Protestant Movement in Ecuador and Peru: A Comparative Socio-Anthropological Study of the Establishment and Diffusion of Protestantism in Two Central Highland Regions. Ph.D. diss., University of California, Los Angeles.
Parillón, Cutberto et al.
1983 *Un análisis de la situación alimentaria-nutricional en el Perú.* Raleigh, N.C.: Sigma One Corporation.
1986 *Acciones contra las causas de la desnutrición en el Perú: Un enfoque funcional.* Lima: Sigma One Corporation.
1987 Nutritional Functional Classification Study of Peru: Who and Where Are the Poor. Prepared for the Office of Health and Nutrition, USAID/PERU. Raleigh, N.C.: Sigma One Corporation.
Parker, Gary J.
1969 *Ayacucho Quechua Grammar and Dictionary.* The Hague: Mouton.
Passmore, R.
1974 *Handbook on Human Nutritional Requirements.* Rome: Food and Agriculture Organization of the United Nations.
Peru
1878 Resumen del censo general de habitantes del Perú, hecho en 1876. Lima: Imprenta del Estado.
1948 Censo nacional de población de 1940, vol. 6. Lima: Ministerio de Hacienda y Comercio, Dirección Nacional de Estadística.
1966 Sexto censo nacional de población; Primer censo nacional de vivienda, 2 de Julio de 1961. Vol. 1, Volumen de centros poblados. Lima: Dirección Nacional de Estadística y Censos.

1972 Segundo censo nacional agropecuario, 4 al 24 de Septiembre, 1972, Departamento de Ayacucho. Lima: Instituto Nacional de Estadística.

1974 Censos nacionales, VII de población, II de vivienda, 4 de Junio de 1972, Departamento de Ayacucho. Lima: Oficina Nacional de Estadística y Censos.

1977a Información basica de comunidades campesinas. Censo aplicado en Mayo de 1977 por SINAMOS (Sistema Nacional de Apoyo a la Movilización Social), Dirección General de Organizaciones Rurales. Lima: SINAMOS.

1977b Comunidades campesinas del Perú; Información censal población y vivienda 1972, Departamento de Ayacucho, series 1, vol. 2. Lima: SINAMOS, Dirección General de Organizaciones Rurales.

1983 Censos nacionales, VIII de población, III de vivienda, 12 de julio de 1981, resultados definitivos, Departamento de Ayacucho, 3 vols. Lima: Instituto Nacional de Estadística.

1984 Hechos y cifras demográficas. Lima: Consejo Nacional de la Población.

1986 Plan departamental de desarrollo de Ayacucho, CORDE Ayacucho. Lima: Presidencia de la República.

1987 Indicadores demográficos y socioeconómicos: Peru 1987. Lima: Consejo Nacional de la Población.

Platt, Tristan
1986 Mirrors and Maize: The Concept of *Yanantin* among the Macha of Bolivia. In *Anthropological History of Andean Polities*, ed. J. Murra, et al., pp. 228–259. Cambridge: Cambridge University Press.

Poole, Deborah
1982 Los santuarios religiosos en la economía regional andina (Cusco). *Allpanchis* 19:79–116.

Price, Barbara J.
1974 The Burden of the Cargo: Ethnographical Models and Archaeological Inference. In *Mesoamerican Archaeology, New Approaches*, ed. Norman Hammond, pp. 445–465. London: Duckworth.

1978 Demystification, Enriddlement, and Aztec Cannibalism: A Materialist Rejoinder to Harner. *American Ethnologist* 5:98–115.

1982 Cultural Materialism: A Theoretical Review. *American Antiquity* 47:709–741.

Pulgar Vidal, Javier
n.d. *Las ocho regiones naturales del Perú.* Lima: Editorial Universo S.A.

Rappaport, Roy
1968 *Pigs for the Ancestors: Ritual in the Ecology of a New Guinea People.* New Haven: Yale University Press.

Rasnake, Roger Neil
1988 *Domination and Cultural Resistance: Authority and Power among an Andean People.* Durham, N.C.: Duke University Press.

Reid, Michael
  1985 *Peru: Paths to Poverty.* London: Latin American Bureau.
  1986 Peru's Shining Path to Perdition. *Guardian,* August 1, p. 9.
Rhoades, Robert E., and Stephen I. Thompson
  1975 Adaptive Strategies in Alpine Environments: Beyond Ecological Particularism. *American Ethnologist* 2 : 535–551.
Riding, Alan
  1989 Peru Fights to Overcome Its Past. *The New York Times Magazine,* May 14.
Rivera, Jaime
  1967 El clima de Ayacucho. Universidad, Organo de Extensión Cultural de la Universidad Nacional de San Cristobal de Huamanga (Ayacucho), year 3, no. 9.
  1971 Geografía general de Ayacucho. Ayacucho: Universidad Nacional de San Cristobal de Huamanga, Dirección Universitaria de Investigación.
Rivera Serna, Raul
  1966 Libro del cabildo de la ciudad de San Juan de la frontera de Huamanga 1539–1547, descrifado por Raul Rivera Serna. Lima: Casa de la Cultura del Perú, Documentos Regionales de la Etnología y Etnohistoria Andinas, no. 3.
Robertson, Hector M.
  1959 [1933] *Aspects of the Rise of Economic Individualism: A Criticism of Max Weber and His School.* New York: Kelly and Millman, Inc.
Roseberry, William
  1983 *Coffee and Capitalism in the Venezuelan Andes.* Austin: University of Texas Press.
Ross, Eric B.
  1986 Potatoes, Population, and the Irish Famine: The Political Economy of Demographic Change. In *Culture and Reproduction,* ed. W. Penn Handwerker, pp. 196–220. Boulder: Westview Press.
Rus, Jan, and Wasserstrom, Robert
  1980 Civil-Religious Hierarchies in Central Chiapas: A Critical Perspective. *American Ethnologist* 7 : 466–478.
Sahlins, Marshall
  1972 *Stone Age Economics.* Chicago: Aldine-Atherton, Inc.
  1976 *Culture and Practical Reason.* Chicago: University of Chicago Press.
Sallnow, Michael J.
  1987 *Pilgrims of the Andes: Regional Cults in Cusco.* Washington, D.C.: Smithsonian Institution Press.
Salomon, Frank
  1973 Weavers of Otavalo. In *Peoples and Cultures of Native South America,* ed. Daniel R. Gross, pp. 463–492. Garden City, N.Y.: Doubleday/The Natural History Press.
Samaniego, C.
  1978 Peasant Movements at the Turn of the Century and the Rise of the

Independent Farmer. In *Peasant Cooperation and Capitalist Expansion in Central Peru*, ed. Norman Long and Bryan Roberts, pp. 45–71. Austin: Institute for Latin American Studies, University of Texas.

Samuelson, Kurt
1961 *Religion and Economic Action*, trans. E. French. Stockholm: Bonniers.

Sanchez, Rodrigo
1982 The Andean Economic System and Capitalism. In *Ecology and Exchange in the Andes*, ed. David Lehmann, pp. 157–190. Cambridge: Cambridge University Press.

Sanders, William T., and Deborah L. Nichols
1988 Ecological Theory and Cultural Evolution in the Valley of Oaxaca. *Current Anthropology* 29:33–80.

Sanders, William T., and Barbara J. Price
1968 *Mesoamerica: The Evolution of a Civilization.* New York: Random House.

Sauer, Carl O.
1948 Cultivated Plants of South and Central America. In *Handbook of South American Indians*, ed. Julian H. Steward, vol. 6: *Physical Anthropology, Linguistics, and Cultural Geography of South American Indians*, pp. 487–543. Washington, D.C.: Smithsonian Institution, *Bureau of American Ethnology Bulletin* 143.

Schaedel, Richard P.
1967 La demografía y los recursos humanos del sur del Perú. Serie Antropología Social 8. Mexico City: Instituto Indigenista Interamericano.

Schneider, Harold K.
1974 *Economic Man: The Anthropology of Economics.* New York: Free Press.
1979 *Livestock and Equality in East Africa: The Economic Basis for Social Structure.* Bloomington: Indiana University Press.

Scott, James C.
1976 *The Moral Economy of the Peasant: Rebellion and Subsistence in Southeast Asia.* New Haven/London: Yale University Press.

Shaw, R. Paul
1976 *Land Tenure and the Rural Exodus in Chile, Colombia, Costa Rica, and Peru.* Gainesville: University Presses of Florida.

Skar, Harold O.
1982 *The Warm Valley People: Duality and Land Reform among the Quechua Indians of Highland Peru.* Oslo: Universitetsforlaget.

Smith, Robert J.
1975 *The Art of the Festival; As Exemplified by the Fiesta to the Patroness of Otuzco: La Virgen de la Puerta.* Lawrence: University of Kansas Publications in Anthropology, no. 6.

Smith, Waldemar
  1977 *The Fiesta System and Economic Change.* New York: Columbia
         University Press.
Snyder, Joan
  1960 Group Relations and Social Change in an Andean Village. Ph.D.
         diss., Cornell University, Ithaca, N.Y.
Sombart, Werner
  1915 *The Quintessence of Capitalism: A Study of the History and Psy-
         chology of the Modern Business Man,* trans. and ed. M. Epstein.
         London: T. F. Unwin, Ltd.
Soukup, Jaroslav
  1970 *Vocabulario de los nombres vulgares de la flora peruana.* Lima:
         Colegio Salesiano.
Stein, William
  1961 *Hualcan: Life in the Highlands of Peru.* Ithaca: Cornell University
         Press.
Stern, Steve J.
  1982 *Peru's Indian Peoples and the Challenge of Spanish Conquest:
         Huamanga to 1640.* Madison: University of Wisconsin Press.
Steward, Julian H.
  1949 Cultural Causality and Law: A Trial Formulation of the Develop-
         ment of Early Civilizations. *American Anthropologist* 51:1–27.
  1950 *Area Research: Theory and Practice.* New York: Social Science Re-
         search Council.
  1955 *Theory of Culture Change: The Methodology of Multilinear Evolu-
         tion.* Urbana: University of Illinois Press.
Stone, Glenn Davis, Robert McC. Netting, and M. Priscilla Stone
  1990 Seasonality, Labor Scheduling, and Agricultural Intensification in
         the Nigerian Savanna. *American Anthropologist* 92:7–23.
Super, John C.
  1985 The Formation of Nutritional Regimes in Colonial Latin America.
         In *Food, Politics, and Society in Latin America,* ed. John Super and
         Thomas Wright, pp. 1–23. Lincoln: University of Nebraska Press.
Tawney, Richard H.
  1958 [1930] Foreword to *The Protestant Ethic and the Spirit of Capi-
         talism,* by Max Weber. New York: Charles Scribner's Sons.
  1962 [1926] *Religion and the Rise of Capitalism: A Historical Study.*
         Gloucester, Mass.: Peter Smith.
Taylor, John G.
  1979 *From Modernization to Modes of Production: A Critique of the
         Sociologies of Development and Underdevelopment.* Atlantic
         Highlands, N.J.: Humanities Press.
Taylor, William B.
  1987 The Virgin of Guadalupe in New Spain: An Inquiry into the Social
         History of Marian Devotion. *Ethnology* 14:9–33.
Thomas, R. Brooke
  1973 Human Adaptation to a High Andean Energy Flow System. Occa-

sional Papers in Anthropology, no. 7. University Park: Pennsylvania State University.

Thorp, Rosemary, and Geoffrey Bertram
1978　*Peru: 1890–1977: Growth and Policy in an Open Economy.* New York: Columbia University Press.

Tosi, Joseph A.
1960　Zonas de vida natural en el Perú. Instituto Interamericano de Ciencias Agrícolas de la OEA (OAS), Zona Andina, Boletín Técnico, no. 5. Lima: Organización de Estados Americanos.

Tosi, Joseph A., and Robert F. Voertman
1964　Some Environmental Factors in the Economic Development of the Tropics. *Economic Geography* 40: 189–205.

Towle, Margaret
1961　*The Ethnobotany of Pre-Columbian Peru.* Viking Fund Publications in Anthropology, no. 30. New York: Wenner Gren Foundation for Anthropological Research.

Troll, Carl
1968　The Cordilleras of the Tropical Americas; Aspects of Climatic, Phytogeographical and Agrarian Ecology. In *Geo-Ecology of the Mountainous Regions of the Tropical Americas,* ed. Carl Troll, pp. 15–56. Bonn: Ferd Dummlers Verlag.

Tschopik, Harry
1947　*Highland Communities of Central Peru: A Regional Survey.* Smithsonian Institute of Social Anthropology Publication no. 5. Washington, D.C.: U.S. Government Printing Office.

Turner, Victor W.
1967　*The Forest of Symbols: Aspects of Ndembu Ritual.* Ithaca: Cornell University Press.

Urton, Gary
1981　*At the Crossroads of the Earth and the Sky: An Andean Cosmology.* Austin: University of Texas Press.

Vallée, Lionel
1971　La ecología subjetiva como un elemento esencial de la verticalidad. Actas y Memórias del 39 Congreso Internacional de Americanistas, vol. 3: 167–173. (*Revista del Museo Nacional* [Lima], vol. 37.)

Vargas Llosa, Mario
1983　Inquest in the Andes. *The New York Times Magazine,* July 31.

Vargas Ugarte, Rubén
1956　*Historia del culto Maria en Iberoamérica y de sus imagines y santuarios mas celebrados.* 3d ed. 2 vols. Madrid: Talleres Gráficos Jura.

Vazquez, Mario C.
1964　*The Varayoc System in Vicos.* Comparative Studies of Cultural Change. Ithaca: Cornell University.

Way, Anthony B.
1976　Morbidity and Postneonatal Mortality. In *Man in the Andes: A Multidisciplinary Study of High-Altitude Quechua,* ed. Paul T.

Baker and Michael A. Little, pp. 147–160. Stroudsburg, Pa.: Dowden, Hutchinson, and Ross.

Weber, Max
1958a [1904–05] *The Protestant Ethic and the Spirit of Capitalism.* Trans. Talcott Parsons. New York: Charles Scribner's Sons.
1958b [1922–23] The Social Psychology of the World Religions. In *From Max Weber: Essays in Sociology,* ed. and trans. H. H. Gerth and C. Wright Mills. New York: Oxford University Press.

Webster, Steven S.
1971 An Indigenous Quechua Community in Exploitation of Multiple Ecological Zones. Actas y Memorias del 39 Congreso Internacional de Americanistas, vol. 3:174–183. (*Revista del Museo Nacional* [Lima], vol. 37.)

Weismantel, Mary J.
1988 *Food, Gender, and Poverty in the Ecuadorian Andes.* Philadelphia: University of Pennsylvania Press.

Weiss, Wendy
1985 The Social Organization of Property and Work: A Study of Migrants from the Rural Ecuadorian Sierra. *American Ethnologist* 12: 468–488.

Werge, Robert W.
1980 *Potato Storage Systems in the Mantaro Valley Region of Peru.* Lima: International Potato Center.

Winterhalder, Bruce, Robert Larsen, and R. Brooke Thomas
1974 Dung as an Essential Resource in a Highland Peruvian Community. *Human Ecology* 2:89–104.

Winterhalder, Bruce, and R. Brooke Thomas
1978 Geoecology of Southern Highland Peru: A Human Adaptation Perspective. Occasional Paper no. 27, Institute of Arctic and Alpine Research. Boulder: University of Colorado.

Wise, Carol
1986 The Perils of Orthodoxy: Peru's Political Economy. *NACLA Report on the Americas* 20, no. 3:14–26.

Wolf, Eric R.
1959 *Sons of the Shaking Earth: The People of Mexico and Guatemala—Their Land, History and Culture.* Chicago: University of Chicago Press.
1982 *Europe and the People without History.* Berkeley and Los Angeles: University of California Press.

Wright, Henry T., and Gregory A. Johnson
1975 Population, Exchange and Early State Formation in Southwestern Iran. *American Anthropologist* 77:267–289.

Yamamoto, Norio
1981 Investigación preliminar sobre las actividades agropastoriles en el distrito de Marcapata, Departamento del Cuzco, Perú. In *Estudios etnográficos del Perú meridional,* ed. Shozo Masuda, pp. 85–137. Tokyo: University of Tokyo Press.

Zuidema, R. T.
    1986 Inka Dynasty and Irrigation: Another Look at Andean Concepts
        of History. In *Anthropological History of Andean Polities*, ed.
        J. Murra, et al., pp. 177–200. Cambridge: Cambridge University
        Press.

INDEX

Abortifacients, 33
Age-dependency ratio, 20, 22–23, 34
Agrarian reform, 52
Agriculture: agricultural calendar, 71–73, 136–137, 168, 204–206; cash-cropping, 10, 13, 28, 42, 43, 86, 93–94, 97, 102, 106–107, 125, 193, 229n4; changes in, 108–109; crop rotation, 72–73, 74–75, 194; cropping methods and soil fertility, 73–75, 207–215; double-cropping, 72–73; ecological constraints on, 23, 28, 35, 37–39, 198; ecological zones and, 39–46, 202–203; fallowing system, 72, 74, 75, 226n2; fertilization for, 68, 70, 71, 73, 108, 209; infields used in, 70, 71; insecticides needed for, 68, 108, 212; interplanted crops (*mellgas*), 73–74; kitchen gardens, 71; labor available for, 62–68, 193–194; labor requirements for, 75–77, 216–219; length of work day for, 67–68; migrants involved in, 102; outfields used in, 70–71; percentage of farmland, 43; percentage of irrigated lands, 71, 72; production costs of, 68–69, 79; production figures, 77–81, 227nn7–10; sex-

ual division of labor and, 48, 211, 213–215; wages for agricultural labor, 63–64, 65, 87, 111, 122. *See also* Irrigation system; Land; *names of specific crops*
Alcohol consumption, 32, 51, 64, 82, 92, 95, 110, 129, 138, 140, 148, 173, 174
Allen, Catherine J., 16, 17, 222n8
Alpine rain tundra zone, 40–41, 44, 202–203
Andahuaylas, 58
Animal herding, 35, 37, 40–41, 44, 59, 63, 88
Animal ownership, 58–61, 225n13
Annis, Sheldon, 18, 196, 228n14
Apurimac, Department of, 230n14
Arnold, Dean E., 223n8
Ayacucho (city): geographic setting of, 3, 6; government workers in, 229n10; growth of, 9, 229n4; highway system and, 123–125; history of, 7; manufactured goods from, 93; migration to, 111, 112; as regional center, 8; religion in, 135; Shining Path movement in, 10, 229n10; temperature in, 39; trade with Quinua, 106; university in, 103
Ayacucho (department): economy of, 99–100, 102; food consump-

Printed and bound by CPI Group (UK) Ltd, Croydon, CR0 4YY

09/06/2025

14685840-0002